Desert War

The Battle Of Sidi Rezegh

Peter Cox

16pt

Read How You Want

LARGE PRINT BOOKS, BRAILLE & DAISY

Copyright Page from the Original Book

TABLE OF CONTENTS

ACKNOWLEDGEMENTS   iii

INTRODUCTION: The Forgotten Desert Battle   vii

Operation   xvii

CHAPTER 1: The First Libyan Campaign   1

CHAPTER 2: Tobruk   20

CHAPTER 3: The Plan for Crusader   42

CHAPTER 4: The Great Approach March   74

CHAPTER 5: The Battle of the Armour   97

CHAPTER 6: Totensonntag: The Sunday of the Dead 123

CHAPTER 7: The Division Moves West   164

CHAPTER 8: The Attacks on Sidi Rezegh and
Belhamed   189

CHAPTER 9: Rommel's Dash to the Frontier   220

CHAPTER 10: Rommel Returns to Sidi Rezegh   238

CHAPTER 11: Mounting Pressure on 4 and 6
Brigades   265

CHAPTER 12: 4 and 6 Brigades Withdraw   289

CHAPTER 13: Wrapping up the Campaign   315

CHAPTER 14: Treating the Wounded   350

CHAPTER 15: For You the War is Over   376

CHAPTER 16: Counting the Cost of Crusader   404

EPILOGUE: Return to Sidi Rezegh   429

NOTES   442

BIBLIOGRAPHY   504

Back Cover Material   531

Index   533

ANZAC BATTLES SERIES

Series Editor: Glyn Harper

The Anzac Battles Series is a collection of books describing the great military battles fought by Australian and New Zealand soldiers during the wars of the twentieth century. Each title in the series focuses on one battle, describing the background to the action, the combat itself, the strategy employed and the outcome. The story is told through the actions of the main protagonists and the individuals who distinguished themselves in the battle. The authors are all respected military historians with specialist knowledge of the battles described.

Already available

The Nek: A Gallipoli tragedy
Peter Burness

Dogfight: The Battle of Britain
Adam Claasen

Maps

The Mediterranean area, November 1941
The main battle area
13 Corps, 21–22 November 1941
Advance of 4 and 6 Brigades, 23–28
 November 1941
Position of forces, 29 November – 1
 December 1941
Gazala area

ACKNOWLEDGEMENTS

I am deeply grateful to the many people who have helped me with the preparation of this book, and those who have provided me with family and personal records, diaries, correspondence and photographs of the men who served at Sidi Rezegh. I was extremely fortunate in being able to talk with some of the veterans, several of whom, sadly, have since died.

I wish to record my sincere thanks to the following:

In New Zealand: the family of Bill Andrew; Wayne Hammond, Dianne Richardson and Bunty Hammond, the family of Phil Hammond; Geoffrey Heaps, Hugh Heaps and Majorie Paterson, the family of Eric Heaps; Graeme McIver, Murray and Judy McIver and Violet Williams, the family of Leslie McIver; Russell and Maryann Nelley, and Sam Nelley, the family of Louis Nelley; Bill Paterson, son of Clement Paterson; Eugenie Gatenby and Marise Perry; Harvey Polglase and Michelle Polglase; Edith Costello; Stephanie Handley;

Nathania Kenny; Alan Lee; Robert Loughnan; John Staveley; Brian Wintle.

In Britain: Diana Carney, Alf Blacklin's eldest daughter; Elizabeth Ramsay and Ruth Stevens, daughters of Randel Heron.

I would also like to thank David Beckingham, Jonathan Forsey, Jan Love and Peter Scott for their assistance; Ian Watt, Professor Glyn Harper and the team from Exisle Publishing for all their work in the production of this book; Fran Whild for her expertise in producing the maps; Anna Rogers, not only for her expertise in editing the book but also for her continuing support and advice throughout the whole process; and my family, Robin, Rebecca and Richard, and David and Kate, for their interest and encouragement – and especially Robin, who was my travel companion on our visits to Libya.

Although every effort has been made to ensure the accuracy of information, one of the considerable challenges I found in writing the book was the amount of conflicting information in the various records. I have tried to use information that I considered to be the most authoritative, but if errors do exist, the responsibility is entirely mine.

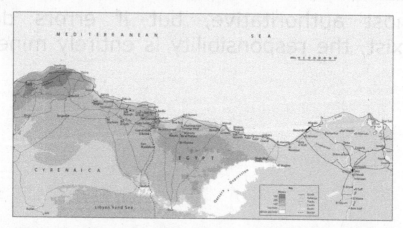

The Mediterranean area, November 1941

INTRODUCTION

The Forgotten Desert Battle

During the night of 18 November 1941, some 20,000 men of the 2nd New Zealand Division crossed the border from Egypt into Libya. As part of the 118,000-strong British Eighth Army, it was the division's opening move in Operation *Crusader.* The campaign had two primary objectives. The first was to destroy German and Italian armoured formations near Tobruk, a Libyan port occupied by the Allies but surrounded by German and Italian forces. The second was to drive the enemy back through Cyrenaica, the eastern region of Libya. If these moves were successful the ultimate objective was the overall defeat of the Germans and Italians in Africa. As the battle unfolded, and as the division's commander, Major General Bernard Freyberg, had predicted at the outset, much of the New Zealanders' battle was fought around a place called

Sidi Rezegh, on a barren and stony desert ridge outside Tobruk. The campaign was partially successful, but at a high cost. By the time *Crusader* ended in early 1942, more New Zealand soldiers had been killed or taken prisoner than in any other campaign the division fought in the Second World War, and more New Zealanders died, were wounded or reported missing than in any other Eighth Army division that took part in the operation. New Zealand casualties totalled 4620: 879 killed, 1699 wounded and 2042 captured.[1]

My interest in Sidi Rezegh arose several years ago when I researched the war history of my father, who fought at Sidi Rezegh. Sergeant Brian Cox was a member of 9 Platoon, 3 Company, 27 (Machine Gun) Battalion. He was only 59 when he died in 1976; he had rarely spoken about his experiences and the subject remained largely dormant until, in 2002, my son asked me what my father had done in the war. That question culminated in my writing *Good Luck to All the Lads – The Wartime Story of Brian Cox 1939–43,* published in 2008. Through the research for that book, including tracking down and talking to several of Brian's wartime mates, it became apparent that Sidi Rezegh loomed very large.

Although Brian spoke little about the war I did recall a couple of times when the name Sidi Rezegh was mentioned. The first was in 1958, when a copy of the newly published 27 Battalion volume of the Official War History arrived at home. I asked my father about a photo of him with the gun team, of which he was the leader, 'on Sidi Rezegh airfield'. Brian is sitting in the middle of the group behind a machine gun, looking relaxed and confident, staring straight at the camera, a cigarette dangling from his lower lip. This seemed a very different man from the father I knew, a quiet accountant heavily involved in local sports administration. Over the years I skimmed the book from time to time but did not really understand the context.

The second occasion was in the mid-1960s. I was reading an article about the Battle of El Alamein and asked my father if he had fought there.

He replied 'No', then paused, and said, 'But I was at Sidi Rezegh.' Although he did not elaborate, I sensed that the name held much significance, but I did not press him to explain.

During my research I learnt more about Sidi Rezegh, and through some good luck made contact with John Black from Auckland, a member of Brian's platoon. He, in turn, introduced me to Phillip ('Phil') Hammond, from Christchurch, who had entered camp at Burnham with my father and was with him at Sidi Rezegh. It was clear that this had been Phil's most significant wartime action. Frequently when I visited him he would recount his Sidi Rezegh story and, once started, would look into the middle distance, reliving the day and oblivious to anything going on around him. If he did address me, sitting beside him, he called me 'Cocky', my father's nickname. Through his reminiscences I became very familiar with the story of the battle.

Eventually my wife Robin and I decided it was time to see the areas where Brian had fought, so we mapped out an itinerary that covered the main areas of his war journey. Fortunately by 2007, when we planned to go, Libya was opening up to tourists and we were able to visit Sidi Rezegh, travelling to Tobruk by car from Alexandria. Our time in Tobruk was limited, and the visit to Sidi Rezegh brief, but it was enough to give me a sense of the battlefield and we were able to go to the little building known as 'the mosque', around which much of the battle for the New Zealand soldiers was fought.

Before we reached Libya we had already been to many of the places Brian had seen with the New Zealand Division. In Cairo we had visited the sphinx and the pyramids, standing in the places where Brian had been photographed, and climbed to the citadel above the city. As we had wandered the bazaar, on the hill above us 'Mohammad Ali's alabaster mosque, uniquely white in this sand-coloured city, sat with minarets pricked, like a fat, white, watchful cat'.[2] We had walked along the Corniche in Alexandria before travelling west through places with names familiar from Brian's war story: El Alamein, Mersa Matruh, Sidi Barrani and Sollum.

Finally we were in Tobruk, having successfully managed the 'Libyan two-step' to acquire visas, made it through the lengthy border checks and survived the madcap drive through the Libyan traffic from the border. The following morning our guide, Mousa Saad, collected us from the hotel. Heading west, we drove through Tobruk until, after travelling some 25 kilometres, we turned onto a rough, cobbled road that led to the entrance to Knightsbridge War Cemetery, Acroma, the last resting place for 441 New Zealand servicemen.

Almost deserted, the cemetery was considerably smaller than the one at El Alamein we had already visited. Although it was a sunny day, a brisk wind sent eddies of dust swirling around the neatly tended headstones and ruffled the many small plants and shrubs. We walked among the headstones, searching for the names of men from Brian's company and leaving poppies on the graves of these and other men whom we had been asked to seek out. Two and a half years later, when we returned for our second visit, some of the poppies were still there, dusty and faded but intact.

It was moving to see all the New Zealand names, and from the recorded dates of death it was apparent that many had been Sidi Rezegh casualties, men who had crossed the frontier with the New Zealand Division on that November night.

***

I was pleased that *Good Luck to All the Lads* seemed to find its way to many of the men's families. While it was very gratifying to know that the book had filled some gaps in their own history, it was even better to be able to meet some of these people and hear their family stories. I also met other Sidi Rezegh veterans, including Clement ('Clem') Paterson, formerly of 19 Infantry Battalion, and other families with fascinating tales of their relatives' adventures. It also became clear that for many of the men wounded or taken prisoner, Sidi Rezegh was the first step of another chain of adventures.

The book's emphasis on Sidi Rezegh seemed to strike a chord, and it was complemented by creating a website, www.sidirezegh.com, with information about and photos of the New Zealand involvement in the battle. A number of people contacted me, wanting more information or providing information about and photos of the New Zealand involvement in the battle. A number of people contacted me, wanting more information or providing further material. I was asked to speak to several groups, and it soon became apparent that few people knew of the battle, and many expressed surprise at the scale of the campaign and the number of casualties. I felt that although Robin and I had visited Sidi Rezegh, there was still some unfinished business there.

So in September 2009 we visited Libya again, seeing a greater area of the country, including historical sites and the Great Sand Sea, and this time travelling more extensively over the Sidi Rezegh battlefield. We drove and walked over the area of the critical phase of the battle, from 23 November until 1 December 1941, which was the centre of my father's experience. The landscape is largely unchanged; it was not difficult to appreciate the challenges the men had faced.

Sidi Rezegh, which has been described by Sir Geoffrey Cox (no relation), as the 'Forgotten Battle of the Desert War', was a complicated campaign from New Zealand's perspective. Before the battle Freyberg had been adamant that he did not want the three brigades of the New Zealand Division split up. However, because of the outcome of the initial encounters in the battle, it was soon necessary for 6 and then 4 Brigades to be diverted, to come to the aid of the British forces and to march on Tobruk, leaving 5 Brigade to carry out the division's original role. Each of these brigades has its own story, as do the individual battalions within them. Indeed every man who fought there has his own tale to tell.

During my research it has been interesting to read many accounts of the battle, although sorting through different versions of events and conflicting material has sometimes been challenging. The British, South African and Australian military histories have provided further insights and helped to place the New Zealand role in some context. Several families have kindly shared diaries, letters or other accounts of the campaign.

When New Zealand's major campaigns of the war are listed, Sidi Rezegh is frequently not mentioned, yet this battle was an important episode in the desert war and a significant victory for the Eighth Army. The New Zealand Division played a major role, at a high cost, and for all the soldiers who fought there it was a big part of their lives. The aim of this book is to tell the story of this often overlooked battle and of the men who fought there using, where possible, their own words.

Operation

EIGHTH ARMY CAMPAIGN OVERVIEW

	30 Corps	13 Corps	Tobruk Garrison
Nov 18	Into Libya	Into Libya	Garrison forces prepare to break out
19			
20	7 Armoured Div engage enemy tanks	Moves into position around frontier	
21			Commence breakout of Tobruk perimeter
22	7 Armoured Div withdraw after heavy losses to reorganise	2 NZ Div and 4 Indian Div isolate frontier forces	Under fire
23	5 South African Brigade overrun		
24			In position at Ed Duda
25		2 NZ Div advances to Sidi Rezegh, Belhamed and Ed Duda	Under fire
26	Enemy armour counterattacks to frontier		
27		2 NZ Div and Tobruk Garrison link up; corridor open	
28	Enemy tanks return to Tobruk front		
29		Final battle for Sidi Rezegh	Heavy fighting in corridor area
30	4/22 Armoured Brigade and 1 S. A. Brigade ordered to support 2 NZ Div		
Dec 1		Corridor severed	

December/January mop-up enemy frontier positions; enemy withdraws westwards through Cyrenaica

Crusader

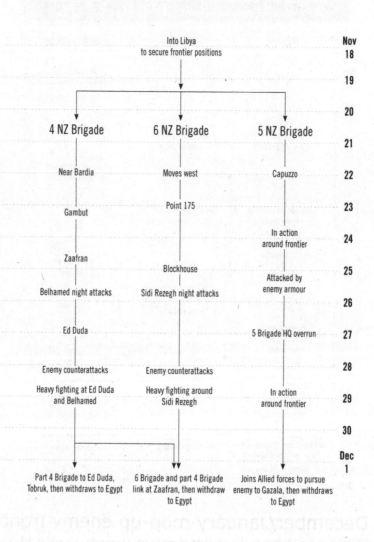

NZ DIVISION 13 CORPS

Into Libya
to secure frontier positions — **Nov 18**

19

20

4 NZ Brigade — **6 NZ Brigade** — **5 NZ Brigade** — **21**

Near Bardia — Moves west — Capuzzo — **22**

Gambut — Point 175 — **23**

In action
around frontier — **24**

Zaafran — — **25**

Blockhouse

Belhamed night attacks — Sidi Rezegh night attacks — Attacked by
enemy armour — **26**

Ed Duda — — 5 Brigade HQ overrun — **27**

Enemy counterattacks — Enemy counterattacks — **28**

Heavy fighting at Ed Duda
and Belhamed — Heavy fighting around
Sidi Rezegh — In action
around frontier — **29**

30

Dec 1

Part 4 Brigade to Ed Duda,
Tobruk, then withdraws to Egypt — 6 Brigade and part 4 Brigade
link at Zaafran, then withdraw
to Egypt — Joins Allied forces to pursue
enemy to Gazala, then withdraws
to Egypt

CHAPTER 1

The First Libyan Campaign

Positioned at the centre of the southern Mediterranean coast, Libya has long been important in the region's flow of trade. Stone Age and Phoenician traders passed through the region, and later there were periods of Greek and Roman occupation. Historically Libya comprised three distinct areas: Tripolitania in the west, Fezzan in the south and Cyrenaica in the east. In 1911 Italy occupied Libya and it was officially ceded to the country shortly afterwards; Tripolitania was quickly subdued but the Fezzan and a strongly independent Cyrenaica took longer to overcome. In January 1930 Italian leader Benito Mussolini, frustrated by the resistance in Cyrenaica, appointed Marshal Rodolfo Graziani Governor of Cyrenaica and over the next few years the Italian regime brutally overcame the resistance. To maintain control, the

Italians were forced to keep a large military presence in the region.

By 1940 Britain and Italy both had a significant interest in the Middle East. For Britain, it meant control of the Mediterranean, the Suez Canal and the western flanks of the vital oil fields and refineries of Iran and Iraq, the loss of which would have had a paralysing effect on the British war effort. For Italy, a significant role in the Middle East meant a place at Hitler's table, as well as access to air bases and cover for its 'fourth shore' – its southern flank.

In this context Libya, and especially Cyrenaica, was significant. From Brega in the Gulf of Sirte in the west, to Al-burdi (also known as Bardia) in the eastern Gulf of Bomba near the Egyptian border, Cyrenaica bulges into the Mediterranean. Whichever side occupied it had use of its airfields to provide air cover for shipping and therefore supply lines in the Mediterranean, something that was especially important for the British as they relied on ships sailing from Malta to Alexandria. This caused tension between the British government, which wanted the air cover maintained, and the armed forces commanders who were reluctant to commit to taking 'the Bulge' without adequate forces and equipment.

In February 1940 the First Echelon of the 2nd New Zealand Expeditionary Force (2NZEF) arrived in Egypt, where it became part of the British Middle East Forces under General Sir Archibald Wavell, Commander-in-Chief, Middle East Forces. He was responsible for an area, vital to Britain, that covered nine countries across two continents – not just Egypt and its Western Desert but a large part of the Middle East, from Iran down to Abyssinia. With only 36,000 men in Egypt, Wavell's forces were minimal, but there were plans to build a base large enough for nine divisions – approximately 150,000 men. As there were no German troops in North Africa when the New Zealanders arrived, they had time to become established and to train. Italy, although not yet at war, was potentially the most pressing threat to Egypt and, although they were not particularly well trained or equipped, had some 250,000 troops in Libya, and others in East Africa. The German High Command did investigate whether there was merit in Germany and Italy jointly attacking the Middle East oil fields by way of Egypt, but this never eventuated. Wavell moved quickly to face the Italian threat. On 8 June Major General Richard O'Connor, appointed to command a Western Desert Force, shifted his base to Maaten Baggush in Western Egypt, to prepare his plans for the defence of Egypt.

On 10 June Mussolini finally declared war on Britain. In the words of the official history of 20 Battalion, 'The New Zealanders' reaction was one of keen delight.' Troops at a concert in Maadi 'broke into cheers on hearing the news and the audience sang the national anthem with a patriotic fervour that stirred and uplifted every man who was there'. Preparations for air raids increased: 'tents were dispersed, dug in and sandbagged, slit trenches were dug and troops stood-to at dawn and dusk "waiting hopefully for Italian parachutists".'[1]

A detachment of New Zealand Signallers had been sent to Baggush the previous day, to take over signal communications for the Western Desert Force. Soon after their arrival a small unit including Sergeant J.M. Browne was sent to undertake a reconnaissance of the forward areas. When they were attacked near Buq Buq, close to the Libyan border, by three Italian planes, Browne was 'so incensed ... that he leaped from the truck and fired three shots with his rifle, an action which he claimed was the first by a New Zealander against the enemy in Africa'.[2]

In late August and September most of the New Zealand troops in Egypt, formed as 4 Brigade Group, moved to Western Egypt as a precaution against an attack by the Italians on Mersa Matruh, some 200 miles (320km) west of Alexandria. Based at Baggush, 30 miles (48km) east of Mersa Matruh, on the Mediterranean coast, the New Zealanders were to assist with the construction of defensive positions while they continued training in the surrounding desert.

Having seen the German successes in Europe, Mussolini impatiently urged

Graziani, with his army assembled in Libya, to take the offensive. Graziani, however, was aware that his forces, although large, were unprepared and ill-equipped. Hitler, concerned to protect Germany's southern flank, offered Mussolini a force of 250 Panzers but Mussolini dismissed the offer, believing he would not need the armoured support until his troops were in Western Egypt. In England, too, now that the risk of the German invasion had receded, Churchill wanted to see the war taken to the enemy. He continually urged the Middle East Command to take the offensive, despite Wavell's concerns about their battle readiness.

On 13 September, after Mussolini directly ordered a reluctant Graziani to attack, the Italian army advanced into Egypt. Although the British harassed the Italians, they were heavily outnumbered and it was fortunate that the Italians did not try an outflanking manoeuvre. By 17 September the Italians had reached Sidi Barrani, 65 miles (105km) east of the Egypt–Libya border but well west of Mersa Matruh. As they advanced the British withdrew, demolishing buildings and dumps as they went. After the Italians arrived Rome Radio proudly announced that 'All is quiet in Sidi Barrani, the shops are open and the trams are running again', which, as one writer has observed, 'would have come as a surprise to the inhabitants, most of whom had never seen a tram in their lives'.[3] Fortunately the reluctance of the Italian army to proceed further allowed O'Connor and Wavell time to strengthen their forces and plan their own offensive.

The Italian air force's attacks on the New Zealand positions at Baggush with 'thermos bombs', which exploded by vibration, resulted, on 13 September, in the first death from enemy action in 2NZEF. Thirty-three-year-old driver George Osborn from Auckland, serving with 4 Reserve Mechanical Transport (RMT), was in a convoy that was bombed; the blast threw Osborn onto a thermos bomb, which exploded, fatally wounding him.

On 28 October Mussolini, seeking further Italian glory, impulsively ordered the Italian invasion of Greece, but after only three weeks the Greek forces, although far weaker, pushed the Italians back into Albania. A furious Hitler told Mussolini that this would affect the campaign in Egypt and withdrew his earlier offer of Panzer support.

By now the British were reading Italian air force signals, which gave accurate information about the strength and disposition of Italian forces. They were also benefiting from German intelligence through the interception of German signals exchanged in code by means of Enigma machines. Through the code breakers working at Bletchley Park in England, the Enigma material, known as Ultra, was combined with other intelligence material received to produce signals intelligence, or SIGINT, which provided the British with valuable, though sometimes limited, information about troop movements, supply difficulties and the location of major formations. It did not, however, help with qualitative information, such as improvements to the Panzer tanks. SIGINT did mean, though, that the Allies knew there were no immediate plans to move German forces into the region.

In Egypt, on 9 December, the British forces under O'Connor counterattacked in a campaign called Operation *Compass,* which was carried out by British, Indian and Australian troops. By 10 December the Italian army around Sidi Barrani was under great pressure. The British infantry, supported by infantry tanks (I-tanks) passed quickly through to the rear of the Italian garrison, which was forced to surrender. Naturally, Churchill was ecstatic with the news, telegraphing Wavell that the Western Desert Force had 'rendered glorious service to the Empire and to our cause'.[4]

With this swift success incurring only minimal casualties, what was originally intended to be just a 'five day raid' now turned into something much greater. This was despite the British forces, at only some 31,000, being far outnumbered by the Italians. Much to their dismay, the New Zealand forces played only a modest part in O'Connor's raid. There was a reluctance to commit the still incomplete division until it was fully formed and trained in accordance with Freyberg's agreement with the government. Despite that, many New Zealanders did participate in this first Libyan campaign, including communications personnel, engineers and drivers.

New Zealand signallers played an important part in ensuring that cables were maintained to keep the communication systems operational. The engineers kept water supply pumps and pipelines operating and the companies of railwaymen had the vital task of ensuring the railways took supplies to the desert depots. But the most significant part was played by New Zealand transport, with 4 RMT attached to the Western Desert Force to move troops and supplies for 5 Brigade of 4 Indian Division.

On 6 December the 4 RMT trucks, each carrying 20 Indian troops, drove off into the desert. Two days later the men were briefed: they would be attacking the Italian camps at Tummar West and Tummar East. The next day they moved to the assembly point, 'and the first New Zealand charge in the Second World War'.[5] After an artillery barrage at 12.30p.m., the trucks with their New Zealand drivers departed and as they approached the Italian camps the enemy artillery opened up. When the Indians responded they were joined by armed drivers 'keen to "go in and get an Eyetie too"'.[6] So keen were the drivers transporting the 1st Royal Fusiliers, fighting with 5 Indian Brigade, that they brought their trucks close to the enemy positions, borrowed bayonets from the platoon Bren gunners and charged alongside the infantry, yelling, 'Come on then, you Pommie bastards!', as they ran.[7] The attacks were successful, thousands of prisoners were taken and a lot of food and other supplies were acquired. But it was also a salutary introduction to the reality of battle. The men were 'shocked at the sight of some of the wounds, realising for the first time what a mess shell fragments and grenades can make of a human body'.[8]

By 12 December 40,000 prisoners had already been captured and all available transport, drivers and support troops were needed to move the prisoners of war. New Zealand mechanics repaired and operated abandoned Italian trucks and on 30 December 4 Brigade group provided transport to convey 19 Australian Brigade from near Alexandria to the outskirts of Bardia, a 350-mile (560km) trip. As machine gunner Bill Andrew recorded in his diary, on New Year's Day 1941 they were

in Western Desert, Egypt. Continued journey in trucks conveying Australian troops to Libya after spending a cold night about 15 miles [24km] past Mersa Matruh. Passed through Sidi Barrani at mid-day and lunched – more bully beef and biscuits. Saw remains of battle through Buq Buq. Camped for the night 5 miles [8km] from Sollum. Bombs dropped at Sollum.

The next day, after a 6.30a.m. start, they climbed 'over Halfaya Pass, Graziani's road very rough and bitterly cold wind on top of hills. Crossed Libyan border (barbed wire) and through Fort Capuzzo and left Aussies 6 miles [10km] from the border'. They could hear 'artillery and naval bombardments at Bardia'. They then returned via 'Sollum to Mersa side of Sidi Barrani.

Saw much abandoned Italian equipment.'[9]

Australian Major General Iven Mackay reported to Freyberg that it was 'a wonderful piece of work ... for they moved us in two days instead of the three ordained'. The New Zealand drivers were 'untiring and were determined to get my men here in spite of the heavy traffic on indifferently surfaced roads'.[10]

Events moved quickly. On 5 January British and Australian forces took Bardia and captured 45,000 prisoners. Four RMT was again busy transporting some 5000 Australian troops from Bardia to the outskirts of Tobruk. On 22 January 1941 Tobruk fell, and Graziani decided to withdraw. New Zealand engineers lifted mines, repaired vehicles and fixed Tobruk's water supply. Attention then turned to Derna, 100 miles (160km) further west along the coast, and on 30 January the Italians started to withdraw back through Cyrenaica. Some New Zealand drivers operated transport services between Derna and Benghazi while engineers restored highways and bridges.

For Lieutenant Colonel George Clifton, the division's chief engineer, the campaign was an opportunity to become familiar with both the terrain and the enemy. He followed the battle, at times coming under fire as he sought to complete his 'military education'. He was with the first group of New Zealanders who drove into Bardia, which had been taken 'thanks to a nice combination of Australian and British troops – augmented by New Zealand trucks'.[11] Clifton and his team continued west, arriving in Tobruk just after 'the first wave of Tobruk looters' had gone through. They 'ransacked the pillaged naval store, filling up our ration boxes with excellent tinned stuff. Evidently the Imperial Italian Navy did themselves well too.'[12] After a brief sortie towards Derna, Clifton returned to Tobruk after a useful reconnaissance over Libyan territory.

On 6 February Australian forces entered Benghazi and the following day, at Beda Fomm, General Annibale Bergonzoli, commander of the Italian forces, surrendered. By the end of February O'Connor's army had overrun the whole province of Cyrenaica, an Italian army of 10 divisions had been destroyed and over 130,000 prisoners were captured. The Allied troops had advanced 500 miles (800km) in 10 weeks, killed or captured more than half of Graziani's army and destroyed or taken two-thirds of his equipment – ships, aircraft and land weapons. British and Australian casualties were 500 killed, 1373 wounded and 55 missing. Italy had lost a huge area of land, pressure on the Suez zone had been relieved and the Italian morale broken.

New Zealand, too, suffered casualties. On 24 December at Sollum, barges bringing water up from Mersa Matruh were being unloaded when 'suddenly about midday Italian aircraft came over to bomb with unusual and devastating accuracy'. The bombs caused the most serious loss yet experienced by the division. Six men from 4 RMT Company and one from 19 Army Troops Company were killed and six from 4 RMT wounded.[13] One of those killed was Corporal Osbert Pussell of 4 RMT Company. On 12 July Pussell, a battery assembler from Wellington, had become the division's first battle casualty when he was wounded during an air raid. Only 23 years old, he died of wounds on 25 December 1940. He was Mentioned in Dispatches (MiD).

On 25 February 4 RMT began its return trip to Helwan camp, but three days before there had been an ominous foretaste of things to come when a convoy transporting petrol was machine-gunned by 15 planes. Three trucks were struck and driver Steve Tripp was slightly wounded. 'These planes, tenacious, daring, meant business. The bold, black swastika was making its first appearance over Africa.'[14]

In a note written to Freyberg on 27 December, Wavell said he could understand the New Zealanders' disappointment 'at not having taken part in the advance on Sidi Barrani or beyond', but explained the reasons, and in particular that 'the New Zealand Government, quite naturally and quite rightly, has always wished that the New Zealand Division should be employed in active operations only as a complete division under its own Commander'. The division's assistance had been 'invaluable, and the recent success could not have been gained without it'. He concluded on a more positive note for the troops: 'their time will come before long, and I have every confidence that their leadership, training and spirit will win them great distinction in any operation in which they take part.'[15] Despite their limited role, the New Zealanders did gain valuable practice in moving troops and supplies, and maintaining supply lines to a rapidly moving attack. They also experienced the terrain in the Libyan border region and the rigours of the winter climate.

With Cyrenaica taken, the way was open to press on west towards Tripoli but it was not to be. The British units were well spread out and reduced in strength, and the transport was worn out: three-quarters of the tanks of 7 Armoured Division were out of action and replacements had not yet arrived. The supply line stretched back some 900 miles (1450km) to the Nile Valley; the port of Benghazi could not be used as it was subject to enemy air attacks, and the Royal Air Force (RAF) had insufficient planes to counter them.

By now the British had information through Enigma decrypts that Germany was preparing to invade Greece and the British Defence Committee eventually decided to divert the Allied forces in Libya to stiffen Greek defences in March 1941, and this included the New Zealand Division. Even if these forces had not gone to Greece, however, it is doubtful, with the supply difficulties, whether further advances into Tripolitania would have succeeded. Despite Churchill having some last minute misgivings, the movement of troops to Greece proceeded and any opportunity that there may have been to push on to Tripoli was lost.

The 'five day raid', the first Libyan campaign, had been spectacularly successful, although O'Connor was disappointed that he was not able to finish it off. It had been, in one historian's estimation,

> a model campaign, opening with a set-piece battle of great originality and faultless execution, continuing with a relentless pursuit with

improvised supply services, and ending with a daring strategic march and a battle of annihilation. Sidi Barrani, Bardia, Tobruk and Beda Fomm – their brilliance sparkles against the darkest setting of the war; hardly rivalled, never surpassed.[16]

It had also given the New Zealanders their first glimpse of Libya.

CHAPTER 2

Tobruk

Tobruk today is a town of about 130,000 people clustered around the harbour that has throughout history been its key feature. Under Italian occupation, Tobruk became an important military base, strategically positioned 90 miles (145km) from the Egyptian frontier. Its harbour, the only sheltered one of any size between Benghazi and Alexandria, was a key facility in the battles for Cyrenaica. The port was not large, at approximately 2 1/2 miles (4km) long and under a mile (1.6km) wide, but it was big enough to accommodate sizeable vessels, although its capacity was limited to about 600 tons a day. Protecting the harbour on the northern side was a high promontory where the Italian garrison lived in a cluster of houses, barracks and military installations; elsewhere were a hotel, some shops, offices and gardens. Importantly there were also two water distilleries and wells, providing plentiful supplies of rather brackish water.

On 1 January 1941 the Western Desert Force was renamed 13 Corps. Operation *Compass* was going well: after taking Bardia, the next target was Tobruk, where the 25,000-strong Italian garrison, under General Petassi Manella, was strong in artillery but weak in infantry, with barely enough men to establish the perimeter defences. Six Australian Division, under Major General Iven Mackay, was tasked with taking Tobruk, by encircling and isolating the town. Following the fall of Bardia, 7 Armoured Division had moved rapidly west, and cut the western approaches to Tobruk. Twenty-four hours later 19 Australian Brigade sealed the eastern side and by 9 January the entire perimeter was surrounded and, by night, patrols went out to assess the defences.

The Australians attacked on 21 January, with artillery supported by naval guns and RAF bombers. Engineers blew gaps in the southern perimeter wire and men from the 16, 17 and 19 Australian Infantry Brigades took up the attack in a series of waves, supported by Matilda I-tanks. After some heavy fighting, at dusk they took Fort Pilastrino, and that evening the command headquarters of the Tobruk garrison fell. The following day Brigadier Horace Robertson received the official surrender of the garrison from Admiral Massimiliano Vietina. To make the town safe, the Allied troops blew up ammunition dumps, cleared mines and booby traps and occupied three large sunken Italian ships in the harbour that were being used as gun platforms. They took 200 guns and the same number of vehicles, but the biggest problem was providing for all the Italian prisoners.

Observing developments following Italy's Greek disaster, Hitler had been increasingly concerned about O'Connor's success. If the Italians were defeated in North Africa, it would free up some of the British forces for deployment elsewhere. Britain would control the Mediterranean and could challenge Germany's southern flank. Accordingly, on 22 January Hitler ordered the dispatch to Tripoli of the Deutsches Afrika Korps (DAK), a small force comprising two Panzer divisions, led by

Lieutenant General Erwin Rommel. The command structure was confused, as Hitler wanted to accommodate the Italian illusion that the Mediterranean theatre was 'their' war. Rommel had been appointed commander of the German troops in Libya, but he would take battle orders from Graziani's replacement, General Italo Gariboldi, a situation that was to cause ongoing tension and disagreements.

On 12 February, when Rommel arrived, the British army was still pursuing the Italians westwards but he immediately began reconnaissance flights to get to know the country. On 14 February an advance guard of the Afrika Korps started disembarking at Tripoli, and immediately headed 200 miles (320km) east to Sirte. Five Light Panzer Division (later renamed 21 Panzer) arrived on 11 March, followed late in May by 15 Panzer.

From information received through Ultra, the British had a good idea of the size of Rommel's forces, but, believing that the German High Command only wanted the British forces contained, they underestimated how quickly Rommel would attack. Wavell later admitted that he made a big mistake in presuming 'that the enemy could not put in any effective counter-stroke before May at the earliest'.[1]

On 24 March the Panzers pounced, first taking the British forward position at El Agheila and then Ajedabia. The British were soon in full retreat and on 3 April the enemy forces were in Benghazi, having attacked, as Rommel wrote to his wife, 'Dearest Lu', 'with dazzling success'.[2] Rommel continually harassed his men, flying across the desert in his Storch reconnaissance aircraft, even dropping notes to the troops, urging them on. The problem of maintaining supplies he left to his staff officers.

On 8 March the Australians had begun reorganising the forces at Tobruk with Major General Leslie Morshead's 9 Australian Division relieving 6 Australian Division. Morshead's first step was to trim down the garrison to 23,000 fighting men; the others were shipped out. Of this total, about 15,000 were Australian, 500 Indian and the rest

British, including tank crews, field and anti-tank gunners and machine gunners.

O'Connor's command of 13 Corps ended with the conclusion of *Compass.* His replacement was General Philip Neame VC, but he had no desert experience and was soon out of his depth against Rommel. Wavell agreed that O'Connor should go back to the desert to help Neame but his visit achieved little and ended in disaster. On 7 April the two generals were in a car heading toward Derna when they lost their way at night, ran into a detachment of German motorcyclists and were captured. For the British the loss of the skilled and battle-hardened O'Connor was a great blow.

By 9 April Rommel's counter-attack was approaching Tobruk. The Australians had had little time to prepare strong defensive positions and many of the men were inexperienced and short of equipment. Morshead, however, was determined. 'There'll be no Dunkirk here,' he told his assembled commanders. 'If we should have to get out, we shall fight our way out. There is to be no surrender and no retreat.'

And 9 Division was determined that it 'couldn't let it be said that the 9th had lost what the 6th had won'.[3]

The Australians worked quickly to build up the town's defences but these were still incomplete when the Germans started their attacks on 11 April, Good Friday. The major attack came on Easter Sunday. Wavell sent Morshead a message, saying that 'defence Egypt now depends largely on your holding enemy on your front'.[4] But by the following day the garrison troops and armour had repulsed the Germans and the battle was over. The Germans found that the defences of Tobruk 'stretched much farther in all directions' than they had thought, and 'the tanks were brought to a standstill in front of an anti-tank ditch'.[5]

A few days later Rommel called off the attacks until further troops arrived, realising that they would not succeed with the men they had, 'largely because of the poor state of training and the useless equipment of the Italian troops'.[6] By the time the Easter Battle was over the Germans had lost 12 aircraft and 17 tanks; in addition 110 men had been killed and 254 taken prisoner. The garrison's losses were relatively light: 20 killed, 60 wounded and 12 missing. Two tanks and two aircraft were also lost.

After this setback more German troops moved up to the perimeter. To ease the pressure on the Tobruk garrison, the British increased their activities around the frontier area, near Capuzzo and Bardia. Rommel then moved some of his forces from the Tobruk area to consolidate the border defences before resuming his attack on the town. He also increased his artillery and tank numbers while Italian troops maintained pressure on Tobruk. Morshead, anticipating more attacks, moved to strengthen the defensive positions even further while the RAF, though very short of fighter aircraft, did its best to disrupt the German preparations. The disastrous Greek campaign had severely depleted the strength of the British forces. With twice the number of tanks and aircraft that he had available earlier in April, plus three Italian divisions, Rommel could attack in force.

On 30 April the next enemy offensive, the Battle of the Salient, was launched in the western sector. However the garrison forces saw off the attack and the Germans made only a small gain, just inside the western perimeter, at a cost of 2000 casualties. This was such a significant defeat that Rommel was ordered not to attack Tobruk again and to hold his present frontier positions. It was a major boost for British morale.

By May the German and Italian armies had surged eastwards to Sollum, the westernmost town in Egypt. Virtually all the ground won by O'Connor had been lost again. Taking Tobruk, the only ground through to Sollum not held by the Germans and Italians, became Rommel's major objective as his supply lines were under great strain. The use of the port would make it easier for him to attack further into Egypt, something of which Wavell was acutely aware.

At the same time Churchill placed great importance on relieving Tobruk and urged Wavell to take the offensive. When Wavell responded that there were too few troops, they were inadequately trained and underequipped, Churchill dispatched a convoy of tanks and Hurricane fighters, code-named Tiger, to Alexandria through the risky Mediterranean route. Churchill pressed Wavell to get his 'Tiger cubs' into action as soon as possible, which was not an easy task as the tanks required modification in order to operate effectively in desert conditions. Ultra decrypts had revealed that Rommel had been ordered not to attack, to allow his troops to recover from the recent actions, which convinced the British that this was a good time to attack. The analysis, however, was inadequate and did not disclose the superiority of the German weapons and tanks; nor did it indicate Rommel's intentions.

Wavell's campaign, code-named *Brevity*, began on 15 May with the objective of regaining the border area and, it was hoped, relieving Tobruk, but it did not succeed. The British forces were not strong enough and their tanks were too dispersed to be effective against a well-organised enemy defence. The only gains were Sollum, the Halfaya

Pass and some prisoners, but Halfaya was lost again shortly afterwards when the Germans counterattacked. Rommel then strengthened the defences around Halfaya Pass with 88-mm anti-aircraft guns deployed in an anti-tank role, and a large number of experienced German and Italian troops to deter further attacks. Maintaining supplies to these areas was difficult; most of them were still coming overland from Tripoli and Rommel pressed the Italians to build a road to bypass Tobruk to avoid having to cross the desert there.

At Churchill's urging, and despite Wavell's reservations about the deficiencies of the British tanks, on 15 June another offensive, *Battleaxe,* was launched. The British forces made a small advance into Libya, but suffered heavy losses, made worse because of the number of breakdowns and casualties. On 17 June a concerned Wavell intervened and called off the operation; the British withdrew to Sidi Barrani. British casualties totalled about 1000, and they lost about 90 of the 190 tanks they had started with. The German casualties were similar but their tank losses were fewer: 12 Panzers lost and others damaged (and later recovered).

The battle highlighted the inadequacies of the British command, especially the use of armour against the experienced German troops, the concentration of the enemy tanks and the anti-tank guns. Rommel believed Wavell's planning for the offensive 'had been excellent', but 'the slow speed of the bulk of his armour was his soft spot'.[7] Churchill was upset with the outcome, and even more so when Wavell reported to London that 'no offensive in the Western Desert would be possible for at least three months'.[8]

Wavell was now worn out by Churchill's constant demands and his wish for aggression without appreciating the difficulties involved. He was replaced as Commander-in-Chief of the Middle East Forces by General Sir Claude Auchinleck. The New Zealanders regretted Wavell's removal, and when he wrote expressing his thanks to the troops he referred to their setbacks in Crete: 'you have been outmatched in numbers and equipment, never in fighting qualities or endurance.'[9]

Auchinleck arrived in Cairo on 30 June 1941 from his previous post of Commander-in-Chief India. A resolute character, he was primarily a soldier and not a diplomat, and it was inevitable that he would have a challenging time meeting Churchill's demands. Churchill was also coming under pressure from the United States, concerned that equipment and arms that would help rebuild its own forces were being diverted to the Middle East. They were also sceptical about Britain's strategy of liberating Europe through the Middle East. And if Germany succeeded with its Russian invasion, the next target would be a full attack on the Middle East, with converging moves through Turkey and Libya.

Churchill immediately urged Auchinleck to resume the offensive while Germany was preoccupied attacking Russia. Auchinleck, however, considered that several matters needed to be addressed first, including establishing a firm base in the region (especially in Syria, Iraq and Malta) and bringing in further reinforcements. In July Auchinleck travelled to London, where he outlined at length the preparations required before the campaign, now called *Crusader,* could start. A lot of reorganisation was needed after the scattered campaigns that had been fought in the region. The two men regarded the operation differently: Churchill saw it as opening a path right through North Africa, whereas Auchinleck saw it as achieving greater security in North Africa by gaining control of air bases in Cyrenaica. Eventually Churchill reluctantly agreed to a start date of 1 November, though this was later delayed by two weeks.

By the end of October 300 British Cruiser tanks, 300 American Stuart light tanks, 170 I-tanks, 34,000 lorries, 600 field guns, 80 heavy and 160 light anti-aircraft guns, 200 anti-tank guns and 900 mortars arrived. Alan Moorehead, foreign correspondent for London's *Daily Express,* travelled to Western Egypt to observe the build-up. West of El Daba his vehicle 'got into a traffic jam that went on and on for miles; tanks, heavy lorries and twenty-five pounder guns, staff cars, transporters, and signal wagons, anti-tank guns and anti-aircraft guns, travelling workshops, water wagons, ammunition trucks and still more tanks.' Together with the 'new aircraft, new tent cities, new dumps of petrol', he was impressed that the 'little piratical force Wavell had sent to Benghazi had become a great army'.[10]

After pressure from the Australian government, and on Auchinleck from General Sir Thomas Blamey, General Officer Commanding, Australian Imperial Force, between 19 August and 25 October most Australian troops in Tobruk were relieved and shipped out; 2/13 Battalion remained. The men of the battalion had been waiting at the quayside at Tobruk on 25 October when news came that their move had been cancelled. One of the relieving ships, the minelayer *Latona,* had been sunk when approaching Tobruk. Replacing the Australians was the British 70 Infantry Division, comprising 32 Army Tank Brigade, 14, 16 and 23 Infantry Brigades, 1 Polish Carpathian Brigade and some divisional artillery and machine guns. Major General Ronald M. Scobie was appointed General Officer Commanding, 70 Division and Commander of the Tobruk fortress.

One of the newly arriving men was Gunner J.A. ('Alf') Blacklin, with x/432 Battery, 149 Anti-Tank Regiment, Royal Horse Artillery. He wrote to a woman friend in England that he was now one of the 'heroic garrison of Tobruk', although initially he and his companions spent most of their time 'manning the perimeter'. The Italians had initially made 'a fine job' of the defences, which with Australian and British improvements were now 'well-nigh impregnable; concrete trenches and emplacements, deep wire defences, mines and 200 yards in front of this a wide anti-tank ditch. We could walk about in the open and sun ourselves, and except for occasional machine-gunning and shelling everything was splendid.'

The garrison, Blacklin wrote, sent nightly patrols into no-man's-land: 'on one occasion I did a fighting patrol with the Aussies – not that I wanted to, I wanted to do a recce one. Fortunately for me nothing serious happened on it, and I felt rather good with a Bren tucked under my arm!' The patrol, 'a dozen of us armed with tommy guns, Bren and anti-tank bombs ... got a few bursts of MG fire, some unpleasantly close and sizzling over our heads or plopping in the ground amongst us', but it was a quiet evening. They were looking for working parties 'but Itie spent that night in bed!'. Also, as Blacklin explained, 'Tobruk used to get bombed at night pretty regularly and the area dive-bombed occasionally during the days. I expect your idea of Tobruk was like mine, a little place getting plastered, but it is nothing of the sort. The average distance of the perimeter from the garrison is about nine or ten miles [14.5 or 16km] so you can see it's a big place.'[11]

During July and August the Allies continued with some minor actions in the border area. Rommel, though, was impatient to take the offensive, and with the Russian campaign initially going well, he was asked to submit a plan to attack Tobruk and subsequently invade Egypt. Further reinforcements arrived and an infantry division, which later became famous as 90 Light Division, was formed. Rommel also improved the border defences so that there would be protection towards the rear when the time came to move on Tobruk.

Rommel had established his Panzergruppe Afrika Headquarters at Gambut, between Tobruk and Bardia. Through the convoluted structure of the Axis forces, the German and Italian forces were led by General Ettore Bastico. Rommel was in command of the German forces, Panzergruppe Afrika, and reporting to him was the commander of the DAK, Lieutenant General Ludwig Crüwell. The DAK comprised the two Panzer divisions, 15 under Major General Walter Neumann-Silkow, and 21, previously 5 Light Division, under Major General Johann von Ravenstein, plus 90 Light Division, under Major General Max Sümmermann, and the Italian Savona Division. Fifteen and 21 Panzer Divisions both had two tank battalions and three infantry battalions. Von Ravenstein was Rommel's second in command. Heinz Schmidt, Rommel's aide de camp, observed that the two men were quite different: 'von Ravenstein the lover of beauty, the gentle, the human, the considerate, for whom life contained poetry; and Rommel, supremely practical, hard, indifferent to the personal problems of others, concerned with personalities only in so far as they affected his military aims, for whom life was plain prose.'[12]

Also under Rommel's command was the Italian 21 Army Corps, commanded by General Enea Navarini. Thus, although subject to Bastico's overall command, Rommel now commanded all the Axis forces in eastern Cyrenaica, except for the Italian Armoured Corps, under General Gastone Gambara, which comprised the 132 Ariete Armoured Division and the 101 Trieste Motorised Division.

Rommel's forces covered both Tobruk and the border area. Fifteen Panzer was based on the coast, about midway between Tobruk and Bardia, and 21 Panzer was just west of Bardia. Three divisions of Navarini's Italian forces – Bologna, Pavia and Brescia, later joined by Trento – surrounded Tobruk, and another division, Savona, was near the border. Because the Axis forces were very vulnerable to simultaneous British attacks from Egypt and Tobruk, Rommel considered capturing Tobruk vital.

His planning, however, was complicated by severe supply difficulties. During the second half of 1941 the British used Ultra information very effectively to target attacks on enemy shipping. To camouflage the source of the information, they used reconnaissance aircraft, which appeared to be making the initial sighting of the convoys. Shipping losses in the Mediterranean were high: between July and November 48 ships carrying a total of 200,000 tons of supplies were sunk. Rommel considered the attack on Tobruk should occur before the supply situation became even worse and eventually the German High Command gave approval for a November attack. Meanwhile, along the coast between Tobruk and the frontier, 15 and 21 Panzer worked intensively, particularly on the co-operation between tanks, anti-tank guns and artillery.

As a culmination of this training, in mid-September Rommel mounted a limited operation, code-named *Sommernachtstraum* (Midsummer Night's Dream) to attack a British dump south of Sollum. Rommel had received reports of British activity in the frontier area; he wanted to know the scale of this and, if necessary, to disrupt it. Ravenstein's 21 Panzer attacked but ran into difficulties. The supply dump that was their objective did not actually exist and the British forces merely withdrew behind a screen of armoured cars until the pursuing tanks ran short of fuel. The German forces retired back westwards, regaining their lines with difficulty. Rommel himself nearly struck trouble when his command vehicle punctured a tyre.

He was misled by the outcome of the raid as it found no signs of preparation for a British attack and some captured papers gave no indication of any forthcoming offensive. For the British, though, it was a stroke of good fortune. Rommel's tanks had actually reached the area where the main Allied supply dump was due to be established in the next few weeks. The results of the raid convinced Rommel that the British were not ready for any offensive and that there was no impediment to his assault on Tobruk, which was set for the latter part of November. By coincidence, then, both sides were simultaneously planning attacks within just a few days of each other.

CHAPTER 3

The Plan for Crusader

Following its limited role in Libya, the New Zealand Division regrouped in Egypt briefly before sailing to Greece in the middle of March 1941. The German invasion began in early April, and the small Allied force was quickly in difficulty. Outnumbered, outgunned and with virtually no air cover, the New Zealanders were forced to withdraw, before being evacuated towards the end of the month, some to Crete and some directly to Egypt. As Prime Minister Peter Fraser found when he inspected the veterans of the Greek campaign in Helwan on 18 May, their morale seemed high; the men felt that, despite their tough times, they had acquitted themselves well, and were 'convinced of superiority man for man over the Germans given equal weapons and air support'.[1]

In Crete, all the Allied troops, including the 7700 New Zealanders, were under the overall command of General Freyberg. Unfortunately the New Zealanders had been forced to abandon and destroy most of their heavy equipment and weapons when they were evacuated from Greece so that, on the island, they were reduced to digging defensive positions with their steel helmets, and had only the personal weapons they were carrying. The Germans launched an airborne invasion on 20 May and just 12 days later the Allied force had been overwhelmed and the men who were not evacuated were taken prisoner.

For the New Zealanders Greece and Crete had been little short of a disaster. Much of the initial work in establishing the division was eliminated and the further repercussions were serious. Most significant was the loss of men: a preliminary estimate in July indicated that the casualties numbered 5816, about a third of the 16,700 men who sailed to Greece. The immediate priority was to absorb the fresh but largely untrained troops arriving from New

Zealand. This could not fully replace the loss of experienced men from the first three echelons but by 10 July Freyberg was able to advise the government that the division was almost up to strength again. It also had to be re-equipped with guns, vehicles and even small arms.

Also to be faced was a review of the division's role and Freyberg's leadership. There was considerable disquiet back in New Zealand that twice in the preceding months there had been the distinct possibility of the total loss of the division. Fraser felt the government had not been properly informed of the risks before the campaign, especially the lack of air support, a factor that would be critical for the future. The prime minister also sought views about Freyberg's performance, partly as a result of criticisms of the general's method of command raised by an exhausted Brigadier James (Jim) Hargest, newly returned from Crete. (Hargest later revised his opinion, however, and on 30 October informed Fraser that, after 'several conferences', his relationship with Freyberg had been restored: 'I was forthright in my remarks and he was splendid about it all – but the results have been good beyond my strongest hopes.')[2] Fraser was reassured, in August, by opinions from Wavell and Auchinleck. The former wrote that Freyberg had 'produced one of the best trained and disciplined and fittest divisions I have ever seen and he must be given full credit for their exploits in Greece and Crete'. Auchinleck agreed: 'it would be a great mistake to move Freyberg from the Command of the New Zealand Division.'[3] Freyberg had received a charter of authority from the government setting out his powers including, in an emergency, ability to make decisions about the employment of the division. Fraser met him early in June to clarify the government's requirements and Freyberg agreed to keep Wellington fully informed.

While the division was being replenished, retraining also began, including work on combined army and navy operations on the shore of the Bitter Lake. Although planning for *Crusader* was well under way, Fraser's first warning about the campaign came only on 13 September. Freyberg had sent a telegram to the Minister of Defence, Frederick Jones, advising that the division was 'trained and up to war strength and is now moving in stages to the Western Desert'. He would head to the desert the following day and everyone was 'in excellent spirits and good health'.[4] He was, though, anxious about the division's next action. As he later explained, 'what we wanted most was a success, but it was most important that we were not employed upon another costly failure.'[5]

Freyberg's telegram caused some alarm back in Wellington. On 16 September Fraser replied by telegram with a list of questions about the campaign, 'in view of the experience in Greece and particularly in Crete'. He asked Freyberg to send, 'at once', information about the division's intended role, its state of readiness and the adequacy of the likely armoured and air support. 'This information is required by the Government to satisfy themselves' and 'to assure the people of New Zealand that our troops have not been committed to battle without every possible precaution and preparation to meet every calculable emergency being taken'.[6] This was followed later by some further questions.

Freyberg drafted replies, which he passed on to Auchinleck, who expressed his appreciation and assured him of his wish to help the New Zealand general keep the government happy. On 19 September Freyberg responded to the prime minister with a rather vague telegram, answering the questions but not providing much specific information: 'We are at present engaged in intensive desert training for defensive or offensive operations' but 'our role has not yet been disclosed.' He did say that the division was 'probably the best-equipped unit in the Middle East' and provided a list of the equipment deficiencies, 'which will shortly be supplied'. He pointed out significant improvement in the position regarding armoured and air support and that the 'attitude to air co-operation between the Royal Air Force and the Army has completely changed'. He concluded by stressing, 'I don't think there is any division in the Middle East superior to ours.'[7]

During July and August, while Auchinleck was dealing with Churchill's demands, planning for *Crusader* continued. The primary objective of the campaign was to drive the Germans and Italians out of Cyrenaica, and ultimately out of North Africa. The relief of Tobruk, though desirable, was not the major focus. At midnight on 26–27 September 1941 the Western Desert Force was renamed the Eighth Army, led by Lieutenant General Sir Alan Cunningham. Cunningham's 'rapid and vigorous command' in East Africa had impressed Auchinleck, who wanted to see a change from the prevailing approach of 'clinging to the coastal strip, and to move freely and more widely against the enemy's flank and communications'.[8]

But Cunningham had no background in desert warfare and had never commanded armour, and there were very few men in the command structure with relevant experience. There was a lot to do in the short time before the campaign was due to start in November: some divisions were still to arrive, most of the troops were untrained and there were mechanical defects in some of the tanks. Twenty-two Armoured Brigade, which had been expected to arrive by 20 September, did not disembark until 14 October.

Divisional and corps commanders and corps and army staff officers were briefed on the *Crusader* plan at Army Headquarters on 6 October. The Eighth Army would comprise a newly formed Armoured Corps (30) and an Infantry Corps (13). The former would cross the border into Libya, heading north-west and bypassing the defences south of Sollum to 'seek out and destroy' the enemy armour to the south-east of Tobruk.[9] This move, it was thought, would force the enemy out from the prepared defences and minefields around Sidi Omar and Capuzzo. Thirty Corps would take the Sidi Rezegh ridge, then link up with the Tobruk garrison, which would break out of the town perimeter to meet them at Ed Duda, another key ridge. Thirteen Corps would cross the border well south of the coast and then isolate the enemy troops in the border area by encircling them from the western side, to prevent them joining the battle for Tobruk. Following this, the corps would advance towards Tobruk. If the opening moves were successful both corps would move west to drive the Axis forces out of Cyrenaica. In addition a small Oasis Group would create a diversion deep in the south.

The corps structure was the subject of much debate. Unlike the German army, which had been practising tank warfare for some years, the British had no precedent for combining tanks, guns and infantry. Should there be a separate armoured corps and infantry corps, or should the forces be mixed? Although it was ultimately decided that there should be an armoured corps and an infantry corps, Cunningham himself had doubts about this and 'sometimes wondered if it were the right formation'.[10] The alternative, mixed groups, was the German system, where a Panzer division was 'a powerful and versatile organisation of tank crews, gunners, engineers and infantry all trained to work in close harmony'.[11]

Thirteen Corps, under the command of Lieutenant General Alfred Godwin-Austen, was the infantry corps, which comprised 2 New Zealand Division, 4 Indian Division and supported by I-tanks from 1 Army Tank Brigade. Lieutenant General Willoughby Norrie commanded 30 Corps, with 7 Armoured Division, 1 South African Division (with two infantry brigades) and 22 Guards Brigade. The Allied forces in Tobruk included 70 British Infantry Division, the Polish Carpathian Infantry Brigade and 32 Army Tank Brigade. The total estimated maximum strength of the Eighth Army was 118,000, compared with total enemy forces of 119,000: 65,000 German and 54,000 Italian. This opposition was formidable, particularly the German 15 and 21 Panzer Divisions, 90 Light Deutsche Afrika Division and the Italian Ariete Division. In a battle where experienced leadership would be essential, it was unfortunate that neither Cunningham nor Norrie had experience in desert or tank warfare, especially when their key protagonist was Rommel, with his recent successful experience in Europe.

Leading 30 Corps were the three brigades of 7 Armoured Division. Although they were fully equipped by 25 October, training was incomplete and there were still reliability problems with some of the tanks. The British had superiority in tank numbers (although actual numbers vary in different reports); in total 30 Corps had 477 tanks, not including I-tanks of various types. The principal models included 210 A15 Crusader cruisers (mainly 155 in 22 Brigade and 53 in 7 Brigade), 173 Stuarts (mainly in 4 Brigade) and 62 old A13 Cruisers in 7 Brigade. In addition 13 Corps had three cruisers and 132 I-tanks (Matildas and Valentines), and the Tobruk garrison 32 cruisers, 25 light tanks and 69 Matilda I-tanks. Originally Auchinleck estimated that three armoured divisions would be required for the conquest of Cyrenaica, but instead it was launched with 'one and a half armoured divisions and one brigade of infantry tanks'.[12]

The Germans had 244 tanks, mainly 139 MkIII and 35 MkIV Panzers, together with 70 light MkII Panzers, and the Ariete Italian Division had 146

M13/40 tanks, giving a total for the German and Italian armies of 390. Despite the superiority of numbers, however, some of the British tanks were either old models or not in good mechanical condition. Others, including 22 Armoured Brigade's new Crusaders, required modification to air and lubrication systems before being desert-ready, while the new Stuarts had a very limited range and needed frequent refuelling. In addition the British tanks were more lightly armed, with only a 2-pounder gun as the principal armament. The Germans had very efficient tank recovery and repair teams whereas Auchinleck was adamant that replacing damaged tanks relied on ample reserves close at hand. The Germans also had more effective antitank weapons. They had a 50mm anti-tank gun and had adapted the 88mm anti-aircraft gun for anti-tank purposes; this was used to great effect in *Battleaxe*. The British relied on a 2-pounder anti-tank gun, the same as its tank gun, coupled with the 25-pounder deployed as an anti-tank weapon. Significantly, the Germans were more experienced in co-ordinating armour, anti-tank guns and infantry, whereas few British officers had experience of handling armour in battle.

The plan proposed dispersing the Eighth Army widely, 'in a way that was daring, to say the least'.[13] After crossing the frontier the two corps would split and essentially be fighting separate battles. For the plan to succeed 30 Corps had to win the initial armoured battle. This was a rather bold assumption, considering the German armour's successful record, and especially since the British would use only two armoured brigades. Brigadier Alec Gatehouse's 4 Armoured Brigade would be deployed guarding the left flank of the infantry corps. The conference minutes record that the two armoured brigades 'would be stronger than the two panzer divisions put together and each armoured brigade would be "slightly stronger" than a panzer division, the basis of the comparison evidently being a mere counting of tanks'.[14]

The initial objective for the New Zealand Division, together with 4 Indian

Division, was to cut off the strong enemy positions in Sollum, Halfaya and Bardia. It was also possible that the division could be sent westwards to help link up with the Tobruk garrison. Freyberg quickly identified this being quite probable, but he wanted it to be the whole division and not just one or two brigades. He attended the 6 October briefing at Army Headquarters where he sat quietly and 'listened in cynically'.[15] What he heard left him with two major concerns: first, who had control over the armour that could protect the New Zealand Division's left (west) flank, and second, the frequent mention of fighting with brigades rather than divisions.

The main point of contention about the armoured support focused on the role of 4 Armoured Brigade, which initially was to be a 'Centre Force' guarding the left flank of 13 Corps while maintaining contact with the right flank of 30 Corps. When Freyberg raised his worries about the protection of his left flank, Cunningham pointed out that 4 Armoured Brigade would be in support, but that 'meant nothing' to Freyberg, as he made clear: 'they would be ordered away in a crisis and under the circumstances ... unless we had tanks under our immediate command we should not be moved across the wire until the armoured battle had commenced. In this I was quite precise. I was not popular.'[16]

Norrie had little input into the plan, which had largely been finalised by the time he was appointed after the 6 October conference. He later wrote that he 'never liked the 8th Army plan and said so both at the preliminary conferences and in writing'. He was not convinced about disputes over control of the armour, and also thought that 30 Corps should have been 'directed to a locality which would force the enemy to give battle'.[17] Norrie considered that the positioning of 30 Corps on 13 Corps' left flank was sufficient protection in itself. Spreading the two corps over a wide area made the infantry very vulnerable unless the initial armoured battle was successful, as protecting the flanks would be too difficult. But separating one armoured brigade off to guard the infantry created a risk that the remaining brigades would not be strong enough to win that battle. Freyberg was also unconvinced about this aspect of the plan and remained very concerned about the vulnerability of his infantry to a full-scale tank attack.

Norrie observed, too, that the plan proposed 30 Corps advance initially to Gabr Saleh, in the desert to the south-east of Tobruk, to await a reaction from the Germans. The plan seemed to overlook the fact that some important ground should be captured and held, but there was no strategic importance in Gabr Saleh and Norrie's proposal was to drive straight for Tobruk. If Rommel did not react it would be necessary to go looking for him, with the risk of further dispersing the British armour and handing Rommel the initiative. Cunningham, who thought the enemy tanks might instead exploit the large gap between the two corps and attack the infantry of 13 Corps, especially since Rommel had split his forces between surrounding Tobruk and protecting the frontier, overruled Norrie's proposal. He thought that by the first evening the German commander's 'intentions would be known, and a decision could be taken'.[18] Norrie, however, would not concede the point, and eventually his reasoning made Cunningham sufficiently concerned that he decided to travel with Norrie to Gabr Saleh in order to be right on the spot when deciding how to proceed.

Another matter for Cunningham to address was Major General George Brink's 1 South African Division. Brink was anxious that it had not received its transport allocation and had spent too much time building defences around Mersa Matruh at the expense of absorbing reinforcements and carrying out training. Supported by Norrie, Brink raised his concerns with Cunningham several times but as the start date loomed he was faced with an ultimatum: either start on the planned date or change places with the experienced 4 Indian Division. Brink ultimately acquiesced, although he 'was not happy about the state of training of my Division'.[19] Cunningham deferred the start date by three days, to 18 November, allowing for further training but adding to Churchill's frustrations.

It was not until 15 November that Cunningham's army was ready, even if, on the eve of the battle, there was still unease about aspects of the plan. For Norrie the upshot was that 7 Armoured Division would attack, with the experienced 7 Brigade (but with a high proportion of the older cruiser tanks) and Support Group leading, towards the strategically unimportant Gabr Saleh, in the hope that Rommel would join the battle there. To the left would be the inexperienced 22 Brigade, recently arrived as the first Brigade of 1 Armoured Division, with newly modified Crusaders. Four Brigade, with their new Stuarts (named 'Honeys' by their crews) would be towards the right rear, but with limited effective range and restricted by the requirement to guard the left flank of 13 Corps. And guarding their southern flank would be 1 South African Division, under strength and with minimal training in mobile warfare. There were enough compromises in all of that for Cunningham and Norrie, and

Freyberg, to be justified in their anxieties.

While reading the plans Freyberg noted 'frequent mention of brigades instead of divisions and the detailed allotment of tasks raised suspicions that Eighth Army was too ready to fight with detached brigade groups, which would reduce the potential of the force as a whole and make inefficient use of the field artillery'.[20] He considered that the enemy's strength around Tobruk was being underrated and that success would require a greater concentration of infantry than attacking by brigades. He told Cunningham that he 'could not see how 30 Corps, with only the 7 Armoured Division and two South African Brigades plus the 22 Guards Brigade, could fight their way through the whole Afrika Korps and Italian Army to relieve Tobruk'.[21] If Cunningham attacked Tobruk, 'which was surrounded by four Italian Divisions, and one German Division, with two South African Brigades he would fail, and it seemed to me that the New Zealand Division would then be ordered to march on Tobruk.' The plan, however, was not changed, though Freyberg told Cunningham that he had made plans to march on Tobruk, and that all his officers 'had been studying the problem'. He doubted that he 'made any impression on General Cunningham. He thought I was over-anxious and I thought him over-confident.'[22]

On 9 October Freyberg wrote a long letter to Defence Minister Frederick Jones, starting another exchange with Wellington. He outlined his views on the overall situation, and the earlier unsuccessful campaigns, and gave his thoughts on the forthcoming offensive. As *Battleaxe* had shown, with the long distances it was difficult to make an 'approach march by night and carry out a dawn attack', especially in the desert with little cover. The Allies had 'employed inferior forces, especially armoured fighting vehicles and aircraft, with little chance of achieving surprise', and accordingly 'we suffered a decided reverse and lost a large number of tanks'. Although, for *Crusader,* the British had more tanks, the enemy had 'decided superiority in numbers in the air', and had reinforced their Libyan front. He summed up by saying that although the campaign was 'difficult' there was 'a good chance of success'. The battle is 'in the first place a battle of machines and exploitation by lorry-borne fighting troops of all arms'. He was confident, too, that the men of the New Zealand Division were the best equipped and trained troops in the Middle East, and in 'excellent physical and mental condition'.[23]

Fraser did not reply until 6 November, noting that the War Cabinet 'appreciated the timely and most useful views'.[24] Concerned, however, about the enemy's apparent air superiority, he wrote directly to Churchill on 13 October, expressing his apprehension 'lest our troops should again, and for the third time, be committed to battle without adequate air support', or without 'the necessary means of defence and offence' in tanks and armoured fighting vehicles (AFVs).[25]

Drawing on an exhaustive study of the respective air forces, which concluded that the British would have 528 serviceable aircraft, compared with the enemy's 385, although both sides had other reserves, Churchill responded on 24 October with a detailed letter intended to allay Fraser's anxieties. He provided numbers of British and Axis aircraft, and was certain 'that we shall have good air superiority unless the situation alters markedly'. And, he wrote, 'General Auchinleck assures me that the New Zealand Division will have all proper protection'. Churchill noted, too, the British superiority in tank numbers: 'much has been risked in delay in order to gather sufficient armoured forces.' He concluded, 'the armoured battle is what matters and we hope to force the enemy to it. The destruction of his armoured force would bring ruin to the rest.'[26]

Freyberg briefed his senior officers on 17 October that the object of the operation was the capture of Cyrenaica but that the relief of Tobruk was incidental. He reported that tank strength was five to four in favour of the British (though he conceded that the German tanks could be better) and that the enemy had air superiority of three to two. Despite his reservations, just after the conference Freyberg told

Brigadier Lindsay Inglis 'at last we're going into a campaign with a good plan'. Inglis was less convinced, and when Freyberg asked why he replied that 'the dispersion of forces it involved made it look as though we though we were fighting half-armed savages or Italians – not Germans'.[27] The meeting also made some decisions about future training that were to prove vitally important, particularly night marching, bayonet attacks, attacking under artillery and planning for the movement of columns with protection from attack.

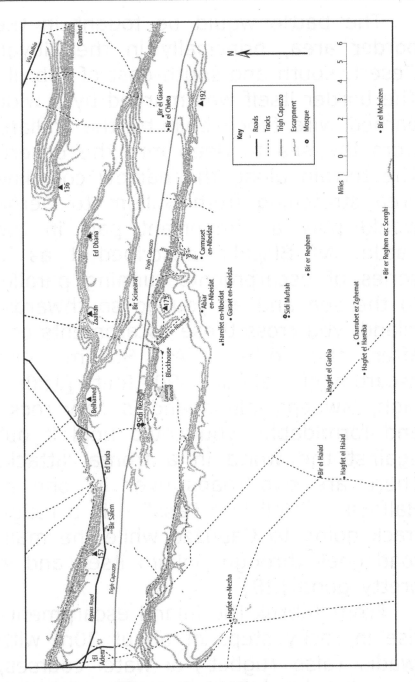

The main battle area

The battle would be fought in the border area, principally in the Libyan Desert, south and south-east of Tobruk. The border itself was marked by a wide barbed wire fence built by the Italians from the sea to deep into the desert. The terrain along the narrow coastline area stretching from Sollum to Derna would play an important part in the battle. Alf Blacklin described it as 'a series of escarpments running parallel to the sea and as you go southwards, inland, you cross these escarpments one after the other'. At Sollum, the escarpment, about 600 feet [180m] high, 'sweeps inland and is very rocky and formidable, you could hold it out against the world in a frontal attack. There are two roads over it; one at Halfaya – "Hell Fire Pass" – is a rough track going to Capuzzo while the main road goes through Sollum itself and is pretty good.'[28]

From Tobruk the inland escarpments rise in rocky steps of about 30m with 'wadis' (also 'rugbet') or water courses, normally dry but occasionally flooded, cut into the faces. The division's engineers built a plaster relief model of the battle area and when Freyberg studied it, he saw that a place called Sidi Rezegh, just a mark on the map 20 miles (32km) south-east of Tobruk would be an important strategic point.

Near Sidi Rezegh there is a series of three escarpments. The most northerly is Belhamed, about 150m above sea level, and 4 miles (6.5km) west of Belhamed on this northern escarpment is the gentle rise of Ed Duda. From here a shallow valley drops gradually southwards some 3 miles (5km) to the second, Sidi Rezegh, escarpment. This is named after a small building, called the mosque, but actually the tomb of a saint and his son – 'sidi' means saint or holy man – on the edge of the 80-foot (25m) escarpment. Finally, about 3 miles (5km) to the south of Sidi Rezegh is the third, southern, escarpment.

The escarpments, strategically vital in such a flat landscape, provided elevation for surveillance and artillery over a wide area, and the wadis gave cover and concealment. Corporal Robert Loughnan of the Divisional Cavalry described the view from the edge of the northern escarpment where, 'from the bottom of the escarpment at our feet the flat and featureless desert with its dull blue-green coat of straggly camelthorn stretched out about four or five miles [6.5–8km] to the coast'. Behind them 'the land suddenly rose in another escarpment, a harsh and rocky one, which provided our skyline'. This escarpment 'was crowned with a little mud-coloured square building with a white dome on top and a shell hole through this; the mosque of Sidi Rezegh'. The escarpments were different heights; the northern one, where they were, 'was not so steep or quite as high as the other one behind us'. Westwards from them the escarpment rose a little towards the rocky knob of Belhamed.[29]

Although the stony terrain meant that vehicles were not so dependent on roads, there were a few strategically important desert tracks or 'trigh', including the Trigh Capuzzo, which ran in an east–west direction south of Tobruk. The Via Balbia, a main road, ran along the coast and during 1941 the Italians built the Tobruk Bypass

Road, which started west of Tobruk, then circled to the south and came back onto the coastal road. At Sidi Rezegh the Trigh Capuzzo and the Bypass Road, both major enemy supply routes, passed close together, so that whoever held Sidi Rezegh, with its slight elevation, controlled the approaches to Tobruk. Freyberg predicted that this area would see the heaviest fighting of the campaign and much of his planning was based on gaining control of it.

South-east from Sidi Rezegh was a rough airfield, and a little further to the east was the only other building on the escarpment, the blockhouse, a resting place for Arab travellers. A track went from the Trigh Capuzzo, past the mosque and towards the airfield. The desert surface was uneven, generally quite rocky with a thin covering of sand, but occasionally solid rock or soft sand, making for challenging driving and creating difficulties for the men digging in. There were a few small rises. Sometimes the maps showed features that appeared to be quite commanding but were really very minor: a 'hill' could be just 1 or 2m high. Some natural features, especially dried-up watercourses and wells ('bir'), as well as some tombs ('gabr') were important because, as Blacklin explained, 'when you get inland there are very few landmarks'.[30]

The desert provided nothing, and bringing in supplies, fuel, ammunition, food and especially water was a major logistical exercise. During the preparatory period the Allies kept the minimum number of troops in the forward area so that supplies could be built up. At one time the vast operation to prepare supply dumps was consuming 180,000 gallons (800,0001) of petrol a day, and the poor quality of the petrol containers meant that 'the loss of petrol between base and consumer came to as much as 30%'.[31] The British supply lines were shorter, greatly assisted by a railhead at Mersa Matruh, 100 miles (160km) east in Egypt, which was extended for a further 93 miles (150km) by November. As the start date of the campaign drew closer, the RAF and South African Air Force (SAAF) stepped up their bombing raids on enemy supply areas and airfields.

Before *Crusader* there was some intelligence from Ultra decrypts, although the information was incomplete. From this source the British learnt of the arrival of 90 Light Division, problems with supplies (including 88mm ammunition), details and locations of enemy formations and tank numbers. As the campaign progressed, although useful information continued to arrive via Ultra, and wireless intercepts, delays in conveying the information to the desert sometimes meant that it could not be used effectively or forces redeployed quickly enough to take advantage of it.

The Allies also intercepted a German intelligence agent operating in Palestine. By maintaining the flow of information, and combining easily verified information with some messages designed to deceive, they were able to create a perception that the British were more interested in the east, an impression reinforced when Auchinleck took a trip to the Ninth Army in Palestine. This news found its way to Rommel, who felt confident that he could continue with his plans to attack Tobruk without the risk of British action.

The Germans, too, had their sources of information, including listening in on operational radio traffic, overseen by Captain Alfred Seebohm. After the enemy obtained a copy of the American 'Black Code', they were able to decipher the extensive reports from British briefings prepared by the American military attaché in Cairo, Colonel Bonner Fellers, and transmitted to Washington. The combined information from Seebohm and Fellers kept Rommel well informed about the Allied forces and their plans.

Rommel was in the final stages of his own planning to attack Tobruk, which was to take place between 15 and 20 November (although the date was later set at 21 November). He was so focused on this that he dismissed intelligence reports that British forces were preparing an offensive, a stance that brought him into conflict with his Italian commander, Bastico. Bad weather on the last few days before Rommel's attack was due to take place prevented any further observations, and in any event the focus by then was entirely on Tobruk.

CHAPTER 4

The Great Approach March

When they returned to Maadi in August 1941, the New Zealanders found it 'rife with rumours as to a move. The commonest of these was that we were bound for Baggush in the Western Desert again', because of the threat that Rommel's forces posed, and the need to relieve Tobruk.[1] In mid-September the division, now up to strength, returned to Baggush to join the Eighth Army and continue training. For a force still smarting after the setbacks in Greece and Crete it must have been very gratifying to see the build-up of equipment and camps as they travelled west. The men would spend six weeks at Baggush, training for the specialised nature of desert warfare; Freyberg insisted on a long period of preparation, to improve the troops' physical fitness, and training on mobility and movement at night.

Freyberg's training plans were disrupted, however, by several requests from Middle East Forces General Headquarters (GHQ) for New Zealand, Australian and South African units to undertake other tasks. For the New Zealanders this included using transport companies as general carriers, which interfered with the need to retain these for mobility training. The division accommodated some requests, including providing anti-aircraft gunners in the Suez Canal area. The New Zealanders were so proficient the British troops in Egypt, to which they were assigned, did not want to return them, but these diversions created conflict between Freyberg and the Middle East Forces GHQ. Australian General Blamey received similar requests but, as Freyberg reported to Fraser, he 'will not lend a single Australian. His policy has made him persona non grata. While we lent everything we were very popular. As soon as we asked for our units back they looked upon me as a Fifth Columnist.'[2]

After the New Zealanders were established at Baggush, training began.

It was quickly apparent that this was based around offensive action, especially attacking a heavily defended fortress protected by wire and mines. Freyberg's instructions for training included practising the movement of large formations, such as a brigade group, which could contain 1000 vehicles, across the desert. The 3-ton truck played an important part in Freyberg's intention to move quickly and achieve surprise where possible.

Fresh equipment was issued, new light tanks arrived for the Divisional Cavalry, Engineers and Signals received a variety of new equipment and new trucks came from the United States and Canada. Moves were carefully planned; they had learnt lessons from the air attacks in Greece – vehicles were widely spaced and slit trenches dug at any lengthy stops. They also trained at night advances, which helped to avoid air attacks and minimised casualties. Crete had shown that, provided there were no wire entanglements, the troops could successfully attack any enemy position at night with the bayonet – hence the need to be able to approach by truck and attack on foot in the dark. Drivers had to learn how to travel over rough ground with minimal lighting on their vehicles.

For further training the engineers built two dummy fortresses in the desert, and wired and mined the approaches to them. These forts, named Sidi Clif (after Lieutenant Colonel George Clifton) and Bir Stella (after the local beer), were constructed on terrain similar to that they would encounter. Starting with 6 Brigade on 9 October, each brigade then carried out a night approach march on these forts of up to 30 or 40 miles (48–65km), in vehicles without lights.

They attacked at first light, advancing under a barrage of artillery and smoke, and cleared a path through the minefields. Then 'tanks' (actually lorries), infantry and supporting units followed rapidly to consolidate and prepare for a counter-attack. The exercise was designed to closely simulate actual battle conditions, moving large groups of men and vehicles, and co-ordinating infantry, machine and anti-tank guns. Unfortunately, there was no training with actual tanks in support. The exercise also showed what speeds and fuel consumption could be realistically expected when moving a brigade across the desert under different conditions. As artillery man Martyn Uren recalled, 'the peak of our training in this form of tactical warfare was reached when the brigades could move 40 miles in a night across the desert.' It was tough going: 'no lights of any sort, and no smoking was allowed. Even silence was ordered, for the purpose of the show was to move by night in secrecy and attack a place at dawn.'[3]

During October and November Corps and Army Headquarters developed the final details of the plan; they digested intelligence reports and training continued, including exercises with air support. They made plans for providing supplies, and managing casualties. Freyberg and his brigadiers knew they were in for a very tough battle, hence their careful consideration of all aspects of the campaign plan. Cunningham and Godwin-Austen paid visits to the division, and both were pleased with what they saw.

On 9 November the New Zealand Division received its orders. On 18 November it would cross the border south of the Omar fortresses, a series of defended enemy strongpoints, and, led by the Divisional Cavalry, head north to cut off the enemy border forces. Four Brigade would move to the escarpment west of Bardia to cover movement between Bardia and Tobruk, and contain any enemy forces in the coastal area by blocking tracks towards the south. Five Brigade would advance to the Trigh Capuzzo and cut the east–west line of communication. Six Brigade would be in reserve, either to support the other brigades or to move quickly west towards Gambut and assist 30 Corps attacking towards Tobruk. Beyond these initial moves, the plans were uncertain, dependent on the outcome of the armoured encounter.

The three New Zealand brigades were in slightly different stages of readiness and experience. Four Brigade, under the command of Brigadier Inglis, included 18, 19 and 20 Battalions, and 2 Machine Gun Company. Inglis, a solicitor, had been awarded the Military

Cross for his part in leading his company in an attack during the 1916 Somme offensive. He later commanded a machine gun company and became 27 (Machine Gun) Battalion's first commanding officer when it was formed in 1939. Also in 4 Brigade, commanding 20 Battalion, was Inglis's old friend, Lieutenant Colonel Howard Kippenberger, who had a short period on the Somme in 1916, where he was wounded. He had commanded a brigade in Crete.

Brigadier James Hargest commanded 5 Brigade which, with four infantry battalions, was the largest, comprising 21, 22, 23 and 28 (Maori) Battalion, and 1 and 4 Machine Gun Companies. Hargest had been a farmer and the Member of Parliament for Awarua before the war. During service in the First World War, he had been wounded at Gallipoli; he later joined the Otago Infantry Regiment and was awarded the Military Cross, Distinguished Service Order and a number of other decorations. Hargest's appointment as brigadier had been controversial; initially he had been assessed as unfit for overseas service, but after the intervention of the prime minister in March 1940 he was given command of 5 Brigade. The brigade had suffered heavy losses in Crete, where it was responsible for defending Maleme airfield. In the view of defence historian John Crawford, Hargest was 'strangely inactive during the vital early stages of the battle for Crete and must bear a large measure of responsibility for the loss of Maleme airfield and thus, ultimately, for the loss of the island'.[4] There were many new faces in 5 Brigade, which had had less time for desert training than the other brigades.

Six Brigade was under the command of Brigadier Harold Barrowclough, with 24, 25 and 26 Battalions, and 3 Machine Gun Company. Barrowclough, another solicitor, had been a member of the New Zealand Rifle Brigade in 1916 when he was awarded the Military Cross and French Croix de Guerre for his bravery in action near Flers in 1916. He was later awarded a DSO and also Mentioned in Dispatches for actions in 1918. Because 6 Brigade had missed the action in Crete it did not require a large number of reinforcements, but the men had less battle experience.

In addition to these three brigadiers, also attending Freyberg's initial briefing of senior officers on 17 October were Brigadier Reginald Miles, Commander Royal Artillery (CRA), Lieutenant Colonel William Gentry, General Staff Officer 1 (GSO1), and Lieutenant Colonel D.T. Maxwell, Assistant Adjutant and Quartermaster General (AA & QMG).

As well as the infantry battalions and machine gun companies, each brigade included a field regiment (artillery), anti-tank battery, anti-aircraft battery, a company of engineers and a field ambulance unit; an effective brigade formation for movement and camps was carefully planned. To provide for rebuilding battalions if heavy casualties were suffered, 10 per cent of the men in the infantry battalions and Divisional Cavalry would be left out of battle (LOB). One of these men from 20 Battalion was Lieutenant Charles Upham, who had recently been awarded the Victoria Cross.

The men knew that action was imminent; they could see the heavy traffic as convoys of water tankers, trucks, tanks, transporters and other supplies rumbled west. Clem Paterson, a lance corporal in Wellington Company of 19 Battalion, remembered that 'rumours were flying about everywhere but when we got issues of emergency rations etc we knew it wouldn't be very long'.[5] Machine gunner Bill Andrew, about to return to Libya for the first time since January, noted in his diary the day of their departure: 'Left Baggush for Libya? A scrap on?'[6] The 28 (Maori) Battalion men were looking forward 'to seek battle on something like even terms with the enemy and with the very definite intention of taking utu for Greece and Crete'.[7]

The division's move to its assembly area was signalled as a 'divisional exercise', and for Uren these words were the giveaway, as their earlier exercises had been by brigade. 'We smiled knowingly at each other when this announcement was made, and prepared for battle.' They were ready for action: 'I doubt whether troops were ever better fitted, and better trained for what lay ahead. We were well acclimatised to desert conditions, and we were trained to a pitch of efficiency in the use of our weapons in the peculiar conditions of desert warfare.'[8]

On 11 November the division started to move out with Freyberg and New Zealand's high commissioner in London, William (Bill) Jordan, bidding farewell to 5 Brigade, the first to leave Baggush. The column followed the coastal road and the Matruh bypass, before heading down the Siwa Oasis Road, then westwards for 12 miles (20km) to the divisional assembly area in the desert at Bir Idwan. When travelling the vehicles were spaced 10 to the mile (1.6km) and travelled at 15 miles per hour (24kph).

The following day 4 Brigade departed, together with Divisional Headquarters Group. Kippenberger, who was leading 20 Battalion for 'the great approach march', later observed that 'until the end of the war it was the opinion of old hands that the morale of the New Zealand Division was at its peak in this campaign. Certainly in the Twentieth it was terrific; we felt like runners, tense for the pistol.'[9]

Six Brigade completed the assembly on 13 November. Freyberg also travelled that day, taking with him 'the bag I carried in Battle of Somme 25 years ago to the day'.[10] The Divisional Cavalry had already moved further west ahead of the division. The commander of 13 Corps was worried about the protection of the left flank after moving over the border, and the Divisional Cavalry had been sent to patrol the frontier south of the Trigh el-Abd to provide early warning of any Panzer activity before *Crusader* began.

By 14 November the whole New Zealand Division, almost 20,000 men, was assembled in a huge laager area in the desert. The trucks, staff cars, guns, light tanks, Bren carriers and ambulances covered an area about 12 by 8 miles (20 by 13km), with approximately 2800 vehicles spaced 200 yards (180m) apart, as a precaution against air attacks (although these did not eventuate). While the troops rested, vehicles were refuelled and repaired where necessary, and provisions were distributed. After all the training over the previous months spirits were high.

All the officers down to company commander level attended a conference where Freyberg briefed them on the campaign. 'No battle is easy', he said. 'This one promises to be a very tough one.'[11] The division's main task was to cut off the enemy border garrisons of Bardia, Sollum, Sidi Omar and Halfaya. They would cover an area on a 30-mile (48km) arc from Sidi Azeiz to cut off movement from the frontier to Bardia, and north-west of Bardia, including cutting the Bardia/Capuzzo water pipeline.

Although he was sure that determined troops would defeat the Germans, Freyberg outlined the enemy's strengths and weaknesses. He knew they would pick their ground well and understood the effectiveness of their armour, but the Italians could be weak links. The Tobruk garrison would have an important role – they might be 'the deciding factor'. They would need to take precautions against the likelihood of attacks from both the air and tanks. He concluded by warning that 'we are in for a tough time'; the 'battle has to be fought out to a finish, in the end ruthlessly. Spirit of British Bulldog wins. You must prepare everybody for it both mentally as well as physically.'[12] Churchill also sent a message to the men of the Middle East Forces (MEF):

For the first time British and Empire troops will meet the Germans with ample equipment in modern weapons of all kinds. The battle itself will affect the whole course of the war. Now is the time to strike the hardest blow yet struck for final victory, home and freedom. The Desert Army may add a page to history which will rank with Blenheim and with Waterloo. The eyes of all nations are upon you. All our hearts are with you.[13]

It was unfortunate, but perhaps not surprising, that his commander, General Auchinleck, was less sanguine about their prospects. Well aware of both the calibre of Rommel and the desert war inexperience of Cunningham, he attempted to dispel any myths about Rommel's invincibility. Although 'not nervous about *Crusader'*, he was aware of the significance of the opening phase;

'how everything hangs on the tactical issue of one day's fighting, and on one man's tactical ability on that one day. It is something quite different to battles as we knew them. All these months of labour and thought can be set at nought in one afternoon; rather a terrifying thought?'[14]

From the assembly area, the New Zealand Division would move westwards in a number of approach marches (by truck), initially by day and then by night, crossing the frontier on the 18th. On the 15th the entire division headed westwards for 50 miles (80km), travelling as one group for the first time. They stopped at Bir el Thalata, where they remained that night and the next day. Fuel consumption was a problem: 25,000 gallons (114,0001) of petrol had been provided, but the slow travel had used 40,000 gallons (182,0001).

Although moving the whole division was challenging, 'there was something fantastic in the view of the dispersed units', according to Captain John ('Jock') Staveley, Medical Officer with 6 Field Ambulance. With each brigade requiring almost 1000 vehicles to transport the men, weapons, ammunition and stores, the division formed a column of trucks, Bren carriers, field guns, anti-tank guns and other vehicles that stretched for nearly 25 miles (40km). But 'moving over open desert, getting stuck and parts of the brigade being lost and turning up in the morning, being enveloped in dust and not being able to see the vehicle in front was a great strain'.[15] Even Freyberg was impressed with the sight of the 'moving vehicles as far as the eye could see – and on the horizon fresh lines of black specks were popping up like puppets on an endless chain'.[16]

Clem Paterson recalled how uncomfortable the trip was: 'like all other MEF troops we are well acquainted with the trays of 3 tonners and I think our behinds must be the toughest in the world. The jolting is terrific.' He was well laden: 'the army has not yet constructed a webbing suitable for Tommy gunners but I lashed a Lewis mag pouch on my left side balancing the water bottle on the right. Ten small magazines filled the pouches (and 250 rounds of .45 ammunition is a hell of a weight) and in addition I carried 3 bombs in my haversack.'[17]

The men's morale was boosted when Freyberg's staff car passed through the column. As intelligence officer Captain Geoffrey Cox reported, 'the men in the trucks had recognised the General ... and had begun to cheer. This was taken up in the vehicles around, and suddenly the whole column was cheering, with men waving from the backs of their three tonners, out of cabs of trucks, from the carriers and the gun quads.'[18]

Amid the excitement there must also have been some pensive moments, especially for married men with families at home. Some wrote letters to loved ones, to be delivered if they did not return. Captain Charles Gatenby of 26 Battalion had left a wife and two young children in New Zealand and found time to write 'a wee note' to his wife, Eugenie:

> You may never get it. I trust you won't, but one never knows. I am writing this as we motor into battle, the outcome of which no-one

knows. In other words darling this may be my last letter to you and there is so much I would like to tell you. Realising how deeply you love and worship me I can imagine the depths of your grief. Darling you must try and get over this, hard though the task may be.

He hoped his son would 'be much as I was' and if his daughter took after her mother 'some man some day will be lucky'. If Eugenie wanted to remarry 'it would meet with entire approval, after all no-one should go through life alone and it is easier for children to have a father, even an adopted father than none at all'. He concluded by writing that he loved his wife 'with all the depth of my being, more than I ever loved anyone ever, far more perhaps than you ever knew. Gladly would I have died for you if it were necessary? Be proud of me darling rather than sad.'[19]

Gatenby entrusted the letter to a fellow officer, Major Henry Horrell, a nephew of Brigadier Hargest, who kept it for the rest of the war in the hope that he would never have to deliver it.

Fortunately, Gatenby did survive, and the letter was passed to his family after he returned to New Zealand. There was one sad postscript. Gatenby died in 1985. On the afternoon of the funeral there was a knock at the door: it was Henry Horrell, hoping to catch up with his old battalion mate.

On 16 November the latest intelligence reports were reviewed, including up-to-date estimates of the enemy's armoured strength, and the brigades received a short visit from Corps Commander Godwin-Austen. As 23 Battalion's adjutant remembered, 'He arrived in a cloud of dust, shook hands all round, bellowing how "that fellow Rommel" would hate to meet us, and how proud he was to command us and tore off in his car before we realized he had arrived.'[20] The visit was not an unqualified success, as Godwin-Austen himself was aware. He later wrote that he did not feel that he had 'gone down' well with the New Zealand officers. 'I expect this was because of my booming voice and the fact that I was "all of a dooda", as I always was with Bernard Freyberg who had been very senior to me in the British Army, which had treated him so badly.'[21]

On the nights of 16 and 17 November the division made two marches of 25 miles (40km), and arrived near the border, well south of the border forts. But trucks travelling without lights created further problems. The route was marked at intervals of about half a mile (800m) with a green lamp facing towards the east to guide the drivers. Even choosing places for the lamps on the uneven ground where they could be seen was difficult. The second night was especially tough, as Clem Paterson recalled. 'It rained pretty hard and we were treated to a night-long display of sheet and fork lightning, lighting up the place vividly. It was dark as hell, the attack having been planned during the first and last quarters.' Paterson's truck 'slipped and slithered and got stuck plenty of times. Unavoidable as hundreds of them had to move along the comparatively narrow way cleared of mines. However we got through safely, stopped, dug trenches and slept until first light then moved into laager positions.'[22] The rough going caused broken springs and breakdowns, and the soft sand meant more problems as the rain flooded the wadis. The weather did, however, keep the enemy air force grounded.

The men of 1 South African Division had a tough first experience of movement by night. Trucks broke down, units became mixed up and petrol consumption was far greater than anticipated. Three petrol tankers overturned, losing precious fuel, something that was to hamper the division for the rest of the campaign. The 'murderous going in the Western Desert' also caused problems for the Stuart tanks of 4 Armoured Brigade as 'the rubber blocks on the tracks of practically every Honey in the Brigade had been chewed to bits', requiring hasty repairs.[23]

By the night of 18 November the New Zealand Division was poised near El Beida, just east of the frontier wire. The move had apparently gone undetected by the enemy; although some aircraft had been sighted it seemed they had either not noticed the movement or not placed any great importance on it. At 10p.m. engineers cut the wire, leaving a 300-yard (275m) gap through which the division poured into Libya. Although some of the men looked around apprehensively, there was no sign of the enemy. It was a 'cold night with keen wind'.[24] They camped in enemy territory for the first time, just west of the border. To the north was 4 Brigade, with 5 and 6 Brigades to the right and left rear respectively.

Shortly after crossing the frontier Kippenberger, leading his battalion, lost the line of lights and went off course, until Inglis came up and said, 'Kip, you're ninety degrees off your course', and they had to execute a circular move to get back on course again.[25] Kippenberger, writing subsequently of 'the great approach march', which would 'always be remembered by those who took part in it', echoed some of Freyberg's thoughts.

The whole Eighth Army, Seventh Armoured Division, First South African Division and the Second New Zealand and Fourth Indian Divisions moved westwards in an enormous column, the armour leading. The army moved south of Sidi Barrani, past the desolate Italian camps of the previous year, along the plateau south of the great escarpment, through the frontier into Libya, south of the enemy garrisons in the Sidi Omars, and wheeled north. Then, just as we were rejoicing in the conception of a massive move on Tobruk, disregarding the immobile frontier garrisons and crushing everything in our path, the whole Army broke up and departed different ways.[26]

CHAPTER 5

The Battle of the Armour

On the morning of 18 November, the division had received a report that the armoured offensive, the critical first stage of the *Crusader* campaign, had begun. The three armoured brigades, 4, 7 and 22, and the Support Group of 7 Armoured Division had started their advance into Libya at 6a.m., initially meeting little opposition. Freyberg was well aware of the move's importance – 'On the success of this sweep depended the next step of the campaign'[1] – and impatient to take the offensive: 'I don't care what the Boche is doing. I would go slap for Tobruk. If we wait he will get his air up. I don't think he knows where we are.'[2]

On the 19th the division remained camped just west of the border, awaiting news of the tank battle. There were several communications from 13 Corps. The first warned that a move northwards was likely, followed in the early afternoon by another suggesting a 'move to the general line of the Trigh el-Abd ... as soon as possible this afternoon'.[3] Orders were given to leave at 3p.m. and it was quite challenging to get the whole division under way at such short notice. The 14-mile (22km) move was plotted to stay out of range of enemy guns at Sidi Omar. It was dark when the New Zealanders arrived at their destination and camped for the night.

They were now, in Clem Paterson's words, 'told the general scheme of things'.

We were to be the 'bait' to draw Rommel's armoured columns southward, not so dangerous to us as it sounds because the I-tanks were ready to meet them. The scheme was successful and we heard the guns for the first time as we made our breakfast. Later on a Jerry recce plane cheekily took a 'shoofti' [look] at us heedless of the Bofors, this resulting in a hurried packing up and shifting of our position in case the Heinkels thought of paying us a call.[4]

In New Zealand, on 20 November the *Evening Post* reported a speech at a businessmen's lunch by Prime Minister Peter Fraser about the campaign opening. To applause, he announced that 'our lads who distinguished themselves so conspicuously in Greece and in Crete, the men of our Expeditionary Force, are once more on the march, but under very different conditions'. There was no 'inadequate Air Force' this time.[5] And the next day, in the Christchurch *Press*, large headlines announced 'British Advance in Libya', '50 Miles Gained In First Day' and 'New Zealand Troops Take Part'. Britain's Eighth Army was sweeping westwards in the Libyan Desert and on the first day 'had penetrated more than 50 miles [80km] on a front 130 miles [210km] wide, from the Mediterranean coast to the oasis of Jarabub'. The move had been highly successful and 'little or no opposition was encountered'. The military correspondent of *The Times,* however, quoted in the report, cautioned that the move was only around the enemy's flank. 'The real battle will come after this move is completed', he warned, 'it may even have begun by now.'[6]

Over the coming days the reports, which took some time to arrive in New Zealand, continued to be positive. The name of Sidi Rezegh appeared in the *Press* on the 22nd, when 'by Wednesday night [i.e. the 19th] advance elements of our forces had captured Rezegh, on the escarpment 10 miles south-east of the perimeter of Tobruk'. That paper also predicted that 'a tremendous tank battle will occur probably in the next two days as the advancing British forces make contact with the two German armoured forces between Sollum and Tobruk'.[7]

These positive accounts did not, however, reflect the reality of the events unfolding in Libya. The initial armoured march on the 18th had been uneventful, and although the advancing forces saw some German tanks and armoured cars covering the Trigh el-Abd, these withdrew, leaving an empty desert. The armoured division arrived at their objective of Gabr Saleh unopposed; they had made their approach march as planned, but there was no sign of any reaction from Rommel. He was still preoccupied with attacking Tobruk, and when reports arrived of a 'reconnaissance in force' in the south he was not immediately concerned. His forces were already dispersed: 15 Panzer was assembled between Gambut and Tobruk, ready to attack Tobruk, while 21 Panzer was near Sidi Azeiz in position to support the frontier garrisons.[8]

With Norrie now seemingly proved correct in his hunch that Rommel might not join the battle, the decision was made for the armoured division to keep pushing on. Cunningham, however, feeling that the battle was unresolved, thought he could not release 4 Armoured Brigade from protecting 13 Corps' flank, leaving just two armoured brigades to proceed north-west. Then 22 Armoured Brigade encountered Ariete Division tanks near Bir el-Gubi on its left flank, which they attacked, 'perhaps rather impetuously', and gradually the whole brigade was drawn away from the main group.[9] The Italians also had anti-tank guns in action and what initially had been seen as an easy target resulted in 22 Armoured Brigade losing 25 tanks.

Now alone, 7 Armoured Brigade continued north-west, capturing 19 Italian aircraft en route at Sidi Rezegh airfield. By evening the brigade was at Sidi Rezegh, but isolated and surrounded on every side except the south. At the urging of Afrika Korps commander General Crüwell, Rommel reluctantly agreed to send a small battle group south but retained the bulk of his forces for the Tobruk assault. Tanks from 5 Panzer Regiment attacked 4 Armoured Brigade at Gabr Saleh and put 23 Stuart tanks out of action. The three British armoured brigades were now well spread out and isolated; 7 Brigade was 25 miles (40km) north of 4 Brigade, which in turn was 20 miles (32km) roughly east of 22 Brigade.

Over the next few days the tank battle intensified. News of the Eighth Army's offensive was broadcast on the BBC, which finally convinced Rommel the British move was significant. He ordered Crüwell to take both Panzer divisions and 'destroy the enemy battle groups in the Bardia–Tobruk–Sidi Omar area before they can offer any serious threat to Tobruk'.[10] The British now had what they originally sought, Rommel committed to the battle, but they received the news with alarm. Instead of having the three armoured brigades of 30 Corps together, they now faced the prospect of the isolated 4 Armoured Brigade being attacked by the Panzers. On the 20th 22 Armoured Brigade linked up with 4 Armoured Brigade, but too late to prevent the Panzers' arrival. In two days the brigade lost 67 tanks.

On the 20th, too, there were further exchanges between 13 Corps and the New Zealand Division about possible moves. Early in the day brigadiers and the Divisional Cavalry commander were warned to be 'in instant readiness' to implement the plan to isolate the border defences. By midday Freyberg, aware that 4 Armoured Brigade was being attacked, contacted 13 Corps to say 'we were ready to go out and help but we should have to move bodily as a force since we could not release artillery without exposing ourselves to attack'.[11] Alternatively they could 'come on to our flank to rally or go to our rear'. If they were ordered to rally 'we can take a strong bump. "We are omnipotent."'[12] Thirty Corps, however, did not think this was necessary.

The division received a warning order at 3p.m. that the division was to move forward about 10 or 11 miles (16 or 18km) at first light on the 21st. Freyberg, keen to press on, rang to say he was willing to move that night. When asked whether he might be nervous about the many enemy tanks around, he replied, 'Oh Good God, we are frothing to go! There's no nervousness here ... We are not frightened of a few tanks.'[13]

That evening Freyberg received a situation report from 13 Corps indicating that the enemy to the north of the division was retiring, and that 4 and 22 Armoured Brigades were being engaged, but 'reports and rumours concerning the armoured battle were many and varied and the real situation was by no means clear'.[14] Freyberg was not too preoccupied, however, to disregard one of his superstitions. As he reported in his diary, he 'saw the new moon: bowed and turned my money over'.[15]

The division's own intelligence summary on the morning of the 21st presented a new picture: 'the enemy this morning reported to be withdrawing west at full speed.' At midday the New Zealanders received another encouraging report from 13 Corps, saying that 'the armoured battle had gone in our favour', and that the German headquarters considered the situation 'one of extreme emergency'.[16]

On the 21st Cunningham assumed that since 4 and 22 Armoured Brigades were together, and the German tanks were disengaging, the tank battle had been won. He ordered the two brigades to attack the German armour, and also released 4 Armoured Brigade from its role protecting the 13 Corps flank. But Rommel, now aware of the looming British threat and thinking that 4 Armoured Brigade had been disposed of, sought to concentrate his forces and defeat the British formations one after the other. He ordered Crüwell to take both 15 and 21 Panzer Divisions north-west towards Sidi Rezegh to attack the isolated British 7 Armoured Brigade and Support Group there. Following Cunningham's orders, 4 and 22 Armoured Brigades pursued them from a distance, delayed a little by refuelling and boggy ground. Not realising that the Panzers were in fact about to attack 7 Armoured Brigade, they reported that the German armour was in full retreat.

On hearing that the Germans were apparently withdrawing, Cunningham concluded that the next phase of the British plan could proceed and rang Godwin-Austen to say that 13 Corps could 'go forward as he pleased, and [he] need not refer unnecessarily to the Army Commander'. He also advised that further orders would be sent for one New Zealand Brigade, the sixth, to be dispatched westwards.[17]

Cunningham also ordered Norrie to help the Tobruk garrison break out. When Norrie replied that he could do nothing to help, Cunningham made it clear that if the Tobruk link-up did not occur 'he would certainly require to see the Corps Commander tomorrow'.[18]

At dawn on the 21st, 70 Division in Tobruk started its move to link with 30 Corps, meeting strong opposition from German and Italian troops, well dug in behind wire and mines and supported by artillery and machine guns.

Some of the toughest fighting was around Tiger position, which was finally taken by troops of the 2nd Black Watch and tanks of the Royal Tank Regiment. Unfortunately the tanks ran into an anti-tank minefield and were late arriving to support the infantry. The Black Watch suffered heavy casualties – 464 out of the 632 who had set out – and the Royal Tank Regiment was also badly hit. By that afternoon the garrison had established a salient about 2 1/4 miles (3.6km) square and had taken some 1100 prisoners.

Alf Blacklin's anti-tank battery 'had been 'saved up' in reserve, but now 'our Battery was the first out'. He saw the Black Watch attack:

> The famous Scottish regiment went out to the skirl of the pipes. They did a marvellous job and broke the main defences of the enemy. I've never seen so many

Jerries all at once when the prisoners came dejectedly back! All went well until Jerry turned his heavy guns on us, things that chucked a projectile 30" by 8" [75 by 20cm] diameter; I saw some of the duds.[19]

New Zealand's 5 Brigade was now ordered to move up towards the Trigh Capuzzo, followed at 1p.m. by Divisional Headquarters and 4 Brigade. Six Brigade travelled at the rear. The Divisional Cavalry led the advance in a series of bounds and gave the all clear before the main body of the division moved. At dusk the cavalry took Sidi Azeiz by surprise, capturing 'four Germans and fifty Italians, among them an officer who had been taking a bath and preferred to wave his towel in surrender rather than to cover his nakedness'.[20] The New Zealanders then established themselves on the escarpment overlooking the Bardia–Tobruk Road.

The main part of Freyberg's plan to take the border area was carried out during the night of the 21st. As he reported,

5 Brigade Group moved by night and 22 Battalion occupied Sidi Azeiz while 23 Battalion moved against Capuzzo. It was a brilliant move and an excellent piece of desert navigation. The attack on Capuzzo was also an excellent piece of planning carried out at dawn with I-tanks. The small force was taken completely by surprise ... Two hundred prisoners ... were captured without casualties to ourselves. The Bardia water main to Halfaya was cut.[21]

The engineers cutting the water pipe were helped by a recently captured major of the Italian engineers, who approached them saying that 'the care of this pipe has been part of my job. Let me show you how to break it.'[22] The New Zealanders also captured the strategically important German Army Signal Exchange at Capuzzo. In the afternoon 21 Battalion occupied Hafid Ridge.

Meanwhile 4 Brigade group advanced northwards towards the Via Balbia. The men had started the day well dug in and resting, and while waiting some, as

Clem Paterson recalled, 'played around ... with a football (though why the news correspondents considered this strange I can't say)'.[23] After passing Sidi Azeiz at midnight they had a muddy trip to the escarpment west of Bardia, taking an enemy camp by surprise on the way. On the following morning they cut the Bardia–Tobruk Road, brought their artillery to bear on a number of targets, cut telegraph wires and took many prisoners. The enemy were taken by surprise and the brigade suffered only light casualties. The attack was successful, and 'the value of these moves was very great as they drove a wedge between the forward elements and greatly handicapped General Rommel in his plans. How great a nuisance it was can be estimated by the number of times our positions were counterattacked.'[24]

On the evening of the 21st, an order arrived for 6 Brigade to move westwards and come under the command of 30 Corps. Significantly, the order from Eighth Army to 13 Corps included the words 'with all possible speed', but this phrase was not passed on and 'no sense of urgency was felt at either Corps or Divisional Headquarters'. Both Godwin-Austen and Freyberg were still under the impression that the battle was going in favour of the British.[25]

The 928 vehicles of 6 Brigade group carried its three infantry battalions, the machine gun company and other units under 6 Brigade command: 6 Field Regiment New Zealand Artillery, 33 Battery of 7 Anti-Tank Regiment, 43 Light Anti-Aircraft Battery, 8 Field Company New Zealand Engineers and 6 Field Ambulance. They were also accompanied by 86 I-tanks from 1 Army Tank Brigade: 8 Royal Tank Regiment with 49 Valentines, and 44 Royal Tank Regiment with 37 Matildas. The brigade was self-sufficient in supply and medical services.

The brigade's objective was to travel 10 miles (16km) west of Sidi Azeiz on the Trigh Capuzzo, ready to move on Gambut. However it struck 'veritable quagmires and tremendous efforts were necessary to extricate vehicles from the mud', and at 1a.m. Brigadier Barrowclough decided though the men were still 6 or 7 miles (10 or 11km) short of their destination, they would halt for the night.[26] The brigade did not reach Bir el-Hariga, 11 miles (18km) west of Sidi Azeiz, until after daybreak. During the night advance units captured a German unit that was using some British trucks which had been captured in Greece, reconditioned and sent to Libya. One of the 26 Battalion HQ Company drivers 'claimed that one of the trucks, an English half-ton Ford, was the one he left in Greece'.[27]

On the 22nd positions were consolidated. Patrols from 4 and 5 Brigades tested the defences of Bardia and the Divisional Cavalry moved west to hold the approaches over the escarpment from the north, supported by a battalion from 4 Brigade and some tanks. One of 22 Battalion's companies had its first encounter with the enemy patrolling between the outer defences of Bardia and Sidi Azeiz. They came under heavy mortar and artillery shelling and although they captured 11 prisoners, four of the company were killed and 15 wounded. At Menastir 20 Battalion was able to disperse an attack by enemy infantry and tanks, and in the afternoon they in turn counter-attacked, supported by tanks, armoured cars and artillery, and captured some 370 Germans, along with some guns. The enemy tanks then withdrew.

Twenty-one Battalion undertook an 'abortive action' against the headquarters position of the Italian 55 Savona Division, which was strongly defended by tanks, artillery and machine guns protected by concrete pillboxes. The battalion suffered casualties – 13 killed and 65 wounded – and Freyberg was 'not enthusiastic' when he heard of the losses in what was intended to be just a show of strength, without tank support and with few field guns. 'Of all the New Zealand attacks in *Crusader* this was the most unrewarding.'[28]

Early that afternoon Freyberg sent 'an appreciation' to 13 Corps, summarising 'the situation on the Bardia front'. He reported that the move north, because of the lack of enemy air activity and because it had been at night, 'was a complete tactical surprise'. He outlined the actions that had taken place and the successes of the brigades. Strong patrols sent towards Bardia had highlighted that it was strongly held 'as far as artillery is concerned' and the patrols were heavily engaged. He felt that 'Bardia defences are garrisoned and firmly held', but that he would be in a better position later in the day to report on the Sidi Omar and Halfaya areas. He was concerned about the lack of ammunition and 'the great shortage of bombardment and barrage guns available'.[29]

Thirty Corps' outlook, however, was less promising. On the 22nd Rommel, now in personal command and wanting to complete the destruction of 7 Armoured Brigade, attempted to force it, together with the Support Group, onto Sidi Rezegh airfield. Here tanks from 21 Panzer, later joined by 15 Panzer, attacked the isolated brigade. Four and 22 Armoured Brigades came to its aid but their attacks were not co-ordinated. Correspondent Alan Moorehead viewed the battle from 'a spit of flat land we were holding just above the Tobruk escarpment. It was ringed with fire.' He witnessed 'the battle of annihilation on Sidi Rezegh'. The British fought gallantly, led by Brigadier Jock Campbell, who 'was like a man berserk', leading his tanks into action 'riding in an open unarmoured staff car.' He stood hanging onto its windscreen shouting, 'there they come. Let them have it.'[30] Alf Blacklin wrote home that 'one of the finest men we had out here was Brigadier Jock Campbell, he got his VC for leading the tanks into action at Rezegh – in a pick-up!'[31]

All three British armoured brigades were in action but the German tanks and anti-tank guns took a heavy toll. In addition 4 Armoured Brigade Headquarters was overrun with the enemy claiming 267 prisoners and capturing about 50 tanks. That evening '30 Corps was compelled to retire, having lost two thirds of its tanks and leaving the garrison of Tobruk with a huge salient to defend'.[32]

Poor communications meant that news of these major losses did not reach Eighth Army Headquarters and it was only the following morning when Cunningham learnt what had happened.

The British armoured brigades had 'obliged [the enemy] by throwing their armoured brigades into the battle in separate units', allowing the Germans to destroy a large number of tanks. For the Germans, this 'eventually led to victory in one of the greatest armoured battles of the campaign, in which the bulk of the enemy's armour was destroyed'.[33]

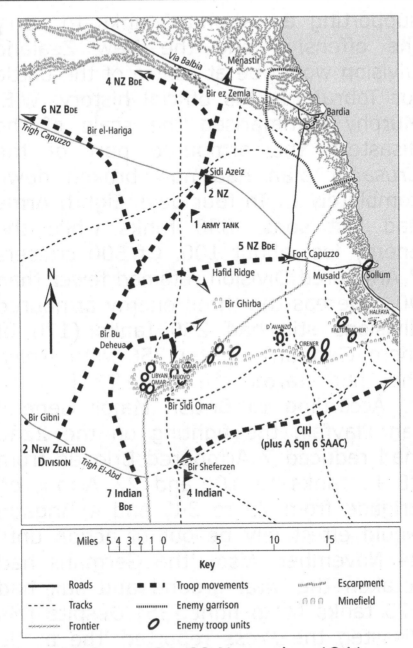

13 Corps, 21–22 November 1941

With the critical tank encounter lost,
it would be over to the infantry,

supporting arms and I-tanks to carry the offensive and the New Zealand Division would be at centre of the battle for Tobruk. In his official history, W.E. Murphy summarised the scale of the disaster: 'the armoured part of the *Crusader* plan had now broken down completely ... In four days Eighth Army had lost some 530 tanks while the enemy lost about 100. Of 500 cruisers 7 Armoured Division retained fewer than 90, whereas the three enemy armoured divisions still had 250 tanks (170 of them German) of the 356 with which they had started the battle.'[34]

According to British Major General Ian Playfair, the fighting on the 22nd 'had reduced 7 Armoured Brigade from 28 fit tanks to 10, and 22 Armoured Brigade from 79 to 34', and 4 Brigade would effectively be out of action until 24 November. Also, 'the Germans had retaken the vital ground and still had 173 tanks fit to fight'.[35] Despite this disaster, the *Press* reported 'the battle is not settled yet. It may last several days. But it is going better than expected. Following Saturday's [i.e. the 22nd] sacrifice of tanks the Germans have lost the chief support of their Panzer divisions.'[36]

At 2p.m. on the 22nd 'things started to develop quickly'.[37] Freyberg received 'an extraordinary telegram' from 13 Corps, requesting that he 'leave minimum troops to observe enemy Bardia and send remainder your troops to clear up North Bardia–Tobruk Road', a request by which 'rather cunningly they have put the responsibility on us to decide what is the minimum number of troops to police Bardia'.[38] Some initial plans were made, but Freyberg instructed the liaison officer to the corps to explain that this 'would mean that we should be very weak in the Bardia area where a counter-attack was possible'.[39] He confirmed his thoughts with a lengthy telegram, setting out his proposal for dispersing his forces and asked for confirmation that this would meet corps orders.

Late on the same afternoon the division received its 'first real news concerning the armoured battle in the west',[40] which was 'so strikingly different from any yet heard that it could scarcely be believed'.[41] The

Support Group was surrounded at Sidi Rezegh and there was an urgent request for 6 Brigade's move west to be accelerated to relieve them. Freyberg, instinctively feeling 'all was not well', contacted the brigade, which was heading westwards towards Bir el Chleta, some 20 miles (32km) along the Trigh Capuzzo.[42] He sent an urgent message to Barrowclough to go to Sidi Rezegh, 'start fighting, and get in touch with [7 Armoured Division commander] General [William] Gott'.[43] Speed was vital; the brigade had already been asked for its tanks to be detached to go to the immediate assistance of the Support Group, but they could not go any faster than they already were. The brigade group overcame some opposition at Gasr el Arid, then halted at 8p.m. for a rest and a meal. The advance was to resume at 3a.m. on the 23rd.

Freyberg, concerned about the division being dispersed, was convinced they 'must get infantry division up to attack Tobruk and get high ground to southeast. Get that and the battle for Tobruk is won.'[44] However it was also essential to contain the area around Bardia, Halfaya and Sidi Omar. Time was of the essence and it was vital the enemy was not given time to regroup and counter-attack while the division was spread out.

In light of these concerns, on the evening of the 22nd Freyberg sent an outline plan to the corps commander, proposing a compromise – send as big a force as possible towards Tobruk, but retain sufficient in the frontier area to prevent any enemy breakout. A modest force would contain the area around Bardia, Capuzzo and Sidi Azeiz and the remainder would join 4 Brigade to 'march on Tobruk'. He also reported that he had 'despatched the 6 New Zealand Infantry Brigade with all haste, complete with Valentines, to relieve the Support Group. I know they will do well.'[45]

That night 4 Brigade was positioned west of Bardia, covering the Bardia–Tobruk Road, and 5 Brigade was covering the eastern flank, around Sidi Azeiz and Capuzzo. Meanwhile 6 Brigade was moving west with all haste along the Trigh Capuzzo with the intention of passing to the south of Bir el Chleta. It would receive further orders at Wadi esc-Sciomar, about 3 miles (5km) east of Point 175, which they expected to reach by 8a.m. There was minimal information about the state of the armoured battle around Sidi Rezegh, and the New Zealanders were not aware that the area was strongly held by the enemy. Their task was to 'secure an all round defensive locality about Point 175'.[46] In freezing temperatures they set off again at 3a.m., and would stop for breakfast as dawn broke.

While the division was successfully containing the border areas, its ability to move on Tobruk in force would be difficult, as it was getting very spread out. As Freyberg noted in his report, 'on the 23rd New Zealand Division less 5 Brigade was divided into five detachments over an area measuring 50 miles by 20[80km by 32] with large forces of the enemy all round them'.[47] With the division being stretched further and further, and the enemy tanks undefeated, there were challenging times ahead.

CHAPTER 6

Totensonntag: The Sunday of the Dead

By the morning of 23 November 6 Brigade was out of touch with the rest of the division. Freyberg, now aware, through a letter from 13 Corps commander, that the situation at Sidi Rezegh would 'remain critical' until 6 Brigade arrived, was anxious to concentrate 4 and 6 Brigades, plus 21 Battalion from 5 Brigade, to move on Tobruk while the enemy was disorganised – 'to attack the Germans before they had time to attack us'.[1] The defeat of the British tanks was exactly the situation that Freyberg had feared; now New Zealand's 6 Brigade was being called on to provide the support badly needed by 30 Corps.

Six Brigade had stopped for breakfast astride the Trigh Capuzzo; 25 Battalion was below the nearby escarpment and 26 Battalion above it. The brigade had planned to pass south of Bir el Chleta, but inadvertently veered to the right. As dawn broke, the men observed a number of fires not far from where 25 Battalion was camped. Then an officer noticed a column of trucks approaching from the direction of Gambut and suddenly realised they were Germans. In fact there was an enemy group camped in their midst, and as it became light Captain Edgar Tomlinson from 24 Battalion watched as 'astonished looking members of the Afrika Korps stared at even more astonished Kiwis'.

Twenty-five Battalion was quickly into action and with them machine guns, mortars and even 25-pounders opened up. 'It was amusing to see the odd soldier endeavouring to hurl a grenade with one hand while holding a cup of tea in the other.'[2] Sergeant James (Randel) Heron, with 3 Company, 27 (Machine Gun) Battalion, recalled that 'we had got the primus stove alight to cook some porridge, when we spotted similar activity taking place a couple of hundred yards away. I believe that we broke all records in getting guns mounted and into action – the

Germans scarpered.'[3] Inadvertently the brigade had stumbled on the German Afrika Korps headquarters; they captured about 200 prisoners, took a number of valuable documents and grabbed or smashed the main wireless links.

Barrowclough, embarrassed that the action had been caused by faulty navigation, was concerned about a possible counter-attack. He ordered 25 and 24 Battalions to resume the march immediately. The brigade climbed up the escarpment and travelled west along the top, troubled occasionally by small-arms fire from the crest on the right-hand side. The brigade halted at the Wadi esc-Sciomar at 10.30a.m. The brigadier's attention then turned towards planning the attack on the first objective, Point 175.

Wanting to move quickly, Barrowclough decided to deploy 25 Battalion, under Lieutenant Colonel Gifford McNaught, supported by a field battery of artillery and an anti-tank troop. Speed was essential, and McNaught had to move fast to brief his officers. He had advised the brigadier that the battalion could start at 11.30a.m., which gave him very little time. He kept reminding himself to 'make it simple, make it simple', but underneath he felt that the attack might be 'a very sticky job'.[4]

Major Harold Wilson, of 29 Battery 6 Field Regiment recalled that although they were not under fire, their observation of Point 175, which they were to attack from the east, was poor. It 'could not be distinguished as a feature, and there was no visible indication that the enemy were in the locality'.[5] Point 175 is the highest point of a gentle oval-shaped rise on a plateau approximately 2 1/2 miles (4km) long and 1 1/2 miles (2.5km) across. The ground rises imperceptibly to the west, where the tiny dot that is the distant blockhouse cuts the horizon about 2 1/2 miles (4km) away. On the right-hand side an escarpment drops away some 80 feet (25m) towards the Trigh Capuzzo. Several wadis cut into the escarpment's north face; to the west and south curls a long, shallow wadi, the Rugbet en-Nbeidat, not obvious as it dips before rising again towards the blockhouse. A few camelthorn bushes were, and are, the only vegetation.

Out of sight, but covering Point 175 from the west and concealed in the Rugbet en-Nbeidat, were enemy tanks dug in hull down, and anti-tank guns with their muzzles just clearing the ground. Surrounding the approaches were machine guns that could provide outflanking fire and another line of infantry and machine guns were positioned just east of Point 175. Twenty-five Battalion was about to get a deadly demonstration, by the experienced men from 361 Afrika Regiment, of the enemy's ability to co-ordinate armour, anti-tank guns and infantry.

The attack's start line faced north-west, between the top of the Rugbet en-Nbeidat and a wadi rising through the escarpment about 2 miles (3.2km) west of Wadi esc-Sciomar. Twenty-five Battalion formed up with B Company on the right, D Company on the left and C Company in reserve. Barrowclough did not commit any machine guns to the attack, either through lack of time or perceived absence of targets.

Since the officers knew little about the enemy's strength, their men were unaware that the area was strongly defended. On the contrary, some of them were told the attack would be easy and McNaught was overheard saying, 'I don't think you will encounter much fire – perhaps a few machine guns.' Not everyone, however, was that confident and there were conflicting opinions about the scale of the German forces. For many of the men, this would be their first experience of action, and as they formed up they speculated about what they were likely to encounter. One felt that 'it won't be much; they're packing up already' while another expected 'a bayonet charge to clear out a few pockets of the enemy about 300 yards to the front'.[6]

The advance began on time, the men moving off towards the objective about 2 miles (3.2km) ahead, while artillery directed fire at what were thought to be some earthworks and machine gun positions ahead. B Company moved along the top of the escarpment but was almost immediately ordered to halt and await tank support. A report had just been received that the enemy forces were stronger than first thought, but the order did not reach D Company's platoons.

Shortly after 11.30a.m. an ambulance of wounded men had arrived at brigade headquarters, and a medical officer from the 8 Hussars gave a graphic account of the now serious situation around Sidi Rezegh and Point 175. He mentioned a heavy enemy concentration around the blockhouse further west, and 100 enemy AFVs on Point 175, together with some heavy guns. There were doubts about the accuracy of the information: some of it was verifiably incorrect. Barrowclough now placed under McNaught's command a squadron of 16 Valentines from C Squadron of 8 Royal Tanks. McNaught rapidly recalled his company commanders and spelt out new orders 'to capture and hold at all costs Hill 175'. Tanks would 'advance in two waves. First wave advance at 15mph and capture objective, will cross start line at zero. Second wave at Inf.

[infantry] pace with C Coy 800 yards [730m] behind forward companies.'[7]

But these orders did not get through to all the men so when the attack resumed at noon most sections were still vague about their objectives and about the likely strength of the enemy. The tanks and carriers advanced at full speed and initially had some successes. They had, however, left the infantry behind, and ran into enemy anti-tank guns concealed in the wadi, with disastrous results. Two infantry companies followed the tanks, both spread out on fronts of 400 yards (365m), but the platoons were hit by heavy machine gun fire, especially in the areas not cleared by the tanks and carriers, and several men were killed. The lack of co-ordination with infantry meant that there were no troops 'to reduce or neutralise' the 'veritable nests of anti-tank guns located at the head of the wadis', which accounted for 12 of the 16 tanks in the attack.[8] McNaught, who had followed the advance in his wireless truck, noticed that the Point 175 feature was 'not as definite as it seemed on the map' and when he arrived 'it was obvious to me that we were most likely in for a sticky time'.[9]

Meanwhile D Company was veering to the left, away from the direction of the cairn and heading toward the Rugbet. As it turned back northwards, it came under heavy enemy fire, but managed to take about 200 prisoners, before attempting to consolidate its position and dig in. C Company, initially in reserve, had now been called forward, and parts of it joined with D Company. Then, as a result of a German counter-attack, McNaught also had to call up A Company, his only remaining reserve. By now McNaught's Advanced Headquarters had moved up close to the cairn, and the area was being swept by fire. His assessment was that their situation was quite good – B and D Companies had made good progress and C and A were available – but he knew that the remaining tanks would be withdrawing. It is also possible that by now Rommel was personally organising the enemy defence, as he had been on his way to inspect the armoured battle.

Shortly after this the situation deteriorated quickly. The men of C and D Companies, in exposed positions, were subjected to heavy machine gun and mortar fire, and they were also short of ammunition. As they sought cover from a few 'very shallow holes and clumps of tussock', enemy tanks overran the two companies and they were forced to surrender.[10] Fortunately the German troops instantly held their fire at the first signs that the New Zealanders were surrendering, quickly searched them and then marched them off down the wadi, into captivity.

McNaught ordered A Company forward, but it was soon 'desperately short of ammunition' and advanced across the plateau with bayonets fixed. 'Enemy fire from concealed positions and tanks decimated the company before 100 yards [90m] had been covered.' Although A Company had fought in Greece and Crete, this was 'the most bitter and hard combat' the men had yet experienced.[11]

Twenty-nine Battery of 6 Field Regiment provided artillery support and successfully shelled some enemy machine gun and mortar positions. Captain J. Malloy, in an observation post on the left flank, 'observed a "Valentine" approaching from the enemy area flying the pennant of 8 Battalion Royal Tank Regiment. He was not at all thrilled when the tank crew opened up on him, and then blatantly waved a Swastika flag.'[12]

Twenty-five Battalion was now in a desperate position. McNaught had already been wounded twice, his Advanced Headquarters was almost in the front line and many of his officers had been wounded. Major Wilson from 6 Field Regiment was with Barrowclough, acquainting him with 25 Battalion's predicament, when McNaught called brigade headquarters to 'send reinforcements 25 Bn right flank urgent'. Wilson contacted both of his forward observation officers, who advised that 'our infantry had been practically wiped out and that their own positions were almost untenable'.[13] Barrowclough committed D Company of 24 Battalion to help, but the men of the 25th did not know they were coming and there was a disastrous exchange of fire between the two New Zealand battalions until they made contact and identified each other.

Barrowclough also committed four machine guns from Brian Cox's 9 Platoon. Many of the men had fought in Greece where 27 (Machine Gun) Battalion had 'gained probably the fullest battle experience of any NZ unit or detachments',[14] but this platoon was in for a 'tough time' at Sidi Rezegh.[15] The machine gunners' trucks took off, directed forward by the intelligence officer from 25 Battalion, but as they passed the artillery, the anti-tank guns and the infantry, they quickly realised they were being taken too far forward.

Phil Hammond, driving the truck for platoon commander Lieutenant Tom Daly, recalled that they 'ran into an ambush and hit the deck in a hurry. The truck was getting peppered and a bullet went through the radiator.' Ordered by Daly to take the trucks back behind the anti-tank guns, Hammond drove 'over the ridge to go along the back of the lines of the Hun machine guns. I just got over the top and the truck gave up.' He jumped onto another truck but then 'over the lip of the escarpment came a crowd of prisoners escorted by two from 25 Battalion then behind came a tank. It looked like one of ours [it was a British Valentine tank that the Germans had captured] until it opened up on the guards and the Hun prisoners took off, then he opened up on us in the transport and gave us hell.'[16]

John Black was also a driver that day, something that 'no doubt saved my life. Whilst awaiting our "call-up" to go into action we came across a "Tommy" 15cwt truck in the middle of nowhere. The call arrived to report to HQ. I asked our platoon commander if I could bring the truck, to which he agreed.' When Black arrived at company headquarters, he found that 'the sergeant's truck had broken down. I was ordered to drive my two mates, "Bun" Prole and "Saint" Farrell into action with their anti-tank rifle.' They headed for the top of the escarpment where 'small arms fire from enemy rifles and machine guns were spitting all around us'.

When Black asked his mates where they wanted him to stop, 'they replied "right here". That is where they were wounded some minutes later, being hit in their buttocks. They both struggled to their feet, put their wounded sides together, linked arms and hobbled out to the RAP [regimental aid post]'. Black then 'took off after the other gun trucks; the enemy machine gun fire was very heavy'. He thought, 'if this is action I don't have long to live. I did not feel any fear, just concentrating on the other trucks and trying to out-manoeuvre the enemy fire.'[17]

By now McNaught had been wounded for a third time. Barrowclough immediately dispatched C Company from 24 Battalion as further reinforcements, together with the battalion's commanding officer, Lieutenant Colonel Clayden Shuttleworth, to take over command of the suffering 25 Battalion, which in the words of Captain Tomlinson of 24 Battalion, seemed 'badly demoralised and disorganised' with men 'streaming off Point 175 hotly pursued by the enemy'.[18]

After D Company of 24 Battalion had stabilised the position on the escarpment, Ray Winfield's machine gun section was able to get its two guns into action, which helped to consolidate that position. Brian Cox's section, however, was 'much troubled by accurate and close-range fire' and also from two tanks, they could not get the guns into action.[19] Cox recalled that 'when the tanks came we went back over the escarpment and stopped there. We didn't get to fire the guns as we couldn't get them mounted. We sheltered around a 3-ton truck and when darkness came retired along a signals line.'[20]

Late in the day Phil Hammond and Laurie ('Pooky') Walker went out searching for New Zealand wounded. As Hammond remembered, 'a machine gun opened up on us. I flattened out and looked up to see Pooky just walking on with dust bouncing up all around him so I thought if he can do it so can I.' They then 'carried on and could hear a New Zealand wounded calling for water and on the way down to him we saw some Huns coming along below us. I thought I saw six but Pooky said only five so said we would handle them.' When Hammond climbed down, 'there was the other Hun looking me in the eye and had me covered with his rifle. I just dropped to one knee and fired at anything but hit him in the left side about the hip and spun him around so I threw his rifle over the ledge and was going down to the wounded chap when Pooky yelled to come quick, a tank was coming up the valley.' Then, in near darkness, they 'ran into a bloke' who they thought was one of their mates, but 'then we realised he was a Hun'. To hurry him along Hammond 'gave him a touch with the bayonet and he took off, then Pooky said, "You silly bastard, he still has his rifle." We soon took that off him then took him to the truck.' After dropping the prisoners off 'we tucked down to a good night's sleep but couldn't sleep for going over the day's doings'.[21]

During the afternoon, with I-tank support, the New Zealanders had taken about two-thirds of the hill, but by evening through enemy counterattacks they held less than half. The hasty planning, poor co-ordination with the I-tanks and lack of covering fire left the New Zealand troops extremely exposed against a well-organised and experienced enemy. It was unfortunate that 9 Platoon's machine guns 'which probably would have been very effective with long-range fire against the wadi and positions beyond, were not detailed to support the attack until mid-afternoon'.[22]

At dusk neither side could consolidate a strong front and as evening fell the area around Point 175 'held some 120 dead or dying New Zealanders, at least as many dead Germans, and several hundreds of wounded on both sides'.[23] That night both Germans and New Zealanders worked to care for the wounded: 'a wounded man bearing as best he could his lonely agonies had about an equal chance of being lifted up by German or New Zealand hands and all were treated with equal compassion'.[24]

The New Zealanders had paid a high price for their small gain. Total casualties in 6 Brigade were 420, 'severe losses by any standard and particularly so against defences which had virtually no field artillery support and very little mortar ammunition'.[25] Over 100 men from 25 Battalion were killed in the afternoon, more in a single action than any other New Zealand battalion in the Second World War. Total 25 Battalion casualties exceeded 350, or two-thirds of those who took part in the attack. Considering that most of the officers and men had little experience of battle, it was 'remarkable that the battalion succeeded to the extent that it did'.[26] D Company of 24 Battalion lost 27 men – C Company lost fewer – and C Squadron of 8 Royal Tanks also suffered: by the end of the day only two of the starting tally of 16 Valentine tanks were left fit for action and 25 of the crew were killed, wounded or missing.

Nine 9 Platoon of 27 (Machine Gun) Battalion had 'given valiant and valuable support to both flanks [and] paid for its devotion in losses tragically heavy for such a small band':[27] 11 men either dead or missing, with 'several more wounded or safe ... though none of the four Vickers guns were lost'.[28] John Black knew that 'having that truck to drive saved my life. I should have been with Lieutenant Daly and Privates Lee and Taylor, all killed that afternoon.'[29]

Kippenberger later described this attack as:

> one of the stiffest in which New Zealand troops have ever been engaged. In broad daylight, on open ground giving every advantage to a determined and skilful defence, the infantry companies engaged took their objective and, despite very heavy losses, held it against fierce counter-attacks. They were gallantly and skilfully supported by an entirely inadequate number of guns and tanks, but in the main they had to rely on their own weapons, and showed what resolute troops can do.[30]

Playfair, however, only briefly records this major action: 'this brigade was hastened on by General Norrie ... it climbed the escarpment and making good speed westwards captured part of

Pt 175 from the 361st Infantry Regiment, with the help of one squadron of Valentines of the 8th Royal Tank Regiment. The casualties were heavy – over 400 in all.'[31]

On the same day, 5 South African Brigade was in a desperate position south of the Sidi Rezegh airfield. At 11.45a.m. Barrowclough dispatched 26 Battalion to come to its aid, meaning that the battalion would be some 6 miles (10km) away from the rest of the brigade. The New Zealanders left immediately, accompanied by four 2-pounder anti-tank guns from L Troop, 33 Battery, 7 NZ Anti-Tank Regiment, and eight 25-pounders from 30 Battery, 6 Field Regiment. They met the South Africans at 12.30p.m. near the southern escarpment.

That afternoon a strong German and Italian force of over 100 tanks and infantry attacked the South Africans. Lieutenant Heinz Schmidt, now released from his role as Rommel's ADC, was with 115 Rifle Regiment of 15 Panzer Division. As the tanks attacked, Schmidt looked around at 'the armoured troop-carriers, cars of various kinds, caterpillars hauling mobile guns, heavy trucks with infantry, motorised anti-aircraft guns. Thus we roared on towards the enemy barricade.'[32] The South Africans, however, fought strongly and 'tank after tank split open in the hail of shells'. Eventually, after fierce fighting, 'tank against tank, tank against gun or anti-tank nest, sometimes in frontal, sometimes in flanking assault, using every trick of mobile warfare and tank tactics', the South Africans were overcome. Schmidt was wounded in the attack. Rommel summed up the battle in a letter to 'Dearest Lu', his wife: 'The battle seems to have passed its crisis. I'm very well, in good humour and full of confidence. Two hundred enemy tanks shot up so far. Our fronts have held.'[33]

Later that day it was the New Zealanders' turn. The anti-tank troop commander, Lieutenant Cyril Pepper, told the gunners 'that the South Africans were being overrun and that German tanks would almost certainly bear down on the New Zealand position. "There are lots of them ... maybe over 150. But don't let that worry you. They are only little ones.'"[34] The gunners were soon in action at close range, firing over open sights at the enemy tanks and lorries. The gunners had a frantic time with two of the L troop guns firing nearly 700 rounds and eventually running out of ammunition. They accounted for about 24 enemy tanks, some of them at the extreme range of 1800 yards (1645m). Barrowclough, who had been receiving reports of the action, now ordered the 26 Battalion group to withdraw back to the main body of the brigade; this occurred later in the evening.

The day's losses were heavy; 5 South African Brigade had 3394 casualties (mainly prisoners) and effectively ceased to exist; about a third of 22 Armoured Brigade's 34 tanks were lost. Twenty-six Battalion group lost 12 killed and about 20 wounded. In L Troop one man was killed and three wounded. Pepper had provided such inspiring leadership that he was awarded the Military Cross, but only three days later he was run over by a staff car that backed into the slit trench he was resting in. Seriously injured, he had to be invalided back to Wellington, where he died, aged 31, on 30 May 1943. It was a tragic loss of a former All Black who had played 17 matches for the team on their tour of Britain and Canada in 1935–36. Another former All Black, Captain Arthur ('Archie') Wesney of 26 Battalion's B Company, who had been wounded earlier in the afternoon, led an attack on some German positions, 'with the same dash he had shown on the football field'. He 'received a burst in the chest and was killed instantly'. The company lost 10 men, seven of whom were killed.[35]

Barrowclough noted that:

this small force had been hotly attacked by an enemy column which had already proved itself strong enough to defeat and overthrow the whole of the 5th South African Brigade Group. That the 26 Battalion and supporting artillery and anti-tank guns were able to maintain their positions and come out of the action with surprisingly few casualties was an eloquent tribute to the high standard of training and fortitude of all ranks.[36]

The official South African war history gives an interesting perspective on Barrowclough's performance. The attack of Point 175 'has been criticised as costly and pointless', it noted, 'but by engaging the attention of 21 Panzer and the Africa Regiment during the critical hours of the day, the New Zealand Brigade played an important part in the main battle, and must have relieved the pressure on the northern face of 5 South African Brigade'. The attack was significant because 'it was the opening action in the second battle of Sidi Rezegh, in which the whole New Zealand Division was to play an important part'. While lamenting New Zealand's high casualties, the South Africans are complimentary about the brigade's achievements: 'improvised infantry assaults in the desert cannot escape loss, and not many meet with the degree of success that Brigadier Barrowclough achieved ... he set about his task with a resolution which was an example to many desert commanders.'[37]

The Germans acknowledged that they had encountered a worthy opponent. The 21 Panzer record of the attack on Point 175 reports that 'the enemy succeeded in making an armoured penetration in Africa Regiment's sector' and that 'Africa Regiment experienced particularly hard fighting, and its most easterly battalion suffered severe losses'.[38]

By evening, 6 Brigade was back close to Point 175, but some distance away from the support of 4 and 5 Brigades and under threat from west, north and south. As the troops regrouped, medical staff attempted to cope with the deluge of casualties. There were insufficient ambulances and the wounded were evacuated in a column of 3-ton lorries that ran into enemy vehicles and had to take off in all directions at top speed, adding to the patients' suffering. The lorries eventually regrouped and came under the command of 30 Corps, which used the vehicles for other purposes. As a consequence, 'for the remainder of its operations [6 Brigade] was rendered immobile and the consequences may well have been serious'.[39]

That evening, in Liddell Hart's words, 'the wide plain south of Sidi Rezegh was ... a sea of dust, haze and smoke'. All around, 'hundreds of burning vehicles, tanks and guns lit up the field of that *Totensonntag'*.[40] The date, 23 November 1941, the third Sunday of the month, is marked in the Lutheran calendar as *Totensonntag,* the Sunday of the Dead, the equivalent of All Souls' Day, when the Germans remember those who died in the First World War. It is an appropriate name for the day that saw one of the heaviest tank attacks in the desert war, and one of *Crusader's* toughest infantry actions.

General Auchinleck talks with General Freyberg, New Zealand GOC, during manoeuvres after the Libyan campaign. (DA-02407-F, Alexander Turnbull Library)

Brigadier Harold Barrowclough commanding 6
New Zealand Brigade in the Western Desert.
(DA-01974-F, Alexander Turnbull Library)

Brigadier Lindsay Merritt Inglis during the Second World War. (DA-01514-F, Alexander Turnbull Library)

Lieutenant Colonel Leslie Andrew, VC, with Brigadier Hargest and General Freyberg at Helwan, Egypt. (DA-13918-F, Alexander Turnbull Library)

Lieutenant Colonel Howard Kippenberger with Lieutenant Charles Upham, Egypt. (DA-02149-F. Alexander Turnbull Library)

Captured film showing Brigadier George Clifton as a prisoner of war in Egypt with General Erwin Rommel. (DA-02894B-F, Alexander Turnbull Library)

Clement ('Clem') Paterson. (Bill Paterson)

Frank Dudman (left) with Bill Andrew. (Andrew family)

Australian troops in the Wadi Sehel, outside Tobruk.

Alf Blacklin. (Diana Carney)

Charles Gatenby. (Gatenby family)

'Aw-Shucks', Tobruk, 1941, by Alf Blacklin.
(Diana Carney)

Randel Heron. (Heron family)

An armoured car at Point 175, near Sidi Rezegh in 1941. (S. Lyle-Smythe photograph, DA-11453-F, Alexander Turnbull Library)

Men of 9 Platoon, 27 (Machine Gun) Battalion at Sidi Rezegh. Back row, left to right: Ted O'Connor, Laurie Walker, Laurie Daly, Bert Hambling, George Woolf, Phil Hammond. Front: unknown. (Hammond family)

Charlie (left) and Lou Nelley with their mother, Mary. (Nelley family)

CHAPTER 7

The Division Moves West

During the night of the 22nd Freyberg reconsidered plans for the division and next morning reported to 13 Corps that although the surrounding area appeared to have been cleared, there was still 'a considerable force of enemy in Bardia' that would need to be surrounded. He thought Musaid and Sollum were occupied. After proposing some moves to reorganise the division, he summarised the position in two phases. In the first all available troops would join 6 Brigade and march on Tobruk; 5 Brigade would come under the command of the Indian Division. In the second 5 Brigade would be relieved and join the rest of the division.[1] Later that day the corps commander replied, agreeing with phase one, but stating that it would be impossible for 4 Indian Division to relieve 5 Brigade for some time.

Also on the 23rd, while 6 Brigade was out of touch, Freyberg received a letter from 13 Corps advising that, probably from the next day, it was to take over the operations for the relief of Tobruk; the letter described the situation at Sidi Rezegh as 'critical'.[2] The Tobruk garrison, 4 Indian Division, the New Zealand Division and 'at least one infantry brigade group of 1 South African Division' would be under command of 13 Corps.[3] Their orders were 'to capture Sidi Rezegh and Ed Duda "at all costs" and to exploit westwards'.[4] Thirty Corps would reorganise: 4 and 22 Armoured Brigades would protect the flank of the New Zealand Division and 1 South African Brigade since the enemy armoured forces were still largely intact and very active. Seven Armoured Brigade withdrew to Egypt, with reinforcements of tanks and crews going to the other two brigades. This letter also instructed the division 'not to get committed North of the main [Via Balbia] road'.[5] The division complied with this, but 'a wonderful chance was missed' as lying there, almost unguarded, were the

Afrika Korps supply dumps and repair workshops.[6]

Freyberg replied by outlining the proposal to move as much as possible of the division westwards; 6 Brigade was already moving on Point 175 and 4 Brigade on Gambut. His object was 'to concentrate whole division less 5 Brigade group north of and in touch with 6 Brigade group', and to 'move as soon as I can by daylight and consider further advance by night'.[7] Five Brigade would remain to cover the Sollum/Bardia/Capuzzo/Musaid area; it was hoped that the Indian Division would relieve them so they could join the move west but this was unlikely. Freyberg was now being asked to march on Tobruk but without being able to commit the full division. Before the campaign he had written to Cunningham, begging him 'if the occasion should arise, to send us as a three-brigade division, and I pointed out the weakness in my opinion of a binary [two-brigade] division in such an operation'.[8]

Having already successfully taken Sidi Azeiz and Capuzzo, Five Brigade moved to secure the border area, 23 Battalion captured Musaid and 28 (Maori) Battalion captured the Sollum barracks, taking about 250 prisoners along with a lot of enemy equipment. As New Zealand's official war correspondent reported in Wellington's *Evening Post,* 'the sound of Maori hakas broke through the dawn as the Maori Battalion swarmed to a spectacular attack near Sollum, on the morning of November 23'. The Maori approached, screened by British tanks that were heavily shelled by German artillery, then, when they were within a mile of the Sollum barracks, 'in the first grey light of dawn, with bayonets fixed and led by the commanding officer ... rushed in to a swift and demoralising attack' – in the face of heavy fire. The Germans finally 'threw their hands up in surrender. Many scattered in confusion and were chased down the road into Sollum township terrified by the blood-curdling yells of the Maoris.' The battle was quickly over: 'when the Germans realised they were up against inspired Maoris who knew no fear, they withdrew from the barracks and retreated smartly down the road'.[9] Although the Maori casualties were initially light, during the day they were shelled by enemy long-range guns from Halfaya, and by dusk 18 had been killed and 33 wounded, including the commanding officer, Lieutenant Colonel George Dittmer.

Reports were now reaching the division that Sidi Rezegh was in enemy hands and that 7 Armoured Division had withdrawn. Leaving 5 Brigade – less 21 Battalion, which joined the group moving west – to secure the Bardia sector, the rest of the division began the march to Tobruk. The situation was urgent. 'By attacking and keeping on attacking,' Freyberg wrote, 'we had a larger enemy force in our area at a disadvantage but we had to keep at him. Surprise and the bayonet were our means and time was the vital factor. We had the legs of the enemy, and in my opinion, would keep the initiative so long as we did not get tied to the ground.'[10]

By nightfall on the 23rd 6 Brigade was on Point 175, but subjected to shellfire and under threat from north, south and west. That day 4 Brigade, excluding 20 Battalion, moved off westwards, keeping to the north of the Trigh Capuzzo towards Gambut airfield but there were several enemy outposts in the vicinity. After a few miles they ran into fire coming down from the escarpment above them. They turned their 25-pounders on the enemy guns, which disappeared behind the escarpment, but the bombardment resumed and continued until dusk. On the morning of the 23rd German mortar bombs and shells were still bursting among the Gambut buildings, but by 3p.m. the brigade took the weakly held airfield where there were some 30 aircraft, mostly already wrecked. They captured about 130 prisoners and also dumps of fuel, food and water. Four Brigade then moved up to be in line with 6 Brigade.

The division was now well scattered and vulnerable; Freyberg later summed up the position:

> 6 Brigade had been ordered up to the Sidi Rezegh position, 45 miles [73km] away from where we were at Sidi Azeiz, to support the

South African brigade, which had become isolated there. We had either to support Brigadier Barrowclough or lose him, for it was obvious that all was not going well. At this time, of course, the Brigadier had been detached from my command and was working under 30 Corps.[11]

On the afternoon of the 23rd Divisional Headquarters, together with 20 and 21 Battalions, started moving west and by 1.30a.m. on the 24th they had reached Bir el Chleta. It was not an easy trip. Twenty-one Battalion ran into the enemy and had to wait for I-tanks from 20 Battalion to support them. Nineteen Battalion was also in contact with the enemy. The going was very rough, flares and gun flashes were visible ahead and on the flanks; in addition there were enemy forces in the area that prevented direct contact with 4 Brigade. By the time the division reached Bir el Chleta the moon had gone down, so positions had to be set in the dark.

On the 23rd Cunningham, shaken by the significant British armoured losses, had sent an urgent request that Auchinleck should fly up to discuss the situation. Auchinleck heard that the initial reports of the German tank losses were optimistic, and also that 4 Armoured and 5 South African Brigades were being overrun. Reports now indicated the British had about 44 tanks fit to fight compared with the enemy's 120, which was a serious concern because of the German tanks' superiority. With the British losses the enemy would be able to attack the British infantry unopposed. The senior officers held a meeting, at which 13 Corps Commander Godwin-Austen gained the impression that Cunningham was thinking of calling off the offensive. But he was adamant: 'I couldn't possibly ask Freyberg and the New Zealand division to call off their attacks – it is absolutely unthinkable.' Norrie shared this view.[12]

The same day Godwin-Austen wrote to Freyberg, who received the letter late on the 24th, putting all the New Zealand troops back under 13 Corps command. He reported that 30 Corps was 'in a bad way', and that 'our own losses have been extremely heavy and though it may be pessimistic to say so, it may well be that we have less tanks (excluding I-tanks) running than the enemy'. There was, however, 'no necessity whatever, I am sure you will agree, to become disheartened over the situation of our 30 Corps. We will meet and destroy the enemy tanks with our guns and I-tanks. I am absolutely determined to relieve Tobruk when we shall automatically get at least 40 more I-tanks.' And he would 'refuse to consider' any withdrawal 'while our prospects on the whole are so rosy by comparison with the enemy's whose mobile German forces are so small and of whom we have already garnered so much'.[13]

This still, however, left the New Zealanders with the formidable task of achieving, with just two brigades (plus 21 Battalion) and such I-tanks as it could muster, what the whole of 30 Corps could not. At a further meeting on the 24th, when Cunningham's Brigadier General Staff, Alexander Galloway, asked Godwin-Austen if 13 Corps could relieve Tobruk, he replied,

'No! But Freyberg will.' The conference ended with Godwin-Austen telling Galloway that 'at all costs this offensive must continue and the latter returned to HQ 8 Army a very much happier man'. According to Brigadier Latham, Godwin-Austen effectively said, 'if you call off this offensive now it will be the greatest disaster the British Army has suffered for centuries'.[14]

Auchinleck, considering that Rommel 'was probably in as bad a shape as we were, especially with Tobruk unvanquished behind him', ordered the offensive to continue.[15] He was convinced that supply shortages would prove the German commander's downfall. After three days Auchinleck flew back to Cairo, leaving behind a strongly worded letter to Cunningham for general publication. He was convinced 'that the determination to beat the enemy of your commanders and troops could NOT be greater, and I have NO doubt whatever that he will be beaten'. After further exhortation, he concluded that 'there is only one order: ATTACK AND PURSUE. ALL OUT EVERYONE.'[16] Auchinleck had also reluctantly decided that an exhausted Cunningham should be relieved of his command, 'because he had begun to think defensively'. On 26 November Cunningham was replaced by Major General Neil M. Ritchie.[17]

On the morning of the 24th, 20 Battalion was ordered to move up to clear out some enemy positions around Bir el Chleta and the Trigh Capuzzo. Kippenberger's plan was to 'make a frontal attack with tanks leading and the infantry following in their trucks, machine-guns, anti-tank guns, and carriers giving covering fire from the right flank'. As they advanced several tanks were hit until the tank commander called Kippenberger, reporting 'I've had seven tanks hit; I'll have to stop'. Kippenberger, seeing the infantry starting to leave the trucks and advance on foot, and now very vulnerable to enemy fire, responded, 'The infantry are attacking; go on or I'll court-martial you.' As he admitted later, 'this was unfair to a very gallant officer, killed a few days later, but it was no time for politeness'.[18]

The battalion took 260 prisoners and captured three 88mm guns, although some enemy troops got away. The men were pleased with their efforts and an exhilarated Kippenberger 'was still rather excited when I met Gentry, the G1, and told him "Tell the General my infantry are beautiful"'.[19] Twenty Battalion then rejoined 4 Brigade, north of the Trigh Capuzzo.

Six Brigade's first objective for the 24th was to clear Point 175, then advance towards the blockhouse. At 4.30a.m. A Company of 24 Battalion advanced and took up positions in reserve behind C Company. At 10.30 B Company attacked Point 175 from about a mile (1.6km) east of the crest. As on the previous day there was no real briefing: one man later recalled that 'B Company was given a "small job of cleaning up a pocket of resistance" while another thought the task was "clearing up a few machine gun posts at Point 175"'.[20] Meanwhile 26 Battalion protected the southern flank, supported by 9 Machine Gun Platoon and some tanks.

B Company did not initially meet heavy opposition and successfully took the cairn, but further west the fire intensified and several men were killed when caught on the exposed western side of the crest. Colonel Shuttleworth ordered B Company to halt as by then it had 'regained the line originally occupied by Col McNaught and from which he had been driven back'. Although 'this was ... a particularly well executed daylight advance', the men were left in an exposed position and suffered quite high casualties.[21]

Now 6 Brigade held some of the Point 175 hill but the enemy held strong positions in the wadi Rugbet en-Nbeidat, and around the blockhouse on the higher ground further west. Barrowclough, watching 24 Battalion's fortunes, realised that taking Point 175 did not give the control he had hoped, because of the lie of the land around the blockhouse and the cover given by the intervening wadi. To consolidate its position on the Sidi Rezegh ridge, the brigade had to take the wadi and then the blockhouse. The brigade had suffered heavy I-tank losses and was low on artillery ammunition, which placed it in a precarious position, as the commander of 30 Corps had warned of an attack in force by enemy tanks. Fortunately, although the 'victorious but battered 15 and 21 Panzer Divisions had laagered for the night not far from the New Zealanders', there was no attack; Rommel had other plans for his armour.[22]

The brigade needed reorganisation; the hard-hit 25 Battalion was restructured into two infantry companies, using any available reserves, including cooks, clerks and drivers. To guard the southern flank Freyberg ordered 4 Brigade's 21 Battalion to join the 6 Brigade group, and it took up position just to the east of 26 Battalion at Point 187. During the day the positions were consolidated, although 24 Battalion was attacked and later some areas were bombed, with minor casualties.

From some captured enemy troops New Zealand intelligence officers had now discovered that in addition to the Italian infantry there was a strong division of experienced German infantry present, of which they had not been aware. This was 361 Afrika Regiment, part of the ZBV Afrika (Special Purposes) Division (subsequently renamed 90 Light), which had only recently arrived.

As the *Auckland Star* reported a couple of days later, 'a radical change is gradually occurring in the Sidi Rezegh engagement'. What was 'originally a mass encounter between armoured vehicles, the engagement is now assuming the guise of a modern pitched battle, with mobile artillery playing a more important part'. The 'tank units', were 'now licking their wounds and taking stock of the position'.[23] The *Evening Post* quoted a tank officer's opinion that 'the Germans seemed confused by the convolutions of the battle, and did not seem to know where they were. "One German motorcyclist, with his companion in a side-car, drove straight into our lines, and, after saluting, asked in German where the commanding officer was ... We quickly collared them both."'[24]

For the next few days Divisional Headquarters occupied a flat area near the base of the escarpment east of Point 175. Nearby a small wadi curved up through the escarpment and a dressing station was established on its eastern side. Over the succeeding days it would treat hundreds of casualties from both sides. Not far away a POW camp was also set up – just a crude cage of barbed wire.

On the 24th Rommel, buoyed with the armoured successes, decided to make a bold attack on the Allied supply lines and ordered his two armoured divisions to make a raid towards the frontier. Geoffrey Cox observed the German exodus, 'the tops of lorries passing along the escarpment [as] a line of vehicles was moving away south-eastwards, in the direction of Egypt'. He thought they were South African: 'it was only some hours later that I realised I had witnessed the Afrika Korps heading for the frontier.'[25]

With some consolidation achieved and with 4 and 6 Brigades now in line, Freyberg summoned Barrowclough and Inglis to plan the next steps. The three men decided to make parallel night attacks with the bayonet; 6 Brigade would move to clear the wadis west of Point 175 and 4 Brigade would move on Zaafran, another slightly higher point north of the Trigh Capuzzo. Approaching midnight Freyberg signalled Godwin-Austen his position:

> Have now formed up as a binary division without Div Cav. Large pockets enemy still in our rear. We are attacking westward and are now on a line running north and south through Pt 175 ... If we had petrol and ammunition we might have been in Tobruk early tomorrow. As it is we hope to get there tomorrow night but impossible to be definite.

Freyberg received a 'cheerful letter' from Hargest, who reported that 'the Army Commander is very pleased with what the NZ Div has done'.[26]

There was now a gap of about 12 miles (20km) between the division and the most forward units of the Tobruk garrison, which had been fighting its way towards Sidi Rezegh, extending the anti-tank ditch, barbed wire and minefields. The original plan had been to join 7 Armoured Brigade. Because the tank offensive had been unsuccessful, General Ronald Scobie ordered the garrison to dig in and await the arrival of the New Zealanders. The junction point was to be Ed Duda, between Sidi Rezegh and the Tobruk garrison positions.

On the 25th the division resumed its advance westward. At 6a.m. 4 Brigade departed with 19 Battalion on the northern flank, 18 Battalion (with tanks from 44 Royal Tanks) leading and 20 Battalion to the south, near the Trigh Capuzzo. The advance only took about an hour and by 7.30a.m. 18 Battalion was digging in on a 2000-yard (1830m) front level with the western end of Point 175. The advance took the enemy unawares, but it did alert enemy forces further west. Twenty Battalion travelled west some 4 miles (6.5km) until it was level with the blockhouse, when it came under attack from an enemy anti-tank gun nearby.

The New Zealanders met with little opposition and broke up enemy counter-attacks with artillery fire, though shortages of ammunition hampered their efforts. Eighteen and 20 Battalions came under machine gun and mortar fire and suffered casualties. During its move 18 Battalion had a short sharp battle with German anti-tank and machine guns, and took about 30 prisoners, although at some cost. By now they were also aware that 24 and 25 Battalions close by had suffered severe casualties. As Kippenberger later wrote, 'Padre [George] Spence went over to 6 Brigade and came back hours later looking very sad. He had buried eighty of our dead. The General came around and told me we had some very hard fighting ahead.'[27] Nineteen Battalion, on the right flank, also came under shellfire from Zaafran. Clem Paterson recalled that

Jerry either ran hard or simply evacuated before we arrived [but] his guns and mortars ... used to make up for it and plastered us a lot. Then it was more comfortable below ground. Our own artillery were pretty good and more often than not could see their target from the guns. We could see the enemy transport scurrying along the escarpment, shells bursting right amongst them.[28]

The plan for 6 Brigade on the 25th was that 24 Battalion would cross the Rugbet before dawn and capture the high ground around the blockhouse, then carry on westwards. Twenty-six Battalion would move on a parallel line to the south, its objective the edge of Sidi Rezegh airfield. Twentyone Battalion would move later, taking the eastern end of the southern escarpment. Colonel Shuttleworth issued the orders to 24 Battalion about midnight – to 'capture feature BLOCKHOUSE and advance a maximum distance of 2 miles'. The starting time was to be 4.30a.m. and 30 minutes later 26 Battalion would set out. Although there would be some anti-tank support when it became light, the advance would largely be an infantry attack with bayonet, Tommy gun, grenade and Bren gun.[29]

The blockhouse, on top of the escarpment, overlooking the Trigh Capuzzo and with extensive all-round views, was strategically important. It was strongly defended with many well dug-in machine gun positions, and little cover for the attackers. Twenty-four Battalion started on time but soon ran into strong opposition: the wadi was a difficult barrier in the dark and German tanks blew up several trucks. Private L.M. ('Lou') Nelley recalled that 'owing to very heavy machine gun fire and mortar we were forced to ground some two hundred yards [180m] from the blockhouse'.[30] The men also came under fire from their own mortars, machine guns and 25-pounders. A platoon from 20 Battalion, which tried to help by attacking the slopes in front of the blockhouse, was driven back after suffering considerable losses.

Meanwhile 26 Battalion was advancing to the south. C Company came under fire from the direction of the blockhouse, but C and D Companies both reached the edge of the airfield and started to dig in. With 24 Battalion in difficulty, B Company, which had been in reserve, wheeled around to the north to come and support them. By now the blockhouse was also being attacked by artillery and machine gun fire. Four Field Regiment, below the escarpment, also joined in, and Martyn

Uren observed the confusion: the enemy held the blockhouse and 'the ridge still further along the escarpment' but 'our troops ... held the high ground immediately above us'.[31]

A platoon from 24 Battalion, supported by Bren carriers, was sent around to the south, supported by a company from 26 Battalion. The combined weight of the attack finally took its toll and after a determined Bren carrier attack, resistance suddenly crumbled and some 200 German and Italian troops surrendered. There was some continuing fire from enemy guns further west, until fire from 6 Field Regiment drove them off and the blockhouse was finally secure. Twenty-six Battalion's losses were four killed and eight wounded, but 24 Battalion had been hard-hit and was now reduced almost to company strength. The 21 Battalion men, en route to the southern escarpment, were able to retrieve a lot of abandoned equipment from the tank battle before digging in, including vehicles, blankets, Vickers guns, mortars and ammunition.

During the afternoon of the 25th 6 Brigade headquarters moved up to 24 Battalion, 25 Battalion headed to the western side of the Rugbet en-Nbeidat and the artillery batteries, and engineers of 8 Field Company were also moved forward. By that evening the two brigades had successfully achieved their objectives and were positioned, in parallel, astride the Trigh Capuzzo and above and below the Sidi Rezegh escarpment. However enemy counter-attacks continued and the artillery was kept busy harassing enemy tanks; both 4 Brigade and Divisional Headquarters were bombed.

Although both Point 175 and the blockhouse were now in the division's hands, there still some distance to cover to join the Tobruk forces and the enemy was still present in force. Six Brigade's gains of the last two days – a modest, barren hill and 'an Arab lodge, a resting place for travellers, solidly constructed of stone and white plaster, white-tiled inside, a peaceful resort and not at all like the concrete strongpoint most men imagined' – had come at a significant cost.[32]

The *Daily Express* correspondent sent a dispatch that eventually appeared in the *Press* on 28 November. He described the south-east approaches of Tobruk:

littered with broken and burning vehicles, overturned trucks, smashed guns and upended smouldering aircraft, while all over the battlefield wounded and lost men are sorting themselves out, trying to find their units. There is no front line. English and German tanks met and wiped out each other. That is all ... both sides have taken thousands of prisoners and have suffered thousands of casualties. It remains now for the remnants of the opposing armoured forces to reform and wait for reinforcements to reopen this, the bloodiest and swiftest battle the desert has ever seen.[33]

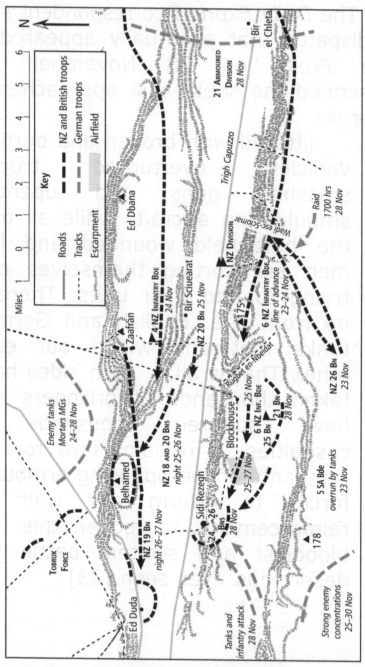

Advance of 4 and 6 NZ Brigades, 23–28 November 1941

Key

- Roads
- Tracks
- Escarpment
- Airfield
- NZ and British troops
- German troops

Miles

Ed Dbana

4 NZ INFANTRY BDE
24 Nov

Zaafran

Bir Scuearat

NZ 20 BN 25 Nov

NZ 18 AND 20 BNS
night 25–26 Nov

Belhamed

Enemy tanks
Mortars MGs
24–28 Nov

TOBRUK FORCE

NZ 19 BN
night 26–27 Nov

Ed Duda

Sidi Rezegh

24 26 BNS
28 Nov

Blockhouse

Rugbet en-Nbeidat

6 NZ INF. BDE

25 BN
25–27 Nov

6 BN
25 Nov

21 BN
28 Nov

5 SA Bde
overrun by tanks
23 Nov

178

Tanks and
infantry attack
28 Nov

Strong enemy
concentrations
25–30 Nov

Trigh Capuzzo

NZ DIVISION

Wadi esc-Sciomar

175

6 NZ INFANTRY BDE
line of advance
23–24 Nov

NZ 26 BN
23 Nov

21 ARMOURED
DIVISION
28 Nov

Bir
el Chleta

Raid
1700 hrs
28 Nov

CHAPTER 8

The Attacks on Sidi Rezegh and Belhamed

By the evening of the 25th, although only two brigades were moving west, the New Zealanders had made good progress towards linking up with the Tobruk garrison. However, only 60 rounds per gun of 25-pounder ammunition remained and there was little chance of that being replenished soon. Other supplies were also running low and there were almost 1000 German prisoners and hundreds of wounded to look after. And there were estimated to be seven or eight German battalions and two Italian Bersaglieri battalions in the Sidi Rezegh–Belhamed area. The battle was now one for control of the three critical escarpments near Sidi Rezegh, the vital section of the enemy's lines of communication where the Tobruk Bypass Road passed close by the Trigh Capuzzo.

That day Freyberg had received a letter from Godwin-Austen congratulating them on their progress – 'you have done splendidly' – and outlining his thoughts about the next steps to achieve a 'definite, firm and secure junction' with the Tobruk force at Ed Duda.[1] This letter was followed by an order as to how the link-up would proceed. Freyberg felt that rather than relieving Tobruk the priority would almost certainly be to join with the garrison around the Ed Duda–Sidi Rezegh bottleneck to repel the inevitable counter-attacks and keep the corridor open.

At 5p.m. that day Freyberg held a conference with his brigadiers, then issued orders to 'attack and capture Belhamed, Ed Duda, Sidi Rezegh'.[2] There were only a few hours to prepare as Zero Hour was set for 9p.m.; this would be another infantry night attack with bayonet and support from I-tanks. The target for 4 Brigade, and 18 and 20 Battalions, was Belhamed, while 19 Battalion would remain at Zaafran. Six

Brigade would attack Sidi Rezegh, with an initial attack over about 6 miles (10km) by 24 and 25 Battalions after which 21 and 26 Battalions would push on to Ed Duda, to meet up with the Tobruk garrison at daybreak on the 26th.

Four Brigade would have a straight advance over reasonably flat ground just north of the Trigh Capuzzo. Six Brigade's plan was 'certainly a formidable one'. The New Zealanders knew enough about the enemy's strength 'to make it perfectly clear that that place would not be won without a stern fight'. And then 'a substantial force had to advance a further three miles [5km] to Ed Duda and engage an enemy garrison about whose strength and composition we had not the slightest information'.[3] There were reports of enemy in front of 4 Brigade but little information about the area facing 6 Brigade, so the former was given two I-tank squadrons in support and the latter only one.

Kippenberger briefed the 20 Battalion men: 'we are going forward tonight to take Belhamed and open the way to

Tobruk.' This was 'the crisis of the battle. We have 6000 yards [5485m] to go and after 4000 yards [3657m] we will have to fight our way. We will go straight in with bayonet and bomb and nothing will stop us.'[4] Kippenberger wished 'every man of you' good luck, and it was 'a very wonderful thing to hear the response: "good luck to you too, Sir"'.[5] Eighteen Battalion's task was 'a straightout silent attack, with the bayonet, infantry face to face with infantry, no trucks, no tanks, no artillery except a few salvoes to help the attackers keep direction'.[6]

Moving in silence, the men departed, 20 Battalion to the left (south) and 18 Battalion to the right (north). They moved through three lines of enemy resistance but after some 3 miles (5km) they came under heavy mortar and machine gun fire and were able to take their objective shortly after midnight, following some heavy fighting. Corporal Ralph Joyes from 18 Battalion knew he would "never ever ... forget that approach march. It seemed endless and I think that most of us were pretty well done when we actually got into the real thing. Even then we saw nothing but tracer which seemed to pass by us on all sides. The noise was terrific with most of us yelling our heads off.'[7]

During the advance, Kippenberger, with a small party and two lorries went astray and ended up on the Tobruk Bypass Road by mistake. They had some difficulty finding their way back to the battalion, as Kippenberger reported to brigade headquarters: 'after much wandering I think the position is that 18th are on the objective but haven't gone far enough and 20th have gone too far. I can't find them anyway.'[8]

On 26 November, a 'bitter breeze followed a very cold night'.[9] Both 18 and 20 Battalions were in very exposed positions on the Belhamed ridge, with 18 Battalion on the eastern half and 20 Battalion to the west. Eighteen Battalion had arrived about midnight and spent the rest of the night trying to dig in. The men had to 'hack out hunks of rock and build sangars above ground, some protection certainly, but poor substitutes for slit trenches'.[10] They were under fire from three sides: enemy infantry appeared to be organising for a counter-attack and were bombarding them with mortars. Both battalions were suffering heavy casualties.

Four Brigade was ordered to support 6 Brigade in taking Ed Duda, but this was later postponed so that the brigade could consolidate its position on Belhamed. It was also apparent that 6 Brigade was in no position to attack Ed Duda, especially in daylight, and there was a strong enemy presence between Sidi Rezegh and Belhamed. I-tanks sent from Zaafran to support 4 Brigade arrived soon after 7a.m. They had some immediate success against enemy anti-tank and machine guns until they were attacked by 88mm guns from the Sidi Rezegh escarpment and several were destroyed or damaged. The attacks on Belhamed continued and because of the number of officers wounded Freyberg was led to believe that 20 Battalion was in a bad position, especially after Kippenberger himself was hit in the thigh by a machine gun bullet. The men had a hard day, with little protection from the continual enemy artillery fire.

It was Four Brigade HQ's belief that much of the fire being directed on Belhamed was coming from enemy troops driven westwards towards Ed Duda. The brigade was able to call up RAF bomber support; that afternoon 17 Blenheim bombers, escorted by fighters, followed later by 18 Maryland bombers, also with a fighter escort, bombed the area south of Belhamed and 4 Field Regiment provided artillery support. But meanwhile British troops from 1 Battalion Essex Regiment and supporting arms attacked Ed Duda. They were fired on as they assembled but eventually took their objective near the Bypass Road. A tragic incident followed. The RAF bombers arrived just when the British troops were advancing and bombed them heavily, killing or wounding almost 40. In fact Ed Duda was not strongly defended and the Italian garrison quickly surrendered.

Although 4 Brigade was quite close to Ed Duda, it was unaware that it had been taken, and Freyberg did not know where the Tobruk garrison troops were. Seeking to get some pressure taken off Belhamed, Freyberg signalled

Godwin-Austen shortly after 1p.m. that 'situation demands Tobruk garrison exerts its greatest pressure as early as possible'. Eventually there was a terse response from Scobie of the Tobruk garrison: 'we are on Ed Duda – ensure NOT bombed.'[11]

Six Brigade's plan was that, in phase one, 24 and 25 Battalions would advance towards Sidi Rezegh and form a box, a defended rectangular position, through which, in phase two, 21 and 26 Battalions would continue towards Ed Duda. They would be supported by artillery (2- and 25-pounders) from 6 Field Regiment, and platoons from 3 Machine Gun Company. Twenty-four Battalion would depart at 11p.m. from a starting line just south of the blockhouse. Its objective was to set positions on the plateau above the mosque, extending some 2000 yards (1828m) east to west, and 1000 yards (915m) north to south. Twenty-five Battalion would extend this box to the south.

Twenty-one Battalion would have a 6-mile (10km) march in the dark over rough ground without landmarks, then have to link up with 26 Battalion, go through the box formed by 24 and 25 Battalions and descend the escarpment near the mosque. The two battalions would then have another 3 miles (5km) to travel before attacking Ed Duda, which would almost certainly be strongly defended. And all this before daybreak. Even getting the attack under way was difficult, to avoid the battalions getting mixed up, and again there was little time to plan. Although several miles apart, 21 and 26 Battalions would have to join up for the assault on Ed Duda under cover of darkness.

Twenty-four Battalion's march started well: the men advanced 3 miles before spreading out in box formation. They were not opposed until they started to dig in and then the firing continued for the rest of the night. They had difficulty forming the box, as it was hard for the separate companies to keep in touch, they had a large contingent of Italian prisoners to guard and there were many enemy both on the crest of the escarpment and in the many wadis. To the south, the men of 25 Battalion forming up their sector of the box and scratching shallow trenches the best they could in the rocky surface, could see bullets flying around to the north near 24 Battalion.

It was nearer midnight before 26 Battalion started out, staying close to the edge of the escarpment. Colonel J.R. ('Rusty') Page thought that 24 Battalion was to have cleared the opposition along the escarpment, so was taken by surprise when the enemy, clearly on alert, intensified their fire along the escarpment. The confusion about where 24 Battalion actually was grew when 21 Battalion arrived above the mosque, expecting to join with 24 Battalion and a guide from 26 Battalion, but found neither.

Despite this setback, 21 Battalion continued trying to move down the escarpment. The battalion became disorganised, however, and was spread out over a wide area both above and below the escarpment. With no chance of reaching Ed Duda, the men were in a dangerous position, spread out but not dug in, and closer to the enemy than they thought. The terrain was playing a big part: although the escarpments offered 'commanding positions', the short wadis indenting them 'provided excellent cover and protection in an otherwise almost featureless expanse of desert'.[12]

At 3.30a.m. Divisional Headquarters, puzzled about 6 Brigade's progress, sent a message to 13 Corps that the brigade had captured Sidi Rezegh and was 'now on the way to Ed Duda'. This was corrected at 5.10a.m., with a signal that Belhamed had been taken but that there was still 'much opposition' at Sidi Rezegh. Since it was obvious that no attack on Ed Duda could be made until Sidi Rezegh was secure, at 5.40a.m. 6 Brigade was ordered to 'consolidate on Sidi Rezegh' and 'make a plan to attack Ed Duda' but not to move until ordered, so the attack could be co-ordinated with the Tobruk garrison.[13]

In agreeing to cancel phase two, Divisional Headquarters had pointed out that 4 Brigade now controlled Belhamed and hoped that 6 Brigade would have secured all the Sidi Rezegh escarpment by dawn. This, however, was not to be; the enemy still held much of it (and in strength), the two brigades were separated by another strong enemy position between the Trigh Capuzzo and Belhamed, and further enemy reinforcements were arriving from the west, accompanied by tanks.

Six Brigade was badly disorganised: 24 and 25 Battalions had become 'inextricably mixed up', even with some of the 26 Battalion troops. By now, as the brigade war diary noted, 'the troops were extremely tired, having been continuously in action for several days and even after repelling the enemy morning attacks all chances of rest was denied to them by the constant shelling and machine gun fire to which they were being subjected'.[14] Barrowclough reported at 9a.m. that he intended to hold Sidi Rezegh with 26 Battalion facing north, 24 Battalion in the centre and 21 Battalion on the left, although that would be difficult as he was out of touch and could not communicate with 21 Battalion. His report did not make clear exactly what the situation on Sidi Rezegh was, and Freyberg wrote in his diary that '4 Brigade reached Belhamed in dawn attack with 18 and 20 Battalions and 6 Brigade reached

Rezegh'. Later reports did explain, however, that '6 Brigade found Rezegh strongly held'.[15] Freyberg felt that the 6 Brigade's position was 'most difficult': it was 'not capable of much further offensive action' and overall 'it was at this stage that we felt the want of another brigade'.[16] Poor communications made planning difficult, especially as his only contact with the Tobruk garrison was through 13 Corps.

Although under pressure on Belhamed, 4 Brigade was established in some strength, but on Sidi Rezegh, where 6 Brigade was trying to consolidate, many units were in difficult positions and with little cover. Snipers and machine guns harassed the 26 Battalion men, who only had the shallow holes they had made during the night, and 'digging new ones was nerve-wracking work'.[17]

But the 'hardest hit' of the supporting arms were the machine gunners: 7 and 9 Platoons, which were forward with 21, 24 and 25 Battalions, 'were involved in very heavy fighting indeed and lost seven of their eight guns in the course of the day, with casualties in proportion'.[18] In 7 Platoon Sergeant Randel Heron's section was 'ordered to follow a telephone line the night before we were taken prisoner and ended up in front of our own artillery and infantry'. They 'were subjected to their fire and that of the enemy the following morning, also enemy tanks'. He also remembered hearing 'wounded Itie soldiers calling "Mamma Mia" behind us': they had 'been wounded by their own artillery which was shelling us at the same time as were our own guns'. It was almost impossible to dig in 'as the ground was so hard. Sand on top but rock underneath.' Then 'a German tank came up from the mosque, with a German officer looking out of the turret. We were machine gunned and had no option but to surrender. One of my men, Private George Capel, had a bullet through his thigh and I dressed the wound with my dressing. That's when my war finished.'[19]

For John Black, with 9 Platoon, going in at night was a tricky business. Very hard ground (even the pick heads turned their points up) and then once the gun was set up and daylight arrived you sometimes found a small rise on the ground just in front of your position which made the gun inoperable. This happened to our gun team that morning, ground was all rocks and some very solid. The enemy (Germans) were not too far away, about 200 yards [180m] and were in darkness during our digging in process, shooting in our direction. Having found a Tommy gun on the truck I put it to good use. This helped to keep them quiet whilst our gun team dug-in ... we were all very tired having had no sleep for thirty-six hours. I knew once my head hit the ground I would be asleep in no time. Later that morning I did slip into 'bye-bye' land. The gun team thought the latest salvo of mortar fire must have hit me. Their method of checking up was to throw stones into my slit trench. That had the desired effect.

During the morning they found they were isolated; their company's 8 Platoon was pulling out. 'They had discovered that our infantry, during the night, had attacked the Germans and had been repulsed. They withdrew under cover of darkness. Here we were; eight machine guns and no infantry protection. No point in staying, we would be prisoners of war in no time.' So under heavy machine gun fire from the enemy they also pulled out, 'having to leave our guns behind' (although they were later retrieved).[20]

Early in the day Barrowclough reviewed as much of the front as possible, and reported that the situation was 'disorganised and somewhat precarious. Every effort was made to organise a defensive system but the difficulties of doing so were tremendous as the whole area was under observation and fire from strong enemy positions.'[21] The Sidi Rezegh ridge had still not been taken and there were several pockets of the enemy in the wadis, making movements dangerous. Even late in the day it was hard to get a reasonably accurate assessment of the battalion strengths, though 21

Battalion was worst hit, with only 15 officers left.

Having received this report about 4.30p.m., Freyberg concluded that it would be impossible for 6 Brigade to move on Ed Duda. He ordered Inglis to take over that responsibility: 'you will join them tonight.' Barrowclough was ordered to reorganise 6 Brigade and 'get secure on top of the hill [Sidi Rezegh]'.[22] Both brigades were committed to another night of attacks with their respective objectives being about 3 miles (5km) apart. Four Brigade's attack was critical, to ensure that the link-up with Ed Duda was secured. The division learnt that 13 Corps headquarters was moving closer to them and Freyberg noted the corps' liaison officer's comment that 'they say that the NZ Div has been the only star in the firmament recently' but that things overall were now considered better.[23]

In 4 Brigade, 18 and 20 Battalions were already committed on Belhamed. Nineteen Battalion, the only battalion still at full strength, was at Zaafran, and was given the important task of moving to Ed Duda, entailing a 9-mile (14.5km) advance in the dark, with I-tanks from 44 Royal Tanks to support them. Inglis proposed a bold plan: the tanks would drive at top speed south of Belhamed directly at Ed Duda, hoping that the sound would discourage opposition. Because of the difficulties of attacking blind, the tank commander 'was unenthusiastic,' but Freyberg, who was attending the briefing, took Brigadier Inglis aside and said, 'Don't let them out of it; make them go.' Inglis assured him that he would. Eventually the tank commander agreed, and from then on 'could not have been more cooperative'.[24] The plan was for 19 Battalion to follow the tanks, but news of the high casualties suffered at Sidi Rezegh led to thoughts that 19 Battalion casualties in this coming attack could possibly be as high as 50 per cent.

Clem Paterson, of 19 Battalion's Wellington Company, remembered word coming about 4p.m. 'that we were to go in that night on a heavily fortified position and break through to contact our forces who had driven in a wedge from Tobruk'. The men's feelings were 'varied, because a large force had failed to make the grade that day. However we had about 13 tanks [to lead the battalion] and got ready.' Three or four tanks would accompany the infantry and each company would have with it only one truck, carrying weapons and ammunition. As Paterson noted, 'tanks hate night operations, being very blind and this was the first organised night attack behind tanks in Army history (or so the tankies told us).'[25]

There was little time to prepare but by 9.30p.m. 19 Battalion was ready. The first wave of tanks drove off, overcame a strong enemy position and only an hour and a quarter after setting out they were at their objective and among friends on Ed Duda. Fifteen minutes after the tanks departed, the battalion followed. 'I wonder can you imagine the scene?' Paterson wrote later. 'A moon nearly full, clouds scudding across the sky. About ten tanks criss-crossing immediately ahead of us and the rest amongst us, tracks screeching and diesels going. Tracer bullets enfilading from side to side and

Verey lights by the dozen, and behind, our whole Battalion pretty close together.'

In the second wave Paterson heard a few isolated shots and enemy listening posts were discovered. It was heavy going and we were dog-tired. Eventually we moved right through the enemy positions – a natural fortress almost, and apart from odd Jerries in dugouts **not a soul** to oppose us! Frantic cries from a POW cage on our right – full of South Africans, captured I think at Sidi Rezegh. I expected any minute that everything would open up at once – it was quite uncanny.[26]

The enemy fire was badly directed and 19 Battalion, 'whose own killing was done almost entirely with the bayonet, so much of it that the troops became sick of it and began calling on the Germans to surrender', took only six prisoners, 'although another 550 were scooped in next morning'. According to Inglis, it was 'the most amazing night attack in my experience, not least because the 19th ... had not a single casualty itself'.[27]

It had been a huge achievement, crossing a rough desert expanse in the dark without losing a man or a vehicle. Nineteen Battalion joined with the Tobruk garrison, made contact with 32 Army Tank Brigade and was then placed in a shallow wadi, 1 1/2 miles (2.5km) east of Ed Duda and 2 miles (3.2km) west of Belhamed. A 16,000-yard (14,630m) telephone line was laid behind the battalion and at 4a.m. on the 27th Inglis received a report that 19 Battalion was on Ed Duda. Despite this, Scobie of the Tobruk garrison was not told about the presence of 44 Royal Tanks and 19 Battalion until 1p.m., and at 3.20p.m. he finally confirmed that those two units were with his own troops at Ed Duda. The communication difficulties between the various units would make it hard to move further westwards, and it was likely they would be facing an armoured counter-attack before long.

As the *Evening Post* reported on 28 November, the link-up with the Tobruk garrison was regarded as extremely important. 'If, as may be expected, the junction is maintained and the breach in the Axis besieging line around Tobruk is widened, Tobruk, with its sea communications may become a valuable base for supplies for the field forces, which are at present maintained by long lines of communications stretching across 200 miles [320km] of desert.' Significantly, 'tanks from Tobruk [were] now available for the main battle in the Sidi Rezegh area'.[28] A war correspondent quoted in the paper next day said 'one picture stands out. It was of a grimy British Tommy and an equally grimy New Zealander, the former from Tobruk and the other from the advancing forces. There was a clasp of hands and "hello, mate, all right?" – "Fine, thanks, how are you?" The men of Tobruk had joined hands with their brothers.'[29]

A few days later, the *Sydney Morning Herald* war correspondent paid 'a glowing tribute to the New Zealanders who hacked their way through the cream of General Rommel's infantry to join the Tobruk garrison'. The New Zealanders 'were attacked by tanks, but beat them back. For a time no supplies could be got through to them and they suffered a shortage of water, food and ammunition, but they tightened their belts and carried on.' He was impressed as 'these veterans of Greece and Crete took revenge for what they had suffered there'. It was quite simple: 'they had been ordered to link up with Tobruk, and link up they did. It was one of the epics of this campaign, and a glorious page in New Zealand's history.'[30]

Six Brigade faced a stern challenge to overcome Sidi Rezegh but it 'was one of absolute necessity and it was clear that at whatever cost it must be undertaken'.[31] All the units were in exposed and overlooked positions and could be counter-attacked. When Barrowclough summoned his commanding officers, they had to meet in 'a hollow no deeper than a dewpond', lying down with the maps spread out in front of them. 'Well gentlemen,' Barrowclough said, 'the General insists that Sidi Rezegh be taken ... 24 and 26 Battalions will attack and capture Sidi Rezegh tonight.'[32] Both commanding officers, said the 6 Brigade war diary, 'recognised the imperative necessity of the contemplated operation and very gallantly applied themselves to the inevitable task'. The troops, exhausted and dealing with heavy losses, were resigned 'to the prospect of another night's heavy fighting against obviously superior odds'. The success of the attack would rely principally on 'the courage and enterprise of the attacking infantry and the well known German inability to stand up to determined troops advancing with the bayonet in the darkness.'[33]

The plan, simpler this time, was for 26 Battalion to attack along the escarpment to the mosque, while 24 Battalion would attack from the south, moving north-west to take an area between the mosque and a lattice observation mast to the south. The recent high casualties resulted in some reorganisation of the battalions: 25 Battalion was left in position to form a base for the attack and one (A) Company and a platoon (from C Company) from 21 Battalion were transferred to 24 Battalion. Colonel Page briefed the 26 Battalion company commanders while sitting on a Bren carrier that was being targeted by an anti-tank gun. Then the men were briefed, and the arrival of a hot stew boosted their spirits for the next phase of the battle.

The battalions moved out at about 11.30p.m. and ran into opposition almost immediately, with flares, tracer bullets and then anti-tank guns and mortars joining in from an enemy that was lying in wait for them. A and B Companies of 26 Battalion fought their way along the slopes, moving from wadi to wadi in the face of heavy small arms fire and grenades. Losses were high: commanding officer Colonel 'Rusty' Page was wounded and Major Thomas Milliken, A Company commander, was killed. Battalion 2IC Major B.J. Mathewson, who had taken command of the battalion for this attack, was badly wounded and his driver killed when their truck struck a mine.

Leading B Company was Captain Charles Gatenby, who had been 'given the honour' after Captain Arthur Wesney was killed on 23 November. As he later told his wife, Gatenby took over at a difficult time: 'bitter fighting went on all the next ten days and casualties were heavy on both sides. Life became a bit of a nightmare.' In this action, his company led the attack twice 'with your foolish husband out in front leading. Someone must have been praying for me because men fell on all sides of me and I always found myself untouched. I still wonder how it was possible for anyone to go through the hail of fire the enemy put down and lived.'[34] Gatenby and his men eventually reached the flat ground below the mosque and formed a front with whoever could be found in the dark.

C Company had to deal with the many pockets of enemy, going from one machine gun post to the next. One of the battalion mortar men, Maurice Cameron, recalled that 'it shook many of the boys to hear the Bersaglieri [9 Bersaglieri Regiment] screaming "Amigo, Amigo" with one hand up and the other on the machine gun. They must have been wondering if it was better to kill or be killed for the devils were forced by Germans behind and hell in front.' In his view it was the 'hardest, bloodiest and most deadly attack ever staged by our unit'.[35] Gatenby agreed: 'the men fought gloriously and I was proud of them.'[36]

Near daybreak on the 27th all four companies of 26 Battalion were close to where they were meant to be but as a counter-attack seemed imminent the officers ordered a short withdrawal back to the crest of the escarpment, a more defensible position. Inadvertently two of the companies ended up right back at their start line, which resulted in the battalion being spread out again, but this did provide men to carry back the dozens of wounded. The two companies returned towards the mosque in the morning and later dug in 'amidst the ghastly mess of the enemy dead'.[37]

Twenty-four Battalion's advance came under fire immediately and then it was 'hand to hand fighting practically all the way to [the] objective'. D Company was caught in a very exposed position on a bare forward slope and 'enemy fire became murderous, machine gun, anti-tank and mortar fire from directly ahead. The company was cut to pieces.'[38] B Company, on the left flank, met little opposition, but Lou Nelley, with C Company, recalled 'very heavy casualties'. The mosque was 'directly in front of us and we thought we could see Tobruk in the distance'. They withdrew to a ridge and dug in facing south, but it was a terrible day for Nelley: 'I had lost my brother [Charlie] and many good pals were missing besides.'[39] A Company from 21 Battalion arrived in support with artillery and charged down to the mosque, and the enemy retired. It had been a hard fought battle but now, apart from the occasional shell, things were quiet and Captain Edgar Tomlinson of 24 Battalion was finally able to report that 'Sidi Rezegh is ours'.[40]

By now 24 Battalion was severely weakened: B and D Companies had only one officer each and C Company had two. Men from 25 Battalion, which had previously been the weakest, were sent to reinforce C Company. In 26 Battalion 23 men had been killed and 61 wounded, nine of whom subsequently died; its total strength was down to a little over 300. After several days and nights of relentless fighting over open ground, against an enemy that was tenacious and well prepared, the two New Zealand brigades had both achieved their objectives. But they had lost many men, they were isolated, short on supplies and ammunition, and they could be attacked at any time.

Barrowclough was aware that the position still needed to be secured. From above the Sidi Rezegh mosque he could see the enemy only 3 miles (5km) to the west and also the flash of shelling towards Tobruk. There was a wide gap between 4 Brigade at Ed Duda and 6 Brigade at Sidi Rezegh, and 5 Brigade was far away to the east. Because 4 and 6 Brigades had come so far, they were vulnerable to attack from north and west, and there was a long exposed southern flank. To protect 6 Brigade's position, 26 Battalion was positioned up on the ridge facing north, and 24 Battalion covered the north and west; the total box covered an area 2000 yards (1828m) from east to west and 1200 yards (1097m) north to south. To the west the Royal Engineers and 1

Essex were strengthening their defences by placing minefields and barbed wire.

At first light on 27 November Barrowclough had gone forward to see for himself the outcome of the attack. The reconnaissance 'revealed how stubborn had been the fighting there' and

it soon became apparent that both the night attack and the subsequent dawn expansion movement had met with the severest possible opposition. The enemy forces comprised a number of Germans and troops of the 9 Bersaglieri Regiment. Both were plentifully supplied with machine guns and anti-tank guns and it was clear that our troops had had to advance right to the muzzles of these guns before their crews were despatched and the guns silenced. There was an enormous number of dead and wounded all over the battlefield.

Despite Cameron's comments on this devastating encounter, the 6 Brigade war diary considered that the Bersaglieri Regiment had fought 'with much greater determination than is usually found among Italian troops and the numbers of their dead and the positions in which they lay showed that they had kept their guns in action to the last'. Several men had reported that the Germans were 'the first to break under our onslaught ... and that the Bersaglieri had been the last to yield'. This was the kind of opposition that had faced 'the exhausted and sadly depleted ranks of 24 and 26 Battalions', who had 'fought their way to victory and their victory was complete'.[41]

CHAPTER 9

Rommel's Dash to the Frontier

While 4 and 6 Brigades were fully stretched on Belhamed and Sidi Rezegh, 5 Brigade was headquartered, under the command of 4 Indian Division since 23 November, at Sidi Azeiz, approximately midway between Bardia and Sollum. The brigade's battalions were covering enemy forces around the border.

Brigadier Hargest had visited the 13 Corps Headquarters, where he learnt of 6 Brigade's tough battles. It had previously been hoped that 5 Brigade would be able to join the rest of the division, but it was needed to deal with the enemy still active in the area. On the morning of the 24th the enemy attacked outposts of 22 Battalion west of Bardia but were repulsed and withdrew. Twenty-three Battalion at Capuzzo was also attacked, but the enemy departed when British tanks appeared. In addition there was still some heavy fighting at the Omars, near the border, where 4 Indian Division was committed.

After the German armoured successes on 23 November, there were differing opinions in their camp about what to do next. Crüwell thought they should wipe out the British tanks altogether while they were in such a weakened state, but Rommel did not agree. The next day, having assumed that most of the British armour had been destroyed, he led Ravenstein's 21 Panzer Division, and Neumann-Silkow's 15 Panzer Division, with Ariete Division protecting the right flank, on a foray to the Egyptian frontier. It was one of the more controversial moves of Rommel's career, made in part perhaps through a lack of good intelligence concerning the exact whereabouts of the New Zealand forces and the British tank losses.

Rommel had two reasons for his dash to the frontier. Because the main British armoured force around Tobruk had been destroyed, he wanted to 'go for the New Zealanders and Indians before they have been able to join up with the remains of their main force for a combined attack on Tobruk'. He also wanted to 'take Habata [the desert rail terminus] and Maddalena and cut off their supplies'.[1] Speed was vital, he was possibly also assuming that a swift attack deep into the back of the British lines would disrupt communications and force Cunningham to withdraw his forces; then he could attack Tobruk. He was optimistic about how quickly this could be achieved: he advised Colonel Siegfried Westphal of Panzergruppe Headquarters at El Adem that he hoped to be back by the evening of the 24th or the following morning.

If Rommel had continued to commit his armour around Sidi Rezegh the New Zealanders, according to Geoffrey Cox, 'would have had a very rough time'.[2] Instead the two New Zealand brigades had a few days' grace to join up with the Tobruk garrison and continue the battle in the west. And 7 Armoured Division was able to reorganise and bring up most of its 200 reserve tanks, while Rommel's men continued fighting.

Rommel's tanks, led by 21 Panzer Division as it was first ready, were ordered drive to the frontier, 'looking neither to right nor left', followed by 15 Panzer Division.[3] Ravenstein noted in his diary that Rommel was so desperate to get under way that the men were ordered to move off at full speed 'even though the battle group was not completely assembled'. Rommel had told him, 'You have the chance of finishing the campaign tonight.' Later the Germans passed a unit from the Guards Brigade but in their haste did not stop to check why they were there.[4] They were guarding two major British forward supply depots, each some 6 miles (10km) square, and according to one military historian, Ravenstein 'passed north of these camps and unknowingly missed a great chance. If he had run across them, the course of the Desert battle would probably have been different. The British could not have maintained the New Zealanders and kept them fighting.'[5] The panicked British forces hastily struck camp and threw gear into trucks as a convoy raced back to Egypt in what became known as 'the Matruh Stakes'.

Rommel reached the border at 4p.m. on the 24th and that evening his forces grouped close by. His plan, to gather his forces and drive 13 Corps towards the guns of the Italian Savona Division, was based on the misapprehension that 30 Corps had been destroyed and that the 13 Corps' two divisions were near the border. He was not aware that the Allied forces were so widespread or that part of the New Zealand Division had already started to move west. When Captain Robert Crisp, with 4 Armoured Brigade, heard of the German commander's move, he thought 'Rommel had gone clean off his bloody head'. There was 'not the slightest doubt that the Afrika Korps had won the first major encounter at Sidi Rezegh, and that if they had stayed in command of that decisive area, they could have fought the Eighth Army to a standstill'.[6]

That night Rommel narrowly avoided capture. His staff car broke down at Sidi Omar, and through a stroke of good fortune he was picked up by Crüwell in a captured British quad gun tractor, which they christened Mammut (Mammoth). Navigating personally,

Rommel arrived in an area under the control of 4 Indian Division, but the vehicle did not arouse suspicion and the Germans spent an anxious night surrounded by British forces. By the morning of the 25th the DAK had gathered at Sheferzen, on 13 Corps' line of communications near the border, but in a state of some confusion as there were two sets of orders, one from Rommel and the other from Crüwell.

That morning Hargest was 'startled' to receive the news of Rommel's border raid.[7] Air reconnaissance reports indicated that a column of about 2000 vehicles, led by 100 tanks, was heading down the Trigh el-Abd. Five Brigade had already heard that some enemy tanks had been seen in the border area, and that some had been destroyed by the Indian Division, but new reports suggested that this force was a lot stronger and it was closing on Sidi Azeiz. And the enemy was nearer than at first thought: the 'gathering gloom' had caused a pilot to overestimate the distance as 20 miles (32km).[8] Hargest told Freyberg he was expecting an attack from tanks that had penetrated the border; he believed they were pushing towards Halfaya and would turn north to Bardia. He was keen for 5 Brigade to join the rest of the division, but in the meantime was 'harassing the enemy' with patrols.[9]

Because of the importance of the Sidi Azeiz airfield, which was the base for patrolling the area, Hargest strengthened his brigade defences with artillery, machine guns and some 600 infantry, which were dispersed around the field. At night they were joined by Divisional Cavalry, who spent their days out on patrol. With the enemy forces growing, 5 Brigade's position was swiftly becoming threatened, partly because the battalions were far apart: 23 and 28 Battalions were near Sollum and Musaid, and 22 Battalion was to the west of Bardia.

By late afternoon on the 25th the German forces were near the border, heading towards Halfaya and the supply dumps behind Sidi Omar. The opposition they encountered at Sidi Omar was far stronger than had been expected; the British forces had regrouped quickly. That night, Hargest wrote later, 'we saw a long line of Verey lights moving slowly towards us from the south, and turning away to the north-west in the direction of Corps Headquarters'.[10]

Soon after first light on the 26th the 5 Brigade patrols saw a large convoy of enemy moving towards Bardia, between 5 Brigade HQ and 22 Battalion, which was further north. A number of New Zealand units were in action that day, including 23 Battalion at Capuzzo and the Maori Battalion at Sollum, and they saw more enemy columns. These were Rommel's tanks, which had refuelled from some of the British supply dumps and were passing through a gap behind the Indian Division, moving quickly either side of 5 Brigade. Most of 28 (Maori) Battalion was at Sollum barracks and sent a section of carriers south on a reconnaissance. About 4p.m. they 'came streaking back at high speed. Their report was: "They're coming in bloody thousands."'[11] Twenty-two Battalion saw a big enemy convoy, estimated at 700–800 vehicles, heading towards Bardia. Another enemy force appeared from the direction of Gambut, but it was driven off by anti-tank guns, which scored some direct hits. That night, the men reflected that they were 'in for a hot time tomorrow. In short, 5 Brigade, intent on isolating the frontier forts, was now thoroughly isolated itself.'[12]

Just when communication was desperately needed Hargest's radios could not make contact with 13 Corps Headquarters, which had shifted west along the Trigh Capuzzo. Although the 5 Brigade guns were in action against the tanks, they were hampered by a shortage of ammunition; Hargest tried unsuccessfully to get assistance from the Indians, but did find some more ammunition. Nightfall brought some respite but Hargest was aware that Rommel would attack next day.

With no new orders from 13 Corps, Hargest's existing instructions, to contain the enemy forces in the border area and protect the airfield, 'made no sense in the present circumstances', but it is impossible now to gauge 'how much was left to Hargest's discretion'. According to Murphy, although Hargest's orders were to 'hold', he was 'free to move his headquarters to a safer place so long as he left the airfield defended'; the obvious place was 22 Battalion's position at Menastir, where the steep escarpment gave some protection against tanks. Hargest considered moving the nonfighting vehicles there and told Staff Captain Wynne Mason that 'if nothing came through next morning we would move at midday'. So the brigade headquarters stayed put and the men spent 'a restless night, with flares much in evidence all round'.[13]

At 6.45a.m. on the 27th the brigade received a message that a large number of enemy tanks was 3 miles (5km) off, approaching from the east. As the men gathered their arms and dived for their slit trenches, shells started falling on the camp. The tanks of 8 Panzer Regiment spread out and opened fire, with a rising sun behind them. Everywhere trucks burst into flames and the camp was sprayed with machine gun fire, but the men of the brigade hit back as best they could with 25-pounders, anti-tank and Bofors anti-aircraft guns. In a hopeless situation, and faced with some 40 tanks, the anti-tank gunners opened up at a range of 1200 yards (1097m); the tanks responded from 1000 yards (915m). One by one the guns fell silent as they were smashed or burned and the men killed or wounded.

No.1 on the P4 gun of 7 Anti-Tank Regiment was Bombardier Michael Niven, who 'gave his orders quietly and calmly, allowing three rounds for each tank engaged, until his gun was hit and its traversing and elevating gears wrecked'. He collected the wounded from all the guns and drove them to the ADS, before returning to put the one serviceable gun back into action. Hargest, from his slit trench nearby 'watched in wonder and admiration' as Niven engaged the tanks until his gun was hit. He then assisted the gun crew of the nearest 18-pounder until that gun was damaged, then a Bofors crew and finally 'was with E Troop, 5 Field Regiment, in its final stand'.[14] When the position was overrun the first thing Niven saw was 'a tank looming over me, and an officer, juggling a luger, was saying "do you kom or do you stay?" I said I guessed I would kom.'[15] However, neither these gallant efforts nor Niven's further acts of bravery as a prisoner of war, including escaping and being tortured by the Gestapo before escaping again and meeting up with the advancing Allied army, were formally recognised.

The 25-pounders were also in action, protected by smoke initially, but eventually the 'thunderous and devastating gun fire' of the German artillery hit two guns and a number of lorries. Second in command Major Arthur Grigg, Hargest's friend and parliamentary colleague, seeking more ammunition, had crossed open ground 'in face of terrible fire' and was bringing back a fully loaded 3-ton lorry when this was hit. As the ammunition exploded Grigg ordered the men to take cover but he went to the one gun that was still firing and took over as gun loader. When the smoke made it too difficult to see 'he stood calmly directing the layer, undaunted by the blazing fury of fire which each round attracted as the tanks picked up the gun flash through the smoke, until he fell mortally wounded and E Troop's last gun ceased fire'.[16] Grigg was later recommended, unsuccessfully, for a posthumous VC.

At 9.15a.m. the battle ended with 5 Brigade Headquarters overrun. Hargest had seen what he thought was a German machine gun post and sought out Brigade Major Thomas Straker to see if a counter-attack was possible. Straker just pointed to a line of enemy tanks attacking in line abreast, followed by more waves of tanks and finally German infantry, shepherding the men into groups and securing them.

As Hargest waited a German tank came up and an officer introduced himself as General Cramer. He complimented Hargest: 'your men fight well ... and fight like gentlemen.' After Cramer agreed that the New Zealanders could get their greatcoats, blankets and food, Rommel appeared. When he sent for Hargest, the latter bowed, but did not salute, which clearly did not please Rommel.

> I replied that I intended no discourtesy, but I was in the habit of saluting only my seniors in our own or Allied armies. I was in the wrong, of course, but had to stick

to my point. It did not prevent him from congratulating me on the fighting quality of my men. 'They fight well,' he said.

'Yes, they fight well,' I replied 'but your tanks were too powerful for us.'

'But you also have tanks.'

'Yes, but not here, as you can see.'

'Perhaps my men are superior to yours.'

'You know that is not correct.'

Rommel then walked off, and shortly afterwards 'the whole motor column set off westwards at a great pace'.[17]

The fact that the battalions of 5 Brigade had been so widely dispersed and were unable to help the headquarters did prevent greater losses, but casualties were still estimated at 44 killed, 49 wounded and 46 officers and 650 other ranks taken prisoner. A dressing station at Sidi Azeiz with about 80 wounded was unmolested, and the worst of the German wounded were also left there. The prisoners were marched off to Bardia, 'a long trudge under a light escort', and Hargest was allowed time to visit the wounded, including Grigg, who was unconscious and died of wounds a few days later.[18] Hargest was later driven off in a heavily escorted car, accompanied by two officers from Brigade HQ, Captain Mason and Brigade Major Straker (who made an unsuccessful attempt to escape before they left), and a driver.

Rommel's forces now largely had control of the area and on the same day attacked 23 Battalion at Capuzzo. The battalion defended strongly with Bofors and machine guns, and inflicted heavy casualties on the enemy. The German troops were only some 300 yards (275m) from battalion headquarters before a determined bayonet attack saw them off. One of the wounded New Zealanders, who witnessed the attack, 'heard the sound of many roaring voices and good lusty New Zealand cursing'. As they went past he 'saw them coming, a long straight line of determined blokes, bayonets fixed and firing from their hips'. Another soldier wrote home that 'in five hours of fierce fighting, our boys were almost right out of the place'.

When everything seemed lost 'they fixed bayonets and in 30 minutes had won back all they had lost, as well as chasing the Germans back two miles and capturing some of their light artillery'. The battalion lost 18 men killed and 36 wounded; some 60 enemy troops were killed.[19]

Less successful were the defenders of 28 (Maori) Battalion's parked vehicles at Capuzzo. They were attacked by a battalion of motorised infantry supported by four tanks and mortars, and with only small arms and no other supporting fire, were forced to surrender. Shortly afterwards, however, their captors released them in the desert north of Capuzzo and did everything they could to ensure the New Zealanders found their way back to their own lines, which they eventually did.

At Menastir, west of Bardia, 22 Battalion was under threat. It could see enemy troops on a ridge a mile (1.6km) to the east, who launched a heavy assault. The battalion, supported by artillery, mortars and machine guns, fought back strongly until nightfall when the Germans withdrew. The following morning, however, on a ridge about 2 miles (3.2km) east of the battalion, enemy troops stepped out of 100 enemy vehicles that were covering an enemy column moving south-west from Bardia, but the column withdrew and the anticipated attack did not eventuate.

Powerless to prevent these enemy movements because it was out of touch with the rest of the brigade and low on ammunition and supplies, the battalion was ordered back towards the south to join 4 Indian Division. To do this it had to pass through enemy-held territory and twice, during the night, the column was forced to stop so that German columns could pass across the track. At one stage an enemy truck briefly attached itself to the convoy.

The brigade was saved by an urgent call from the German acting commander of the Tobruk sector, Colonel Westphal, who had been unable to contact Rommel, for the tanks to return west. Rommel, not knowing the situation around Sidi Rezegh, was initially furious when he heard of the order, thinking it might be a fake sent by the British. Thirteen Corps intelligence officers intercepted a message from Westphal complaining that they were being attacked, and asking over the radio, 'Where are our tanks? Get going as fast as you can.'[20] Accordingly, 21 Panzer left from near Bardia and 15 Panzer from Sidi Azeiz.

Auchinleck considered that Rommel's raid 'inflicted little material damage and the moral effect was almost negligible'. The New Zealand Division had 'been able to fight through to Tobruk which they might never have been able to do if the weight of the enemy armour had been thrown into the scale against them'. The enemy had used up a lot of reserves, had met stiff opposition from 4 Indian Division and had been heavily bombed by the RAF. Rommel's attempt had, however, come 'as a rude shock' and Auchinleck was relieved to hear that the German commander was heading back towards Tobruk.[21]

CHAPTER 10

Rommel Returns to Sidi Rezegh

By 27 November the New Zealanders controlled the high ground covering the south-east approaches to Tobruk. Six Brigade had secured Sidi Rezegh while 4 Brigade had taken Belhamed and linked up with the Tobruk garrison at Ed Duda. Neither brigade, however, was secure; both were well spread out and vulnerable to counter-attack on the southern flank.

Fortunately the day was reasonably quiet for 6 Brigade but not for the dispersed 4 Brigade. On Belhamed 18 Battalion had a 'vile day – steady shelling from the north and west, mortaring all round the compass, machine gunning on fixed lines from the south.' It was, the men recalled, 'horribly typical' of this period on Belhamed: 'days spent lying as flat as possible in your cramped slittie, getting up to stretch your legs only at night or in the early morning.' The enemy shared their discomfort: the New Zealanders could see them shaking out their blankets or coats first thing in the morning just as they did, before, about 9 or 10 o'clock, putting in 'another day hugging the ground and cursing'.[1] Things were also fairly quiet for 19 Battalion, although they were subjected to some shelling when preparing defensive positions, and they rounded up some prisoners.

On the 27th the Germans counter-attacked both 18 Battalion and 20 Battalion. I-tanks that had been sent to Ed Duda returned and helped to clean out some enemy pockets. Two companies from 20 Battalion were sent to attack an enemy position south of Belhamed but they had little support and came under heavy fire. By nightfall 35 men had been killed or died of their wounds and 62 were wounded. Thirteen Corps Headquarters ordered the New Zealanders to secure the positions at Sidi Rezegh, Belhamed and Ed Duda and then continue to move westwards, but the priority was to hold what had already been won. The Tobruk garrison would be responsible for establishing the corridor and keeping it open.

Clem Paterson was with the first group from 19 Battalion to join up with the Tobruk tanks and infantry, 'and you can imagine how pleased they were to see us. They had been waiting four days at that spot.' The next day, the 28th,

> we had trenches dug below the escarpment known as Ed Duda – just in time. From then on we had enough shell-fire to keep most of us going for some time! The fact that the tanks dwelt amongst us was mainly the reason. He had a few 6 inch guns but I never saw our I-tanks hit or damaged by their shells the whole time we were there. Ed Duda became quite an important spot and there were some pretty big tank battles every day.[2]

Alf Blacklin was with the first British anti-tank battery to arrive at Ed Duda where they 'stopped and laagered up for the night and the next day we were on rock and could only dig ourselves in about 9 inches, and we got a bad knocking'. That morning the enemy 'ran over a crest with a battery of five-nines and we were shelled at point blank range'. They were isolated and suffered casualties: 'no tanks or infantry with us, just us on our own and we were practically surrounded by these guns. Personally I don't know how we got away with it.'[3]

To create the impression that the New Zealand forces were stronger than they actually were, a squadron of I-tanks continuously swept from side to side across the southern flank. As reports of enemy movements came in, the tanks were dispatched, 'like a stage army from our rear to the Southern flank according to the direction the enemy happened to be threatening us from'.[4] This movement prompted General Karl Böttcher, who thought he was being surrounded by the British armour, to call for the return of Rommel's tanks, so on 27 November the commander broke off the border action to bring all his armoured forces back to the Tobruk front. As it was his 25th wedding anniversary, however, he took time to send his wife an affectionate message.

The pressure on the New Zealanders continued on the 28th. General Ritchie, acknowledging Freyberg's heavy losses and that 5 Brigade was not available, ordered 1 South African Brigade to join 13 Corps, but they were unlikely to arrive until the 29th. The division also now received an urgent message from 13 Corps that Rommel, now aware that the Tobruk corridor was open, had ordered his armour back from the border.

It was Geoffrey Cox who relayed the news to Freyberg, while the general was washing his face. It included an intercepted enemy message giving the map reference at which 15 and 21 Panzer Divisions would rendezvous, then 'destroy the New Zealand Division' and move on Tobruk. When Freyberg asked where that map reference was, Cox replied that, according to his reckoning, 'it is about the second tussock from where we are standing'. After requesting Cox to repeat the message, Freyberg replied thoughtfully, 'destroy the New Zealand Division'. Then 'a note of cheerful defiance came into his voice, and he said, "We won't let 'em, Cox. We won't let 'em.'"[5]

Tanks of 7 Armoured Division attacked the returning 15 Panzer Division and both sides suffered losses, but the British tanks were unable to 'prevail against an enemy possessing, in all probability, an equal number of tanks, better armoured and mounting better guns'.[6] Panzer Lieutenant Schmidt, commanding a rearguard of two companies that were 'continually pestered by tanks and reconnaissance cars', found the battle 'a strange action fought in reverse' as attacks could come from all directions. His companies 'took it in turns to leap-frog each other', to protect against roving 'Jock Columns', which were 'a nuisance' but 'never really strong enough to do irreparable damage'.[7] The British withdrawal at dusk provided some respite for the Germans and effectively gave up the ground fought so hard for that afternoon. RAF Hurricanes used their air supremacy to harass the returning Panzers. Four and 22 Armoured Brigades were given the additional task of protecting 1 South African Brigade, which was moving up to help the New Zealanders.

Four Brigade planned to clear some remaining enemy positions between Belhamed and Sidi Rezegh. The single uncommitted company from 18 Battalion carried out the attack, accompanied by I-tanks and Bren-carriers, and supported by artillery and machine guns. The attack was successful; the battalion inflicted hundreds of casualties, captured over 600 prisoners and destroyed many enemy weapons, at minimal cost. After the battle, one of the prisoners, the German commander, asked Brigadier Inglis 'how many battalions I had used against his and I told him the actual size of the force, he said it was impossible and wept'.[8] After reaching Ed Duda the New Zealanders circled northwards and took further prisoners. Later in the afternoon the enemy counter-attacked Belhamed but were beaten back with help from 10 tanks from the Tobruk garrison and another 400 prisoners were taken. On the afternoon of the 28th, 19 Battalion was split into two groups; one half went to

Zaafran, and the other half remained at Ed Duda.

Meanwhile, at Sidi Rezegh, action continued for 6 Brigade, as it mopped up a miniature fortress with 'a veritable nest of machine and anti-tank guns and a garrison of 157 men'; the men took 70 prisoners and released 23 New Zealand prisoners. These, however, 'were the only cheering incidents in the course of the afternoon'.[9] The troops had dug in around the escarpment, but were shelled and pockets of the enemy were still causing trouble. When General Freyberg 'went up to see how 6 Brigade were getting on' he was forced to 'take to slit trenches for several minutes during heavy shelling'.[10] The brigade was now surrounded, under attack from the west, east and south, and the enemy also overlooked, and fired on, the guns and parked trucks. Nine I-tanks from Divisional Reserve were sent to assist.

By now the battlefield had become a sea of confusion as numerous separate actions broke out without a defined front line; it was almost impossible to distinguish friend from foe.

The *Press* on 29 November carried the story of a British major with a tank unit pursuing German armoured cars.

The unit had reached British headquarters. The major said that since leaving Sidi Rezegh he had crossed four different British and German lines. 'The forces seem interwoven everywhere,' he said. 'One moment we seemed to be cutting them off and the next moment they seemed to be doing the same to us. I saw British in German vehicles and Germans in British. The only people you can recognise are the Bedouins, and you can't be sure of them.'[11]

The enemy attacked 24 Battalion and overran its forward companies. The New Zealanders mistook the approaching troops for South Africans, only realising when they were close that they were Germans, and by then it was too late; only the reserve companies held. The position at nightfall was 'precarious'.[12] All the brigade's battalions were severely depleted; 24 Battalion 'was practically wiped out' and the others were 'less than a third of their normal establishment'.[13]

Because of this, Barrowclough suggested that all brigade vehicles should withdraw into the Tobruk perimeter, and that 4 and 6 Brigade troops should take up positions with their backs to Tobruk, and face eastwards. Corps orders, however, required the corridor be kept open; accordingly the brigadier reorganised his forces, sending 8 Field Company of Engineers along the escarpment south-east of Sidi Rezegh, 25 Battalion to cover the blockhouse and the remnants of 21 Battalion to Point 175. These, together with the remnants of 24 and 26 Battalions (overlooking the mosque and the valley towards Ed Duda), had the daunting task of trying to hold 8 miles (13km) of the Sidi Rezegh ridge. Since 1 South African Brigade was reported to be moving towards the southern escarpment, Barrowclough was less concerned about that flank.

Twenty-one Battalion had been badly hit. The commanding officer, Lieutenant Colonel John Allen, another New Zealand

MP, had been killed, the second-in-command was wounded and the battalion was very short on supplies and ammunition. There was no medical aid available and at night the men would go out scavenging, 'to salvage ammunition for the next day's how-do-you-do'.[14] On 29 November (although recorded in Freyberg's report, and others, as the 28th), after a night march, the men of the battalion's intelligence section, under Lieutenant Jack Money, were digging in to establish an observation post with D Company in support on their right rear about 400 yards (365m) away. The commander of 21 Panzer, Major General Johann von Ravenstein was on an early morning reconnaissance when his staff car inadvertently drove into the intelligence section's area; the troops watched his car approach slowly from near the escarpment, about 200 yards (180m) in front of them.

The patrol and D Company's machine guns immediately opened fire, causing the vehicle to stop and the occupants to dive into a nearby slit trench, but one person in the car had been hit. After a short engagement the Germans emerged with their hands up and when Money noticed that the epaulets on one man's shoulders belonged to a general, he quickly realised that the man was Ravenstein. As he recalled, 'Twenty-first Battalion "I" section had, all unconsciously, bagged some very big game indeed.'[15] Money stripped the general of his Luger pistol; the other men found a collection of maps and papers, and also provisions, including tinned goods, cigarettes, brandy and rum. When Ravenstein asked that the wounded man be cared for and demanded to be taken to the commanding officer, he was curtly put in his place. The captors, though elated, were also very conscious that 21 Panzer would soon be looking for their general.

Anxious to secure the prisoners, after checking with battalion headquarters the men drove off to brigade headquarters, but the general's car had been damaged and the engine seized, leaving the group stranded. Money sent off an urgent request for a Bren-carrier, then the New Zealanders waited anxiously for it to arrive. In a mixture of French and German, Ravenstein suggested they have something to eat so, while closely guarding the general, they opened the back of the car and found, in a previously overlooked compartment, bread, butter, cheese, raisins and figs. As they enjoyed a slightly bizarre desert picnic, Money was nervously aware that the general kept glancing towards where the enemy must be. Fortunately the carrier arrived before the Germans could reclaim their general, and Ravenstein, his staff officers and driver were all safely delivered to brigade headquarters; the general was then delivered to divisional headquarters.

There, intelligence officers Geoffrey Cox and Robin Bell interviewed Ravenstein, who initially called himself Müller. They did not believe him, there being no general of that name in their intelligence records. Bell thought that Ravenstein was a professional soldier of the Junker or privileged landowner class who would not want to be associated with the Nazis, and suggested to Freyberg that they call Ravenstein to appear before him. With an armed guard and much ceremony, Ravenstein was brought forward and introduced to the New Zealand general. He then admitted his real name.

Cox and Bell closely examined the seized documents, and especially the maps, as they showed the German positions and plans. They were suspicious, however, that the maps might deliberately show false information to entice the New Zealanders to alter their own positions, a trick that the Kiwis themselves had used. One map showed the enemy's intentions for their armoured divisions, which gave an ominous signal of what could be expected now that Rommel's tanks were returning. The establishing of Ravenstein's identity made it clear that the information was genuine.

The maps indicated that 21 Panzer, with lorried infantry, was on the Trigh Capuzzo to the east, and its path would take it through Belhamed to attack the northern flank of the Tobruk corridor. Fifteen Panzer, tracking further south, would head west towards Sidi Rezegh and then cross the flat ground to Ed

Duda. The map also showed the gun and minefield positions to the north. Fifteen Panzer was already moving westwards on the route as shown, south of Point 175 where Ravenstein was captured. Its actual path was slightly modified; rather than attacking Sidi Rezegh it went further west, down the escarpment to attack Ed Duda. Meanwhile the Italian Ariete Division would split into two columns; one would follow 15 Panzer and the other would target Sidi Rezegh. Rommel was committing all his tanks to the attack, including those that had been recovered from the battlefield.

The maps were then passed on to Divisional Operations staff, and Bell and Cox did not see them again. This warning of the German plans was a tremendous stroke of good fortune for the New Zealanders. Or was it?

Murphy suggests that this map and other documents were not as much use as had been thought because Ravenstein had missed an early morning conference at which some changes had been made to the plans. The maps foreshadowed a large assault coming from the east, whereas in fact one of the attacking parties, 15 Panzer, was already some miles west of Sidi Rezegh, and moving towards Ed Duda.

Cox disputed these conclusions and especially the anticipated 'tremendous assault from the east', noting that the map showed only 21 Panzer attacking from that direction, and 15 Panzer from the south, with no other unit committed to the east. In his view it was clear that 6 Brigade at Sidi Rezegh, 4 Brigade at Belhamed and Divisional Headquarters on the Trigh Capuzzo were all under threat.[16] Freyberg's subsequent report stated that Ravenstein's map warned them of what to expect, which suggests that he had found it useful.

Ravenstein was temporarily in 4 Brigade's custody. According to Brigadier Inglis, despite claiming that he did not speak English, Ravenstein had confidently pointed out the location of the enemy forces, then said he had a complaint to make. After being captured he had wanted to get his coat from the car and did not feel that his guard was 'very correct'. Having told the guard, 'Me General. Mein Mantel im Auto',

Ravenstein 'took a short step towards the car'. At this point, in Inglis's words, 'the general who had denied speaking English repeated perfectly what the soldier had said – "I don't care if you're effing Adolf Hitler, don't you move a bloody foot"'.[17]

Later, when Bell was transporting Ravenstein into Tobruk, they came under fire from artillery. Bell could see the MkIV Panzers of 15 Panzer giving covering fire while MkIII tanks were positioning to attack; behind them lorried infantry also had their weapons ready. A confident Ravenstein told Bell that in an hour's time their roles would be changed, but the attack was repulsed. In the afternoon the Germans attacked again and once more Ravenstein, although 'greatly interested and perhaps impressed' with the resistance shown by the New Zealanders, again said that 'in one hour's time you will be my prisoner'. Again the attack was unsuccessful.[18] With the setting sun behind them, the Germans attacked for a third time. Ravenstein once more reminded Bell that he would shortly be captured, and invited him to dine in his mess that evening. Once more, however, the defenders fought off the attack. After dark they were able to make contact with the Tobruk garrison, and Ravenstein, the first German general to be captured in the war, was sent in.

On 28 November No.1 Troop of Divisional Cavalry's C Squadron, along with two other troops, was patrolling at Zaafran, guarding the rear of the New Zealand positions. From the edge of the northern escarpment they overlooked the Via Balbia coastal road; behind them on the Sidi Rezegh escarpment, units of 6 Brigade were desperately maintaining their position and further west 4 Brigade was on Belhamed's rocky knob, also 'bitterly hanging on against counter attacks'. With the troop was Corporal Robert Loughnan, gunner-operator in the troop leader's tank. Fortunately, they were far enough away from the two brigades and the nearby Divisional HQ not 'to be constantly suffering the steady mortaring and shelling that they did'.[19]

The battle had, in Loughnan's words, developed into a dog-fight. 'Neither friend nor enemy really ever knew in what direction they would be fighting next. There are tales of the gunners getting a sudden 180-degree switch. There was hardly a gun in the division which during that week had not had occasion to engage targets, usually tanks too, over open sights; as often as not from a quite unexpected direction.'

Their duties that day had been 'to report convoys of any size passing along this [Via Balbia] road'. About half an hour after any report 'a Desert Airforce squadron of Marylands would arrive flying in close formation, they flew straight to their target and at a given signal dropped their loads in one shower. You could see the bombs fall. A highly satisfying job this had been.'

Shortly before dusk C Squadron started moving back towards the east. The three tanks in Loughnan's troop were flanked by two Honeys that had been captured by the Germans, then abandoned when they ran out of fuel. Two artillery officers waved them down and asked for help to deal with a German convoy of tanks, anti-tank guns, trucks and half-track carriers off which enemy troops were leaping to join the attack. The artillery had been under attack for two hours without any support but when Loughnan's squadron arrived 'the skirmish didn't last long. By and large the Squadron brought down a pretty concentrated barrage of small arms fire which effectively broke up the attack and slewed it off to the left.' They were then ordered 'to disengage and pull out'. It was obvious, however, that the enemy was close by 'so nobody was surprised when we were ordered to "stand-to" for the night'.

Loughnan's troop spent a quiet night in the laager, but in the early morning a German armoured car sped right through the middle of the group 'treating us to a burst of machine-gun fire as it disappeared into the gloom'. The men who had been on picquet duty 'swear that it had been there right in the middle of the laager all night, its crew blissfully ignorant that it was not among friends all the time. Such a chance was not in the least improbable in such a melee as the Sidi Rezegh battle.'

The New Zealanders chased the intruder but ran into an enemy anti-tank troop, and that 'set in train quite the fiercest hour or so taken by C Squadron that week ... the whole action was sudden, fierce, disastrous, and took only minutes it seemed'. Two of the tanks were knocked out, their drivers killed, and all of the rest of the crews, except one, were wounded. While Loughnan was watching 'a ball of green light coming straight at us seemed to veer away, turn into a flash of white light about a foot long, and shoot past the far side of our tank, hit the ground and go straight upwards'.

Now isolated, 'we were still advancing, though slowly, alone. Not until many months later did I know that at that moment three men in a single little tank were shaping up to a whole Panzer division', as all the other tanks had been called back. Loughnan aimed a long machine gun burst at one of the anti-tank guns and silenced it, but that burst presented the enemy guns 'with a good bright muzzle blast from us to lay sights on and no gun-fire to keep him blinking either'. Then he paused, which was 'disastrous. There came another gun-flash and emerging from it that same swelling ball of light. But this time it developed not into a white streak but into a perfect white circle swelling up. It only had to travel 200 yards [180m] but in that time I was able to notice the difference and think: "My number's on this one." It landed right behind the guns. To me there was no sensation of sound – of explosion – just a blinding flash.'

Loughnan was momentarily dazed; 'my next conscious thought was of surprise that I was sitting sideways in my seat, hunched up in what seemed a silly drunken attitude'. He was able to sit up and 'with that came the courage to look down. Other than a little hole in my jersey, nothing seemed to be amiss. No blood. No nothing.' His relief was 'exhilarating'. He then tried to reach the guns but his right hand would not work, as 'diagonally across the back of it was stuck a large piece of metal'. He tried to remove the metal with his left hand but 'the end of my thumb seemed to be missing and I could not see my middle finger, hidden as it was from sight behind a piece of metal. My index finger was a shapeless pulp, and burnt jet black.' Fortunately the driver, Stanley ('Shorty') Gollan, was unhurt and the crew sought cover at Squadron Headquarters.

Loughnan was given morphia for the pain and a doctor attended to his wounds before he was taken to a regimental aid post (RAP) where his hand was stitched up. Nearby 'mortar bombs were exploding close-handy enough for me to see the places where shrapnel was piercing the hamper of medical supplies up on the deck of the 15-cwt truck'. He was aware that

the whole of No.1 Troop seemed to be there as casualties. There were only two of us not killed or wounded. It had been an expensive fight for us but I knew that the guns of our tank alone had evened the score. We silenced that gun so we must have silenced some crew as well. So with that satisfaction I gave up struggling against the morphia in my brain.

He was later transferred to a big marquee near the Sidi Rezegh mosque.

There, the wounded were lying on stretchers around the tent walls and surgery was being performed on a table in the middle of the tent. In the afternoon, still under the influence of morphia, he noticed someone coming round the stretchers. 'The more seriously wounded were being picked out to be carried outside. I was taken out as my wounds included one in the chest.' He was happy to move 'as not very far away a battery of 25-pounders was barking away, and plenty of mortar fire arriving back. A wall of canvas was but poor shelter against stray shrapnel.'

Outside, orderlies were digging slit trenches, which puzzled Loughnan. The sergeant major in charge 'insisted on having all the "slitties" in straight lines. He seemed also to be exercising some form of punishment too as he had some men digging holes and others apparently filling them in. I thought him rather odd if he could not postpone the punishment until clear of the battlefield.' Loughnan, however, was 'content to lie there gazing at the little old mosque on the hill just above us'.

During the evening of the 28th the enemy overran the medical dressing station (MDS) and the POW cage east of Point 175 (see Chapter 14, p.157). The Divisional HQ, only about 600 yards (550m) away over the escarpment could have been taken too but for the onset of darkness. Corps Headquarters, now almost in the front line, shifted into Tobruk, as did New Zealand Division's Administration Group. Poor radio reception, especially at night, made it increasingly difficult for the division to communicate with corps.

The position was becoming grave: the division, except for 5 Brigade still masking the frontier area, was virtually surrounded. The enemy was constantly shelling the division area and harassing the various positions. The German 15 Panzers were covering the south and west, and 21 Panzer the east. Patrolling further south-east was the Italian Ariete Division; remnants of the Afrika Korps were to the north of Belhamed. Although the Tobruk corridor was still open, there were four Italian divisions surrounding it: Brescia, Trento, Pavia to the west and Bologna to the east.

From the 6 Brigade's positions it was apparent that the enemy forces overlooking them from the southern escarpment were strengthening, and 1 South African Brigade had not arrived. With the large number of vehicles to control, the South Africans frequently had to halt and change direction and were making slow progress. On the 28th [,] when it was still 12 miles (20km) south of Point 175, 'there was a muddle – which cannot be explained – between the two Corps about a message, and it halted for the night'.[20]

During that evening 'alarms and excursions continued as darkness came on'.[21] As Freyberg reported,

the situation was most difficult. Our supplies, and in particular our 25 pounder ammunition supplies, were very low; Sidi Rezegh could not be held if 1 South African Brigade did not arrive, and finally General von Ravenstein's maps gave us a clear picture of the scale of attack we would have to meet. During the night Divisional Headquarters moved closer to 4 Brigade and everything possible was done to meet the coming attack.[22]

Interestingly, the South African history gives a far more positive perspective. Although the New Zealanders were under threat, there were British tanks concentrated close to the rear of 15 Panzer, with 1 South African Brigade and the artillery of the Support Group nearby. Perhaps optimistically it notes that these forces 'were capable of a powerful blow' especially if coordinated with the New Zealanders. 'On the whole the situation favoured the Eighth Army.'[23]

CHAPTER 11

Mounting Pressure on 4 and 6 Brigades

With the enemy now closing in, it was obvious, by the afternoon of the 28th, that an attack was imminent. In the words of the 18 Battalion official history, 'A large enemy force, armour and all, on the highest escarpment on the Division's southern flank, was nibbling at the edges of 6 Brigade, clearly with the intention of pushing through to the north and smashing the Tobruk corridor.'[1]

As a misty dawn broke on the 29th a large convoy could be seen driving directly towards the New Zealand positions, about 280 trucks with an escort of 15 tanks and some armoured cars. Initially the New Zealanders thought that this could be the South Africans coming to their aid, but enemy shellfire trained on the new arrivals gave the game away. Brigadier George Clifton, now Chief Engineer of 30 Corps, had volunteered to lead a convoy through the night and through the German lines, and here it was, bringing much-needed supplies: petrol, water, rations and, most importantly ammunition. Shortly afterwards another convoy arrived from Tobruk, with 25-pounder ammunition.

That morning 15 Panzer and the Ariete Divisions continued to move west and there were some unsuccessful attacks on the corridor. Six Brigade saw considerable enemy movement and fired its artillery whenever the Germans came into range. There was some encouraging support from the RAF, with bombers escorted by fighters making raids on enemy tank and transport positions. Four Brigade had a fairly quiet day, their artillery dealing with any enemy movements, although 18 Battalion was battered by shellfire, even if it did little damage. Many of the shells were 'duds', but even these 'were nerve-wracking, ricocheting and skidding all over the place with a noise like a train going through a station'.[2] From their positions the men could hear the noise of the battle taking place at Ed Duda away to the west.

The Australian 2/13 Battalion, the last Australian unit still with the Tobruk garrison, had initially been positioned at the Wadi Sehel west of Tobruk, but were later shifted back nearer the town. On the 27th it was sent to the El Adem road, but by the 28th the position in the corridor was so desperate, with the German Panzers making a number of thrusts, that at 6p.m. the battalion was ordered to move to Ed Duda. Scobie's parting words were: 'Ed Duda must be held at all costs.'[3] On the 29th German tanks and infantry attacked Ed Duda at 1p.m., and two companies of 1 Essex suffered heavy casualties.

That night 2/13 Battalion counter-attacked. Shortly after 10p.m., as they started moving up, a stray shell landed in the middle of 10 Platoon, killing or wounding 18 of the 26 men. Tank and artillery support was called up and as the remaining Australian infantry attacked, their commanding officer, Lieutenant Colonel Frederick Burrows, called out, '"The Australians are coming!" And come they did – with a bayonet charge that would chill the most iron-hearted.'[4] They overran the German positions and took 167 prisoners at a cost of two killed and five wounded. Shortly after the German gunners retaliated and Ed Duda was raked with heavy artillery fire.

From Ed Duda Alf Blacklin could see the New Zealanders under attack further east. 'The sky was filled with columns of smoke, gun flashes and shell bursts, and at night flares went up continuously.' Just how hard the fighting had been was evident: 'the battleground now looks a terrible sight as up to a week ago the dead had not yet been buried.'[5]

The enemy, who had moved in from the east below the escarpment, shelled New Zealand Divisional HQ, but I-tanks from the Divisional Reserve kept them at bay; there was minimal damage and few casualties. 'As the day [29th] went on,' Inglis reported, 'the situation warmed up. The 15 and 21 Panzer Divisions, the Afrika Division and the Ariete Armoured Division were closing in and beginning to stab at us from most points of the compass.'[6] That afternoon, enemy attacks on 6 Brigade, which was spread extensively around Sidi Rezegh with minimal troop numbers, began in earnest. Ed Duda, Sidi Rezegh and Belhamed were all being attacked by 15 Panzer and Ariete Divisions and the only British forces in any position to support the New Zealanders were 1 South African Brigade, and the tanks of the remnants of 4 and 22 Armoured Brigades, which were operating as a composite brigade.

Both of these were positioned south of Point 175 but efforts to get them to advance further were failing. Although the division was anxious to see the South Africans move up, the latter felt that a concentrated drive by the brigade, the armoured brigades and the Support Group was needed. Inglis was sceptical that the South Africans would ever arrive 'because we knew from our R/T intercepts that the South Africans were fiddling about in the desert instead of coming on'.[7]

Twenty-one Battalion on Point 175 had seen off two attacks, but the enemy took some positions and captured some men. In the afternoon

D Company was taken by surprise. When an armoured car appeared the men, on watch, thought the South Africans were arriving. They saw vehicles steadily approaching from the south but could not positively identify them so sent out a carrier patrol to check. As a column of tanks came into view the men held their fire to identify the occupants, who were wearing black berets and waving a greeting from the tank turrets. Suddenly, though, they slammed down their turret lids and opened fire. A frantic call went out for artillery support, but none was forthcoming, and by now the tanks, a column of the Ariete Division, possibly using captured British tanks, was right on top of the New Zealanders. The enemy overran Point 175, although some New Zealanders were able to escape below the escarpment. This gave the enemy control over a key observation point and further depleted 21 Battalion.

By the evening of the 29th the South Africans were in sight of Point 175, but on finding that it was in enemy hands Brigadier Dan Pienaar postponed any further advance until daylight. One of their armoured cars, equipped with wireless, made it through to the New Zealand Divisional HQ, but the wireless broke down. The several messages sent to the South Africans from Army, Corps and Divisional Headquarters were 'evidence of a strong desire to help the New Zealanders' while trying to avoid a repetition of the disaster that had befallen 5 South African Brigade, but 'they added to the general uncertainty instead of clearing it up'.[8] It was not certain whether Pienaar had been ordered forward. Norrie's 'clear recollection' was that the South Africans told him Freyberg cancelled their move forward, but 'this was subsequently denied by 2 NZ Div and must have been due to some misunderstandings or mis-hearing on RT'.[9]

That night, with German artillery overlooking the rear of the New Zealand positions, enemy troops were moving closer and it began to seem, because of pressure around Ed Duda, that it would not be possible to keep the corridor open. In Inglis's view 'it was a damned draughty corridor with nothing to go through it anyway'. Following a briefing from Barrowclough, Freyberg reported to 13 Corps HQ that the division was virtually surrounded and it appeared that the enemy was trying to separate the New Zealand forces and the Tobruk garrison. Inglis 'had by no means the same faith' as Freyberg that the South Africans would help and thought 4 Brigade should consolidate east of Ed Duda.[10] As Freyberg wrote in his diary, Inglis 'recommended that Div HQ should follow 13 Corps into Tobruk but cannot agree so only chance of holding Sidi Rezegh and Belhamed depended on co-ordination of plans with SA Brigade. Sent orders to 1 SA Brigade to attack Pt 175'.[11]

In the darkness 15 Panzer moved north and took Ed Duda but lost it again during the night. Shortly after midnight a message arrived from Corps HQ – it had been sent at 7.40p.m. – advising that there had been some successful armoured attacks to the south and west of Bir el Chleta, and also that 4 and 22 Armoured Brigades were attempting to reach Sidi Rezegh.

The South African Brigade was also trying to break through. The corps communication ended with the helpful message that 'Corridor will be kept open at all costs'.[12] A survey of the fighting force of 6 Brigade revealed that 24 Battalion had only four officers and 159 other ranks, 25 Battalion 10 officers and 235 other ranks, 26 Battalion 10 officers and 260 other ranks, and the hard-pressed 21 Battalion had only one officer and 91 other ranks remaining.

The night of the 29th passed reasonably peacefully, but as it became light on the 30th, Divisional HQ could see a mass of vehicles on the escarpment around Point 175. Was it the South Africans? Freyberg turned to Major Ian Bonifant of the Divisional Cavalry and told him that 'we aren't sure who those chaps are. We want you to find out.'[13] Bonifant set out but was soon back, pursued by gunfire from the escarpment, giving Freyberg the answer he was seeking.

In anticipation of this Brigadier Reginald Miles, commander of the New Zealand artillery, had already positioned his guns and 'a moment later the skyline erupted with flames and dust and smoke as our guns opened up. This bombardment smashed several trucks, and chased the rest away.'[14] Unfortunately it was not enough to dislodge all the Ariete infantry and gunners, who were well dug in. During the day the division came under heavy artillery fire from 105mm guns positioned on the southern escarpment, several of the guns of 4 Field Regiment were put out of action and there were several casualties. The New Zealanders did, however, succeed in blowing up an ammunition dump on Point 175, disabling and destroying some enemy tanks and forcing the infantry to disperse. A further communication from Corps HQ confirmed that 'orders are to hold this position at all costs'.[15] There was news, too, that the Ed Duda position had been consolidated.

Both 15 Panzer and 21 Panzer attacked 6 Brigade and Divisional HQ, using tanks, lorried infantry and 88mm guns. The guns of 21 Panzer shelled Divisional HQ during the morning, forcing it to shift a mile (1.6km) further west and close to where 6 Brigade HQ was situated, near the mosque. From there more gunfire could be heard to the west, and bursts of earth and flame were thrown up by the shell bursts; this was 15 Panzer mounting an assault. The attack on Sidi Rezegh came at 4p.m., with 51 tanks advancing fast from the west towards 24 Battalion, followed by another attack from the south-west of 26 Battalion. Behind the tanks were large numbers of infantry. It was hoped that lorries could fetch 25 Battalion from the foot of the escarpment but before that could occur another attack came in from the south and the troops had to remain where they were. With the attacks coming from all directions, and the anti-tank guns knocked out, the outcome was inevitable. Conditions were very difficult for the defenders, with the dust and sun in their eyes making for limited visibility. Soon the enemy had overrun whole of 24 Battalion and A and B Companies, half of 26 Battalion.

In 24 Battalion, Lou Nelley's platoon by now 'numbered only twelve and one Lieutenant'; the rest of the platoon 'had been either killed or wounded in the advance'. They were confronted by tanks that 'started to close in and we were forced out of our positions and obliged to give ourselves up'.[16] Some 24 Battalion men who were either concealed or in rear positions escaped, but others were taken prisoner, including Colonel Shuttleworth, who was 'taken away but refusing to acknowledge defeat by putting up his hands'.[17] The survivors, three officers and 60 other ranks made their way to Brigade Headquarters, and another 23 found their way to Tobruk.

Although some tanks attacking 26 Battalion were taken out by 25-pounders, the enemy was too strong; the final message from the battalion commander was that 'The tanks are within fifty yards of us'.[18] Men from C and D Companies of 26 Battalion watched helplessly as most of A and B Companies were captured. About 80 C and D Company men ran back along the escarpment out of sight of the enemy. The battalion's losses now were significant: nine officers and 217 other ranks had been captured. Total casualties by now were 449, or three-quarters of the full complement, including 89 who had been killed or subsequently died of wounds.

Captain Charles Gatenby was among the B Company, 26 Battalion men captured. 'It was obvious that the Germans were putting in another attack and we had little or nothing to defend ourselves with. The Germans were going to use about 40 or 50 tanks to overrun our position.' When he saw the tanks advancing he 'rang back on the field telephone to the brigadier for permission to withdraw, because the position was untenable'. But Barrowclough 'explained that was impossible, we stayed there whether we liked it or not because a corridor to Tobruk had been established; the longer we could delay the advance of the Germans, the more people could get through, the rest of our division plus other support troops. So he said goodbye and good luck!'

As the Germans approached, Gatenby's batman, Arch Tutbury, suggested they surrender and that Gatenby should wave a white flag. Gatenby replied, '"Arch you know bloody well I haven't got a white flag." After a minute or two hesitation he said, "Wave a white handkerchief, boss." I said, "You know damn well all my hankies are khaki." There was no response, the tanks got closer then Tutbury said, "I've sorted it out, boss. You wave your white maps, which I know you've got."' But Gatenby, unwilling to submit, said, 'Arch, in about 10 seconds you and I are going to make a dash for that wadi, jump over it and take a chance.' This they 'duly did, and jumped into the arms of a detachment of Germans who were using the wadi to advance on us'.[19] Fortunately, 'the Germans in the tanks gave us every consideration and did not needlessly slaughter which they could have easily done had they so chosen'. Despite that, 'it was a bitter blow, but there was no alternative'.[20]

On Belhamed, watching 'dimly through the smoke and dust' the men of 18 Battalion could see the 'awful, depressing sight'. That evening, looking at 'the macabre glow of fires for several miles along the escarpment [they] knew that they themselves would be next, and that they would need all their "guts" to face what was coming next day'.[21] Until now, 18 Battalion's transport, which was further east, had been largely out of trouble, but now they were heavily shelled. That night all of 4 Brigade transport went back through the corridor to Tobruk. At Zaafran, the 19 Battalion group was also attacked by enemy armour.

During the day, a group of vehicles spotted to the south was again the subject of conjecture – might this finally be the South African Brigade? The latter's movements were 'a complete mystery': at 10.30a.m. 'they were reported by wireless to be 4 miles [6.5km] away to the east and advancing towards Hill 175' but a later report placed them to the south and making for Sidi Rezegh.[22] By midday on the 30th wireless communication with the South Africans was restored and Freyberg spoke directly to Pienaar, urging him to 'push on, push on with the bayonet'. Except for a strong point around the blockhouse, Sidi Rezegh was lost, and that evening Barrowclough urged that the division should withdraw back into the Tobruk perimeter: that was the only way that the rest of 6 Brigade could avoid annihilation. As far as Freyberg was concerned, only the arrival of the South Africans 'on the flank of 6 Brigade could save the situation'.[23] Barrowclough, however, felt there was little chance of help from that quarter.

At 7.45p.m. Freyberg sent a message to 13 Corps Headquarters that '6 Infantry Brigade have been overwhelmed and enemy has Sidi Rezegh'.[24] At 9.15, wireless having failed because of the atmospheric conditions, Freyberg sent Bonifant and another officer to deliver a message to the South Africans. The order read: 'Sidi Rezegh was captured by the enemy this afternoon. Our position is untenable unless you can recapture it before dawn 1 Dec. You will therefore carry out this task at once.'[25] Freyberg had told Bonifant, 'I don't care how rude you are to him, we want him here in the morning.' The two New Zealanders covered the 25 miles (40km) to the South African Brigade, but Pienaar dismissed Bonifant as a 'cheeky young bugger' and marched him before 30

Corps commander Norrie who, however, 'fully supported Bonifant and ordered Pienaar to comply with Freyberg's request'.[26]

Since Sidi Rezegh and Point 175 had been lost, Freyberg asked Godwin-Austen if the remainder of 6 Brigade could be sent into Tobruk, but this request was turned down because it was still hoped that the South Africans and armoured support would be arriving early next morning. However, 'these hopes', as Playfair notes, 'were not to be fulfilled'.[27] Freyberg also decided that he would only retain a small Battle Headquarters, which would move to a position between 4 and 6 Brigades. All other unnecessary transport and personnel, together with secret papers, should be sent to Tobruk, accompanied by Brigadier Miles to report on the situation to 13 Corps HQ. Six Brigade's transport was shifted closer to Belhamed.

Six Brigade HQ felt that 'it could not do more than point out the utter impossibility of the situation. The responsibility for the decision to leave us in that situation must be accepted by Corps HQ', but it was 'doubtful whether the Corps Commander really appreciated how vitally important it was' for both Sidi Rezegh and Point 175 to be captured and how 'improbable it was that both of them could have been taken simultaneously by the South African Brigade which was still apparently miles away from both objectives'.[28]

But Norrie, concerned at Pienaar's delay, was 'determined to apply ginger' and handed over command of 30 Corps to Gott 'in order to devote himself exclusively to this task'. He ordered the South Africans to attack Point 175, then went off to await the advance; he 'got very impatient with the apparent delay and sent rude messages back to hurry the bde [brigade] up'. From the South African point of view, however, if 'the armoured brigades, reinforced by the bulk of the South African artillery, were incapable of penetrating the screen imposed by the Ariete, the South African Brigade cannot be blamed for failing to attempt it'. After the decision was made to send the brigade to join the New Zealanders, the return of the

German armour had changed the shape of the battle significantly.[29] The South Africans recommenced their advance but paused when east of Point 175 and finally attacked by moonlight, only to find the position was strongly held by enemy troops supported by tanks. At dawn they were still nearly 2 miles (3.2km) short of their objective. Pienaar sent a reply back with Bonifant outlining their attempts to take Point 175 and concluded by stating that he was 'trying to isolate Point 175 tonight if I cannot succeed to capture it'.[30]

Six Brigade was now very weak, with only 8 Field Company and 25 Battalion on the escarpment, but vulnerable to attack. In darkness enemy tanks advanced on 8 Field Company along the ridge, then retired when fired on. Twenty-five Battalion repulsed an attack from the south and another from Point 175. The other battalions – 21, 24 and 26 – consisted of only a few survivors and headquarters units. Although there was still artillery support it was within machine gun range and could not remain in action. The remnants of 4 and 22 Armoured

Brigades were also stretched and could not assist as they had to patrol the Tobruk corridor and protect the flank of 1 South African Brigade, advancing towards Point 175.

Brian Cox's 9 Machine Gun Platoon was now on the edge of the Sidi Rezegh airfield with the engineers of 8 Field Company covering approaches from the south – well placed for Major Jack Luxford to follow the day's events. The men knew that 24 and 26 Battalions had been overrun and that half a section of 8 Machine Gun Platoon which was with them had evaded capture. John Black remembered that it was 'much quieter here for a while but later we did have our moments. The enemy tanks rounded up two of our battalions down in the wadis below us and it certainly looked ominous to us – we would be next.'

They were approached by 'a small three man Italian tank with its gun pointing down – in a non-firing position, an Italian soldier was sitting on the outside waving our guns down'. Black held his rifle at the ready, but the Italian 'greeted me with a big smile. In part Italian and part English he explained that his tank commander was badly wounded. I noticed this Italian had a watch, something I needed, so suggested he give it to me. He pointed to his wedding ring and pleaded to keep it. When I said that's ok you keep it he threw his arms around me and gave me a big hug.' Black 'was quite embarrassed, first time a man had hugged me'.[31]

When three men from 26 Battalion were moving towards 8 Field Company they ran into the German 33 Reconnaissance Unit and were captured. The Germans continued eastwards, but were suddenly engaged by four Vickers guns of 9 Platoon, and a section of engineers made a successful bayonet charge. They rescued the three prisoners and captured several useful vehicles and much equipment, including some welcome antitank guns; the German unit fled. This was probably Brian Cox's last action during the campaign.

In the *Press* a few days later Australian war correspondent, John Hetherington, reported that 'little has been heard of [the New Zealanders] because nobody has been able to get through. They had been out on their own with pockets of enemy tanks, guns and troops separating them from other British and Empire troops.' After travelling in with an armoured convoy, Hetherington 'spent all Saturday [i.e. the 29th] with the New Zealand Division in the midst of one of its fiercest battles, with tanks, infantry and guns on both sides hammering and surging for mastery'. The desperate situation was obvious. He quoted an officer who declared, 'It's going to be a sticky day. If we can hold on until nightfall we shall have them where we want them.' As Hetherington noted, the New Zealanders, using tanks, 'did hold the enemy, but for a few hours it was very sticky indeed. Everybody at New Zealand headquarters breathed freely by nightfall.'[32]

The next day the *Press* included a tribute to the division from 'military circles in Cairo': 'the New Zealanders were superlative troops and were fighting magnificently, "putting up a marvellous show". Throughout the operations New Zealand infantry has shown superiority over the best the Axis has to offer.'[33]

Luxford summed things up in the 3 Company War Diary: 'things were now pretty sticky and we were expecting a busy night. By now the company had suffered severe casualties.' That night 'after dark some vehicles were heard moving just over the edge of the escarpment between us and the Brigade HQ'. A couple of anti-tank guns went to investigate and opened fire: 'it turned out that they were three 3-ton lorries of ammunition towing two or three enemy guns. We had a great fireworks display out of it.' As he concluded, however, 'The prospects were gloomy for the morrow if the South Africans who had been expected for the last two days, did not arrive by morning.'[34] At 6 Brigade HQ, too, there was a resignation that 'we had to remain in our positions with a fairly settled presentiment of disaster on the following day'.[35]

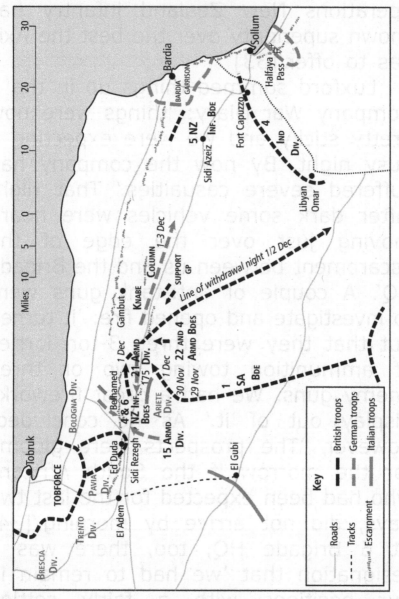

Position of forces, 29 November – 1 December 1941

CHAPTER 12

4 and 6 Brigades Withdraw

'The misgivings of the previous evening were soon proved to have had a sound foundation': there was no sign of the South Africans.[1] Miles returned from 13 Corps HQ at 3.30a.m. on 1 December with orders that the corridor must be held, and a message had gone to 30 Corps: 'Enemy captured Sidi Rezegh and has been attacking New Zealand Division on West and East with tanks. Consider it absolutely essential 7 Armoured Division concentrates every effort to destroy enemy tanks East and West New Zealand Division position.'[2] General Freyberg was 'up at first light and made everyone dig again'.[3] More enemy attacks were anticipated and no support had arrived from either the South Africans or 4 and 22 Armoured Brigades.

Shortly after daybreak the attack on 4 Brigade at Belhamed began. The

Germans knew that the division had suffered 'but was still unshaken in its fighting strength'.[4] Tanks of 15 Panzer Division, supported by artillery, moved forward under cover of dust and smoke, and turned their machine guns on the artillery and anti-tank guns. After waking to heavy shellfire, the 18 Battalion men watched as the German tanks 'seemed to be coming straight for them' but they veered off to the east, and 'the noise of the battle rose to an unbearable racket as they clashed with New Zealand artillery two miles [3.2km] away. This epic slogging match, tanks against field guns at point-blank range until the guns died fighting, holds a place of unique tragedy and honour in the Division's history.'[5] But, as Inglis later reported, the 6 Brigade transport had been 'parked right on the place where we had arranged for the 4 Field Regiment's fire to be brought down', and soon 'columns of smoke began to rise from burning vehicles'. It was 'impossible, therefore, for the 25-pounders to open on their pre-arranged zones and equally impossible to put down any observed fire because the smoke hid the German attack'.[6]

The shortage of 4 Brigade troops made any meaningful counter-attack impossible, though the few remaining I-tanks from 44 Royal Tank Regiment were able to provide some support. By 7.30a.m. the 20 Battalion anti-tank guns were engaging enemy tanks at very short range but the odds were stacked against them. I-tanks were sent forward but came under heavy fire and could not proceed; 20 Battalion, which had gone through five changes of command in three days and suffered heavy casualties, surrendered shortly afterwards. 'The enemy had taken Belhamed, and 370 of the 20th, ten of them officers and a lot of wounded, had been captured.'[7]

The battalion was without Kippenberger, who had already been captured. He watched 'sadly and anxiously' from an MDS in a wadi as 20 Battalion was overrun. It 'took some time before we were able to get a reliable account of what had happened after I was wounded' but later he could write that the battalion, 'which then had nine officers and 286 men, with four two-pounders, was attacked by forty-eight tanks and some hundred lorried infantry and after ninety minutes resistance was completely overrun, one man escaping'.

Kippenberger also had 'an odd conversation' with a German artillery officer.

He came up and said: 'We have retaken Belhamed, and our Eastern and Western Groups have joined hands.' I expressed regret. 'But it is no use; we have lost the battle,' he went on. 'I am glad; it has been a pleasure to meet you. You have fought well,' I said. 'That is not enough. Our losses are too heavy. We have lost the battle,' he answered and went on his way.'

After the battle, there was an incident 'that left a good deal of bitterness'. While attending a parade of the new 20 Battalion, Inglis made 'some handsome remarks on the performance of the unit up till 1 December' but then said that 'it surrendered too easily at Belhamed'. This greatly upset Kippenberger, who later tried to piece together just what happened. His statement about 48 tanks may have overstated the number, but 'inquiries among prisoners after the war have only confirmed my opinion that when surrender took place there was no possibility of continuing effective resistance or of running away'.[8] There was, however, speculation on whether Kippenberger's leadership would have made a difference, and whether he had erred by standing with a group in an exposed position at Belhamed when he was wounded. Inglis later acknowledged that 'the effect of what I said was not good'. He subsequently spoke to the battalion again and said, 'I myself would never be captured unless the enemy knocked me helpless first. This was more than I ask of others; but I think it was an assurance that it was right to give under the circumstances.' He was, however, 'thankful that I was never put to the ultimate proof'.[9]

The New Zealand artillery had been under great pressure; ammunition was low, and communication and observation were both difficult. On 30 November both 4 and 6 Field Regiments were in action. Manning one of the 25-pounders was Robert Loughnan's brother, Ian. While he was brewing tea in the morning, 'suddenly a large group of German tanks appear over the edge of an escarpment. They are less than half a mile from us. We take little notice of them thinking they are ours.' But 'they open fire and all hell breaks loose'. Almost immediately Loughnan was hit 'in the neck by a bit of shrapnel the size of a one cent piece', from a 75-mm shell, also wounding one of the other men. Then 'the next shot takes out the rest of the gun crew. I am now out of the war and a prisoner of the Germans.'[10]

During the armoured assault on the 6 Brigade positions, the artillery suffered heavy losses. On the night of the 30th, Colonel Weir took the 6 Field Regiment's guns some 2 miles (3.2km) to the north, just east of Belhamed, to be beyond machine gun and mortar range from Sidi Rezegh. The following morning the artillery were in an exposed position when they saw a force approaching from the south. They thought these were the South Africans, but they were

Germans, who knocked out or overwhelmed several of the guns of 30 Battery and then 47 Battery. Other batteries also suffered the same fate; many men were killed and others captured. Brigadier Miles had been calling to the gunners to 'fight over open sights', when he was wounded by a shell splinter; shortly afterwards 'the German infantry then enveloped us' and he was taken prisoner.[11]

This was 'New Zealand Artillery's most tragic action'. Six Field Regiment's casualties, including those of 47 Battery attached from 5 Field Regiment, were 57 killed, 113 wounded and 96 taken prisoner; 23 of its 32 field guns were lost.[12] The final shots were fired by 27-year-old Bombardier Francis Marshall, from Auckland. He had been captured in Greece and subsequently escaped, vowing he would never again be captured. 'He remained true to his word and kept on firing the gun single-handed until a tank ran right over it and killed him.' It was an act of extraordinary bravery and one the Germans respected; 'they took the trouble to bury him in the short time they occupied this feature and put up a cross inscribed "An unknown British soldier" – the only New Zealander on Belhamed they bothered to inter.'[13]

At 7.45a.m. Freyberg sent a message to 13 Corps, explaining that the division was 'being heavily attacked from South and West. 1 South African Brigade failed to take Point 175 last night, but are going to try again this morning.' Then, at 11.55 he reported 'enemy now have Belhamed'.[14] The withdrawal of the Divisional Battle HQ had 'been left perilously late': the men were under fire (Gentry's driver was killed) and around them they could see columns of smoke. When the word went out that 'the gunners already have their hands up – no more than 150 yards away', Freyberg finally ordered the group to go east and rendezvous at 4 Brigade Headquarters at Zaafran.[15] On the way, Freyberg was 'grazed by a shell splinter in the leg' when he stopped to watch some I-tanks at Belhamed preparing to make a counter-attack.[16]

When the enemy tanks turned to attack 18 Battalion some of the men who had seen 20 Battalion surrendering started to climb out of the trenches with their hands up, but their mates quickly stopped them. Artillery support was called up and fired on the tanks, which promptly moved off to the south. Eighteen Battalion then withdrew. The Tobruk corridor was now severed and 4 Brigade was split into two groups. Lieutenant Colonel Joseph Peart led an intact 18 Battalion, under fire, to below the escarpment, and it took up new positions west of Belhamed. Both 18 Battalion, to the east, and two companies of 19 Battalion, to the west, were on Ed Duda, and in touch with the Tobruk garrison. On the other side of the wedge, all that remained under the command of 4 Brigade were the other two companies of 19 Battalion, 6 Field Company, a machine gun company, 90 South Africans from 5 South African Brigade and the remaining I-tanks.

Describing the loss of the corridor, the *Evening Post* reported on 5 December that 'the German tanks were the deciding factor' but that the New Zealand troops 'inflicted terrific casualties on the Hun'. According to the NZEF Official News Service, 'for the New Zealanders it was a bad day but the general situation is good. Reserves are rushing up to attack the badly-weakened enemy forces.' The report concluded that 'the Germans have no reserves, and the blows struck with smashing force by the New Zealanders who throughout were the spearhead of the attack, may well be the deciding factor in this grim Libyan desert campaign'. The article also quoted Ravenstein: 'This is not like the Russian war – this is a war between gentlemen.'[17]

In the same newspaper three days later, the Cairo correspondent of the *London Daily Express* wrote: 'if you have any admiration to spare, offer it to the New Zealanders, who almost alone met the full shock of the panzers on the rising ground outside Tobruk. They were driven back by anti-tank guns, and it was, indeed, a battle between the German anti-tank guns and the New Zealand infantry.' One New Zealander said 'the battlefield was like the [1931] Napier earthquake'.[18]

Divisional Battle HQ was now close to 4 Brigade HQ at Zaafran. The enemy attacked the area around Zaafran from all sides but were beaten back by fire from the 25-pounders and I-tanks. Because of the resistance the tanks turned their attention to Sidi Rezegh instead. As one bombardier remembered, there was an artillery troop 'on the fringe of the division without any infantry support, and consequently our 25-pounders were relied upon to repel attacks, if made in that area. The enemy attacked but was successfully thrown back, although on occasions our guns were firing over open sights at advancing tanks and infantry.' The situation was so confused 'on the last day we held out there, "F" Troop had two guns firing in one direction while the other two pointed exactly the opposite way'.[19]

When the enemy mounted a heavy attack on Sidi Rezegh from the west with tanks and infantry, setting fire to many vehicles, it looked as though 6 Brigade could suffer the same fate as 4 Brigade. But just as the attack was launched a large force of tanks and artillery approached from the east: it was 4 and 22 Armoured Brigades under Brigadier Alec Gatehouse, with 115 tanks. Although 'certain facts can be established' as to what occurred next, as Playfair writes, 'the accounts of what followed, as recorded by commanders on the spot, are in many respects contradictory'.[20]

Despite his brigade's difficult position, Barrowclough saw that the enemy infantry also appeared to be on their last legs and the arrival of the British tanks was enough to make them raise their hands in surrender. Then 'the broken remains of 6 Brigade, including drivers, orderlies and everyone went forward with the tanks without waiting for any instructions. They were only too eager to get even with the enemy.'[21] In his mind's eye, Barrowclough compared the 'huge assembly of British armour stretching out around 8 Field Company ... with the German elements he had to contend with near the Trigh Capuzzo, many of them jaded and bedraggled'. This made him 'more anxious than ever to stage an immediate counter attack'.[22]

Lieutenant Colonel H.D. Drew of 5 Royal Tank Regiment, leading 4 and 22 Brigades, met Barrowclough to prepare a plan of action, but said he 'would do nothing without instructions from his brigadier'. Barrowclough, in his later description of events, said he immediately went to Gatehouse, who was in a tank on the top of the escarpment, and urged him 'to make some effort to recover the prisoners from 4 Brigade and my own 6 Field Regiment' and offered the support of his troops. Gatehouse, however, 'refused to undertake any offensive action. He said that he had been sent forward to cover my withdrawal, and that he could not undertake any more serious action.'[23]

In his account, Drew asserted that Barrowclough agreed with his opinion that the New Zealanders' position was 'quite untenable and that it would be best if he [Barrowclough] could withdraw his Bde to the south on top of the escarpment whilst we covered his withdrawal'.[24] Gatehouse, too, had a different recollection, telling historian W.E. Murphy in 1960 that he was 'quite sure that [he] did NOT meet Barrowclough on that day'.[25] In the end, though, 'it was realised that discretion would be the better part of valour and the disappointed Kiwis accepted their lot'.[26] Barrowclough concluded that he 'had no option but to elect to withdraw to Zaafran where I knew I could join up with Inglis'.[27]

Freyberg, who saw Barrowclough later that morning, recorded in his diary that 'it was a bitter blow for the men could not have done more and now they have lost all the ground they had won'. He also noted Barrowclough's comment that 'whoever gave the order for us to remain on Sidi Rezegh yesterday took a heavy responsibility on his shoulders'.[28] Freyberg later wrote of British Brigadier Scott Cockburn, who had come up to him after the battle and said, 'The New Zealanders will never forgive the British tanks for today.'[29] Murphy decided, in the official history, that it was 'not flattering to his [Gatehouse] brigade that the remnants of a German tank battalion could turn about from a very severe action and appear to drive away a fresh British force which outnumbered it in tanks by about nine to one'.[30]

Whether a counter-attack could have succeeded is debatable; both Kippenberger and Inglis considered that Barrowclough had a good sense of a battle, and that if he thought it was possible, he was probably right. The Germans were worn out and demoralised and the British armoured force was formidable. Gatehouse, however, was quite sure that 'the poor chaps we endeavoured to bring out of that sort of cauldron were in NO state to even think of counter attacking', a view with which Drew concurred.[31] Gatehouse's objective was to 'render what help he could to the New Zealand remnants and then withdraw the whole armoured Brigade right away from the treacherous escarpments to some point in the south where it would be free to manoeuvre without the restraint of terrain'.[32]

The 6 Brigade men found 'the whole episode was puzzling', not helped by poor, sometimes apparently inconsistent and misunderstood communications.[33] For Freyberg it must have been a bitter moment. After battling hard, at a high cost, to break through to the Tobruk garrison, the New Zealanders had held their positions while under attack from the two Panzer divisions and other enemy forces. During these last days 'an unscathed [South African] infantry brigade and an armoured formation with over a hundred tanks manoeuvred gravely in the far reaches of the desert without, as far as he could see, attempting to do anything to help him'. It was not surprising that this did nothing to raise his opinion 'of the reliability of armoured formations', that 'he did not regard Dan Pienaar with much affection', and that 'his wireless conversations with his Corps and Army Commanders were curt and much to the point'.[34]

It was now clear that the New Zealanders' salvation would not come from either the British or the South Africans. During the day Freyberg had been in radio contact with the commanders of both 13 and 30 Corps. An intercepted exchange between 13 Corps HQ and the South African Brigade, ordering the South Africans to move south, made it clear 'that Pienaar had abandoned all pretence at coming to our support' and that the division's only cover would be some tanks from 30 Corps.[35] Because of the strength of the enemy, a withdrawal back into Tobruk was unlikely to succeed. Following a conference with his brigadiers, Freyberg felt that the division should head in the opposite direction, first east and then south. Unable to contact Godwin-Austen at 13 Corps, Freyberg spoke with 30 Corps Headquarters by radio, and outlined his plans to Norrie.

The conversation was overheard by Sergeant H.L. Smith, who 'listened in horrified silence' while Freyberg 'described his plan in the plainest of plain language, quite unblemished by the merest pretence of RT procedure or security precautions'. Smith went over to a nearby officer yelling, 'Did you hear what he said? Did you hear?' Without waiting for an answer, he continued, 'Tiny [Freyberg] said that we are going to break out at dusk – four miles east, nine miles south-east over the escarpment and then flat out for the wire! *And all in clear!*' Pointing to the sinister black shapes squatting on the distant skyline to the north, he turned and peered earnestly into the face of Lieutenant Colonel Agar, who had come up to see the fun. 'And what does he think those bastards out there are going to do about it, sir?' As he sauntered off dejectedly, fragments of his mournful soliloquy floated back to his hearers: '...nine miles to Point 192 ... east to the wire ... nine miles to Hell, more like...'[36]

After talking with Norrie, Freyberg dispatched the following message to 13 Corps: 'Remnants New Zealand Division concentrated at Zaafran and after dark will attempt to break out in direction Bir Bu Deheua. If unsuccessful will attempt break out West. Have made contact with Norrie, who is helping.'[37]

For the remaining 21 Battalion men, withdrawal meant clambering into as few trucks as possible, but even that resulted in 16 further casualties. Twenty-six Battalion took advantage of the tank protection but there were more misunderstandings about the direction of the withdrawal. First they headed south-east up the Rugbet en-Nbeidat but ran into heavy fire, so they turned about and headed north. Twenty-five Battalion also moved to Zaafran. After being shadowed across the plateau by enemy artillery firing from Point 175, what was left of 6 Brigade took up a position on the eastern flank of Zaafran, under armoured protection.

As Luxford, the 3 Machine Gun Company commander, later wrote, 9 Platoon 'had no transport with us so our tanks whipped through the position and the chaps clambered up on to them. The Brigade Group moved off in an EASTERLY direction but had not got very far when it ran into an ambush.' There was a hasty change of direction: 'the whole group turned NORTHwards and there was a wild stampede of trucks across the desert. Control was gone. The Group eventually ran through the 4 Brigade area and stopped. The time would then be about 1200hrs.' As Luxford succinctly put it, 'as a fighting unit the Brigade was useless and so late in the afternoon orders were received to move back to the frontier'.[38]

Phil Hammond and Laurie Walker were out on 9 Platoon's left flank when along the bottom of the escarpment came a heap of tanks we all thought were the Poles from Tobruk. The Huns were dropping the odd shell near them which made them look like ours. A Pommie anti-tank officer came charging in shouting 'man the guns' and kept repeating it but the artillery were all limbered up ready to move so the tanks were in amongst them and they didn't have a chance.

They ran to Hammond's truck and headed for the escarpment. They were about to start up when a tank started coming down so we changed our plans in a hurry. We didn't know where to head so followed along the base of the escarpment and eventually came upon a dozen or so trucks and their crews. While there an officer stood up on the bonnet of a jeep and said, 'If you fellows want to get out of this follow me.' We would have followed a dog to get out of there.

They took off but 'there were troops standing up in their trenches and blasting hell out of us at point blank range'. Then 'the outfit' of which they were part 'swung left and headed for some trucks away on the horizon. Not knowing who they were, anybody was better than the ones we had left', they joined 4 Brigade group at Zaafran.[39] Inglis watched the 6 Brigade men arrive: 'fast as the move was, it was no panic flight. The troops seemed to be enjoying themselves thoroughly. Grinning soldiery standing on the tailboards of the trucks were waving to us and "chiacking" as they passed like char-a-banc parties out on a spree.'[40]

With about 3500 men and some 700 vehicles, only some limited ability to defend and no chance of taking any offensive action, it was fortunate that there were no serious attacks. Late in the day, with the sun at their backs, the enemy again attacked. Artillery, anti-tank guns and the few remaining I-tanks turned the attack back, and some British tanks provided support.

At 5.30p.m. the vehicles of the two brigades and Divisional Battle HQ formed up. Four Brigade led, with 6 Brigade and the remaining I-tanks acting as rearguard. Although still under attack, the group disengaged from the action and then departed, keeping an anxious eye out for the enemy. As they started to make their turn to the south a flare bursting just ahead of the column raised the alarm, but it was just the British units alerting Norrie's armoured forces on the escarpment to the division's imminent arrival. As Freyberg recorded that night, 'having moved out of the jaws of what appeared to be a pincer movement we hoped Ariete and the German troops would run into one another in the dark. It was a great disappointment to leave the area so hardly won but the position was untenable.'[41] However the Germans learnt from an intercepted wireless message that the British forces had suffered such heavy losses that they intended to temporarily break off the battle.

By the early hours of the following morning, 'with uncanny ease', the column had reached Bir Gibni, well south, unmolested by the enemy.[42] On the way they passed through the perimeter of 1 Transvaal Scottish Battalion, who observed that 'the drawling New Zealanders were dead beat but still cheerful'.[43] A group of Italian prisoners had joined the New Zealand convoy. Because of a lack of transport, the New Zealanders had turned the prisoners loose to let them return to their own forces nearby, but they had tired of the battle. They found a damaged truck and trailer and worked quickly to get it running so that they could stay with the convoy.

Norrie, who watched part of the withdrawal, was 'much impressed by the discipline of the NZ troops in spite of the very rough time they had had'. Freyberg's response was typical: the men 'had had a baddish time and were very tired, but otherwise were in good fettle'.[44] Auchinleck noted that 'two thirds [i.e. two of the three brigades] had been cut to pieces, and had to be withdrawn to refit'. That night they withdrew 'with the survivors of the 1st Army Tank Brigade, the partner of their successes, and reached the frontier in the early hours of the 2nd of December, exhausted but in good heart.'[45] As one New Zealander was overheard to say, 'My morale is alright but it's had a hell of a fright'.[46]

On 5 December the *Press* reported on the recent fighting. On 30 November 'Sidi Rezegh, which has been in the centre of most of the terrific fighting of the campaign, was recaptured by the Germans with a vicious tank attack. One of our infantry brigades, depleted in numbers, could not repulse this furious attack.' Next morning 'the Huns launched a major offensive with tanks believed to have been led by General von Rommel. They overran and overwhelmed our infantry. As the tanks crashed through the lines with guns blazing support was racing to the unit but it could not reach the New Zealanders in time.' The men of 4 Brigade 'fought against hopeless odds, and soon were split. Some linked up with the Tobruk forces, who still hold Ed Duda. The remainder were forced to withdraw to the east, where they linked up with oncoming reserves.'[47]

By now the New Zealand Division was divided into three parts: the column on its way to Baggush, the forces with the Tobruk garrison or in Tobruk that would eventually move back to Egypt, and 5 Brigade Group, still in the border region. The Eighth Army situation report of 1 December summarised the position: 'Very heavy fighting all day in the Belhamed-Zaafran–Sidi Rezegh area has resulted in the splitting of our forces with Tobruk and the withdrawal southwards of 4 Armoured Brigade. We still hold Ed Duda, but Belhamed and Sidi Rezegh are in enemy hands.'[48]

By the end of the campaign, as Hammond recalled, in 3 Company, 27 (Machine Gun) Battalion 'there were 38 out of the 134 who started out for this party at Sidi Rezegh'.[49] Their trip to Baggush took four days and by 5 December the remnants of the two brigades were back at the camp. For 26 Battalion, 'it was not a happy homecoming. The sight of so many empty dugouts brought back only too vividly the loss of so many friends who had left Baggush with such high hopes.'[50] Twenty-six Battalion losses were 449: 89 killed or died of wounds, 134 wounded and 226 prisoners of war. The 25 Battalion men who had been left out of battle 'were shocked by the big gaps in its ranks'. Its losses totalled 402: 120 killed or died of wounds, 140 wounded and 142 prisoners of war.[51] Twenty-four Battalion's losses were also high, totalling 523: 101 killed, 145 wounded and 277 prisoners of war.

Freyberg concluded his formal report on this phase of *Crusader:*

> So ended the New Zealand part of the battle to keep the Tobruk Corridor open. This battle in the Western Desert was not primarily however a battle to hold positions, but a battle to destroy the German forces. I believe we went some distance towards achieving this in our attacks at Sidi Rezegh, Belhamed and Ed Duda. I think the German Afrika Korps will bear me out in this.[52]

CHAPTER 13

Wrapping up the Campaign

After 4 and 6 Brigade's withdrawal, there were still New Zealand forces scattered from Tobruk to the frontier. In the corridor were more than 1000 men from 18 Battalion, two companies from 19 Battalion and gunners. There were already 3500 men in Tobruk and others who were wounded. Five Brigade still had 3200 men stationed outside Bardia and there were more wounded in the captured MDS.

Towards the end of November a New Zealand war correspondent drove into Tobruk with a convoy transporting German and Italian prisoners and described the scene. 'Scattered over the wide expanse of the desert perimeter are hundreds of derelict Italian tanks and motor transport of all kinds. Stone buildings overlooking the harbour, which once were reflected in the blue waters of the Mediterranean are now tangled debris.' Occasionally 'a shell from the German long-range guns crashed into a nearby hillside' and at night 'the moon, two days from full, lit up the desert and harbour. In the distance the machine-guns rattled. Artillery on both sides was silent. The New Zealanders were still gallantly holding out.'[1]

With Belhamed and Sidi Rezegh in enemy hands, Rommel had control over the escarpments south-east of Tobruk, but New Zealand troops were still on Ed Duda. Eighteen Battalion was on the northern edge of Belhamed, where it had made contact with 2/13 Australian Battalion, while two companies of 19 Battalion were on Ed Duda, including Clem Paterson, whose 'section post adjoined that of the Essex Regiment', under whose command they had been placed.

They had 'moved off in darkness to take over new positions from the "Lost Battalion" of Australians (the only Aussies left in Western Desert at Tobruk)' and were placed under the command of 2/13 Battalion. Just as they arrived, 'a plane came overhead. It was very low and a bi-plane, a very old model [actually a British Swordfish]. The blighter dropped flares until the place was like day and we felt as naked as we were born.' While they watched 'he climbed, circled, cut off then zoomed down straight for us. We kept as still as statues but he must have seen us all right. However he only machine-gunned once to our left and then cleared out – to our relief!'

Their job at Ed Duda 'was mainly night work, chiefly patrols'. Nearby was a wadi containing a large German camp and a lot of battle debris, including many damaged trucks. German trucks 'used to go up and down during the daytime, to the delight and occupation of our machine-gunners, and we used to go abroad at night. The tents yielded some quite good loot and we took some prisoners, who seemed to stray about. Also our platoon successfully ambushed and shot up a number of trucks.'[2]

On 1 December the Germans and Italians made a joint attack on the Tobruk front but it was unsuccessful. Rommel was still confident but his forces were weakening, and nearly all the tanks needed overhauling. The

Australian battalion was shelled early in the morning, and during this attack Lieutenant Colonel F.A. ('Bull') Burrows was badly wounded; shortly afterwards the battalion withdrew through the perimeter to the El Adem Road.

Ritchie was keen to resume the offensive, 'undeterred by the loss of the positions which the New Zealand Division so gallantly won and defended, or by the renewed isolation of Tobruk'.[3] Auchinleck flew up to Ritchie's Advanced Headquarters to plan the future campaign. There were reserves that could be brought in to reinforce the British forces, including an armoured car regiment from Syria, an infantry brigade from Cyprus and three Indian infantry battalions. In addition, 1 Armoured Division had just arrived from Britain. The enemy, by contrast, was unable to introduce fresh troops.

Scobie was worried about the length of the perimeter the Tobruk garrison was trying to hold, especially if there was to be no support from either 30 Corps or the remnants of the New Zealand Division. He and Godwin-Austen decided that if the New Zealanders could not hold their position the Ed Duda appendix might have to be abandoned and the garrison retire to the original perimeter. Because such a withdrawal would have relinquished the key passages, the Trigh Capuzzo and the Bypass Road, to the enemy, army headquarters asked them to hold onto their positions for as long as possible.

The Essex Regiment was more positive. Commanding officer Lieutenant Colonel John ('Crasher') Nichols signalled that 'Ed Duda growing stronger every hour, feel confident we can resist attack from any quarter. Strongly deplore any suggestion of withdrawal.' The Ed Duda positions were not relinquished, but they were subjected to shellfire for some days, and occasional attacks. Enemy losses were mounting, but the New Zealand forces suffered relatively light casualties.[4] They repulsed a second, halfhearted German attack on Ed Duda on 4 December.

The New Zealanders from Tobruk helped by providing working parties and overhauling vehicles while guns were brought up in support. Ritchie ordered a new plan to relieve the town, using

Indian and South African forces, and some from 30 Corps, and south of Sidi Rezegh roving 'Jock' columns with armoured cars harassed the enemy. With the change in plan, and the fact that the bulk of the New Zealand Division had returned to Baggush, it was decided that all New Zealand personnel still in Tobruk, except fighting forces, would be evacuated as soon as possible.

On 1 December 18 Battalion, under the command of the Tobruk garrison, was on the escarpment near Ed Duda. The men sheltered in Italian sangars near the Bypass Road; nearby was a well-equipped RAP and the remains of an Italian field hospital. From this position it was easier to move wounded into Tobruk, and to receive supplies and food. By now Tobruk was 'a huddle of dusty ruins, a landlocked harbour full of wrecks, bombed nightly, the water undrinkable – what a dump to fight for'. Over the next few days the battalion, in what Colonel Jan Peart described as 'positions of extreme difficulty with three sides open to attack and with little support available', came under frequent attack.[5]

On 3 December the enemy attacked with artillery support, but a late counter-attack by I-tanks sent them back. The following day the heaviest German attack took place, with tanks and heavy artillery fire, followed by infantry, supported by machine guns and mortars. But 'one of Jerry's own mines did a job its layers never intended – it blew a track off one tank, and the Polish anti-tank gunners finished the cripple off and drove away its companion'.[6] Faced with increasing pressure, and a counter-attack by the Border Regiment, the Germans withdrew.

Suddenly the men were able to move around, 'revelling in their freedom'. They then returned to Belhamed and the 'scenes of terrible desolation, dead Germans and Kiwis, burnt-out Jerry tanks, the gallant New Zealand gunners still lying round their guns'. There were many German dead 'very close to the old New Zealand positions, gruesome witnesses to the fury of the fight that had taken place'.

All the dead were buried, 'friend and foe – there was no time to waste pity or regret on them, it was of necessity a callous, unceremonious burial'. On 10 December 18 Battalion moved to Tobruk, and by 13 December it had returned to Baggush.[7]

For 5 Brigade near Bardia, the departure of Rommel's tanks had removed the immediate threat of attack and it had been possible to reorganise the positions. On 28 November, with supplies running low, 22 Battalion, which was remote from the rest of the brigade, withdrew to an area a few miles north of the Omars. The following day a convoy of much-needed supplies got through to 22 and 23 Battalions, now close together in the Capuzzo area. Meanwhile, at Sollum, 28 (Maori) Battalion 'fought its one and only naval engagement' when the men saw a submarine approaching the pier 'and the MG section and 3-inch mortar in C Company fired on it'. It then headed back to sea and very soon the enemy guns at Halfaya opened up with 'a fifteen minute hate on C Company. The enemy was probably expecting mail and supplies and appeared very upset over their non-arrival.'[8]

Following the loss of Brigadier Hargest, Lieutenant Colonel Leslie Andrew VC from 22 Battalion assumed temporary command of 5 Brigade, and was ordered to hold a line from Capuzzo to Upper Sollum. A few days later the brigade was relieved and sent back to Menastir, to patrol the Bardia–Tobruk road and prevent supplies from Bardia reaching the Afrika Korps, and vice versa. For 28 (Maori) Battalion that meant a gruelling 14-mile (22km) march.

On 1 December Rommel ordered an attack towards the Sollum front, where the enemy forces had only two days' food left. Two groups were sent: a Geissler Advance Guard would proceed along the Via Balbia, and further south, a second group, the Knabe Advance Guard, would travel down the Trigh Capuzzo. As they headed east they found the areas to the west and south-west of Bardia more strongly guarded, by the Divisional Cavalry and 5 Brigade on the Menastir ridge, to block the approaches to Bardia.

The enemy column ran into these forces and 28 (Maori) Battalion, alerted by the Divisional Cavalry, took a heavy toll. Holding their fire until the enemy was almost on top of them, they inflicted heavy casualties, estimated at about 470, including some 250 killed, at a cost of only one killed and nine wounded. In Freyberg's words, 'the rough handling they received was sufficient to discourage any further efforts to link up with the garrison of Bardia'.[9]

Between 4 and 6 December Rommel suffered several setbacks. First, the second attack on Ed Duda had failed, partly because the British now had fresh troops to bring to the battle, and he decided to withdraw from the eastern half of the Tobruk perimeter. Then the attack towards Bardia had also failed, and there was an unsuccessful attack against 30 Corps near El Gubi. Finally the GOC of 15 Panzer, Neumann-Silkow, was mortally wounded by a shellburst.

Rommel's forces were now under considerable pressure. On 4 December he heard that he could not expect improved supplies of transport and reinforcements until late December. The men were tired and bedraggled; water, food, fuel and ammunition were all in short supply. Some German units had already started to withdraw. When British columns from Tobruk attacked positions around El Adem, they encountered solid resistance in some places, but others were unoccupied.

During the first few days of December 5 Brigade made a number of moves around the border area. On 1 December the brigade and the Divisional Cavalry moved back to Menastir to patrol the Bardia–Tobruk road, where they took some prisoners and vehicles, and destroyed dumps. Although it had constantly been in action and its vehicles needed maintenance, the Divisional Cavalry was operating with 2 South African Division, actively harassing the enemy west of Menastir.

Two nights later the group shifted again, this time to the Capuzzo–Sollum area, to relieve 5 Indian Brigade. During the move, an Indian force shelled 22 Battalion between Sidi Azeiz and Bardia, fatally wounding a driver. On 8 December Brigadier Allan Wilder took over command of 5 Brigade, which that evening received orders that it should be prepared to form part of 13 Corps Reserve for action west of Tobruk. By now the enemy were withdrawing toward Gazala; for a short period the brigade, camped at Sidi Bu Amud came under command of Tobruk's 70 Division, but on the 11th, back with 13 Corps, it advanced through El Adem to Acroma.

To assist the pursuit west, 13 Corps needed to organise transport, and the New Zealand troops in Tobruk provided 30 3-ton lorries, 50 other small vehicles and 50 motorcycles. On the 8th another convoy of over 2000 men, and 500 vehicles, mainly from Divisional Headquarters and other administrative staff, returned to Egypt. Remaining in 13 Corps were 18 Battalion, part of 19 Battalion, some artillery and anti-aircraft units, 4 RMT Company and 5 Brigade.

Twenty-three Battalion was ordered to proceed along the Via Balbia towards Gazala, while the rest of the brigade spread out across the track heading west from Acroma. The brigade encountered some enemy units, which took a while to overcome. Twenty-three

Battalion was dive-bombed by Stukas but, with the help of British supporting fire, captured the Mingar el Hosci ridge and took 497 Italian prisoners. The ridge was renamed 'Thomson's Ridge', in honour of C Company's Captain Frederick Thomson, who led the attack and was wounded in it. Thomson, from Timaru, was later promoted to major and was awarded the Military Cross and Mentioned in Dispatches. He was twice wounded, and died of wounds in Tunisia on 8 March 1943. Twenty-three Battalion's casualties, including two killed, were minimal, considering that two enemy battalions held the position.

The casualties were surprisingly light as there had been plenty of resistance. Private Leonard Diamond described the Italian artillery barrage: 'big stuff and small stuff, it whinnied and whined, whispered and whanged over our heads and in our ranks. The Boys went through it like veterans.' Sergeant John Hargreaves saw 'that thin line moving steadily forward into a hail of lead, with shells of all sizes ... bursting all around ... the fact that the ground was sandy saved more casualties'. They were now close enough for a bayonet charge: 'it made the blood sing to see the boys leap forward, a steady line of gleaming steel backed by grim faces. Nothing short of death could stop them now.'[10] The Italians quickly surrendered. At the same time, despite heavy shellfire, 28 (Maori) Battalion captured Mgherreb with a determined bayonet charge. The Italians quickly surrendered and 1123 were captured. The Maori losses were five killed and 11 wounded.

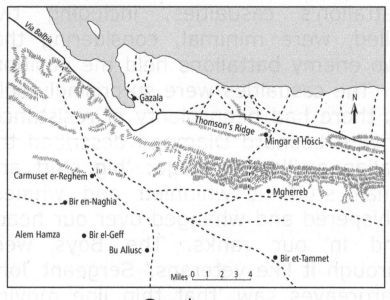

Gazala area

On 9 December Rommel wrote to his wife that he'd 'had to break off the action outside Tobruk on account of the Italian formations and also the badly exhausted German troops'. They moved west and reached the Gazala line by the 12th.[11]

In the face of continued shelling that day, the brigade continued west towards the enemy positions in the Gazala box. The German dive-bombers were also active but caused no damage; the anti-aircraft gunners shot down three Stukas. The Italians had planned good defensive positions at Gazala: there were well-positioned, effectively camouflaged trenches, and machine guns, anti-tank guns and 88mm guns that were difficult to see.

On the 11th most of the New Zealand troops that had gone into Tobruk departed to return to Baggush. Clem Paterson described the scene as he and his companions were withdrawn to Egypt via Tobruk. 'Broken guns, battered tanks and trucks, a few dead mules lined the roads and nowhere does one seem to find desert without tank tracks and occasional burnt out wrecks.'[12]

By the evening of the 12th, 5 Brigade had reached a north–south line just to the east of Gazala, some 40 miles (65km) west of Tobruk, near the coast. Twenty-three Battalion was covering the Gazala landing grounds and coastal areas on the right flank, 22 Battalion was on the left flank at Bu Allusc, and 28 (Maori) Battalion was in the centre, on the escarpment, about 2 miles (3.2km) forward of Mgherreb at Point 182. Masking the German-held Hamza, but out of touch with the New Zealanders, was 4 Indian Division, and to the south 7 Armoured Division was making a wide sweep to come round and cut off the enemy retreat. The Polish Brigade, approaching from the left flank, was to carry out the attack.

The following morning both 22 and 28 Battalions attacked. The former, together with I-tanks and artillery support, overcame an enemy strongpoint, taking 100 prisoners and capturing four guns. Only one man was wounded. The Maori Battalion had to overcome strong resistance before taking Point 181. After a daytime attack during which they were held up by artillery fire, they patrolled the area at night and the following day successfully attacked with a bayonet charge under an artillery barrage. They took a further 380 prisoners.

By now pressure on the Italian and German forces was causing dissension between their respective commands. Rommel was convinced that withdrawal was essential but the Italians did not want to retreat and face further humiliation. Owing to logistical difficulties caused by Ultra decrypts and Royal Navy and RAF successes, Rommel's supplies had dried up, his troops were battle weary and the loss of his 13,000 troops in the border areas, Bardia and Sollum was almost inevitable. On the 15th and 16th the British armour had the opportunity to mount a major attack but missed the chance through delays and failed to bring the campaign to an end. Instead they would have to pursue the enemy across Cyrenaica, easing Rommel's supply problems and making things harder for themselves.

The scale of the Allied attacks was escalating. On the 15th a coordinated attack by the Polish Brigade and 5 Brigade was planned and partially implemented. Heavy fire stymied a 28 (Maori) Battalion attack, causing quite heavy casualties, but the Poles captured Carmuset er-Reghem and Bir en-Naghia. Further south, the Indian Division repulsed an enemy tank attack. At 7.30a.m. on 16 December the Australian 2/13 Battalion, the last to leave Tobruk, drove down the El Adem Road and continued to the frontier, en route to Palestine.

Five Brigade continued west along the Derna road, but was ordered to hand over its troop-carrying transport to help transport supplies to 22 Guards Brigade, which was about to pursue the enemy and hopefully cut off its retreat. Because of the supply difficulties, the Eighth Army did not want any more troops than necessary, and Freyberg was anxious that 5 Brigade should return to the division.

On 19 December Padre Kahi Harawira held a memorial service in memory of the Maori Battalion's fallen. For Private Iver Whakarau, 'this was the saddest day I ever experienced in my life. Saw the hardiest of men shed tears during the sermon, in fact I couldn't hold back myself. Happened to be wearing a pair of goggles so I just pulled them up over my eyes so that no one would see me.'[13] The battalion's casualties were 78 killed or died of wounds, 151 wounded and 13 prisoners of war.

On 23 December, following some maintenance work in Tobruk, 5 Brigade moved back to El Adem en route for Baggush, where it arrived on 29 December. Twenty-two Battalion returned to Baggush; its casualties for the campaign were 23 dead, 44 wounded and 10 prisoners of war. Twenty-three Battalion 'had one short period facing the German soldiers – and it proved its worth in the defence of Fort Capuzzo – but, otherwise, it had fought Italians who had not offered very strenuous opposition'. Twenty-five were killed in action or died of wounds, 68 wounded and 17 prisoners of war.[14]

However, the campaign was not yet over. Four Indian Division, 22 Guards Brigade (transported by New Zealand's 4 RMT company) and other units pursued the retreating enemy forces around the coast, through the Jebel Akhdar (Green Mountains) and into the southern desert. The Oasis Group also made a sweep up from the southern desert. Benghazi fell on 24 December, and the Eighth Army reached Ajedabia by 27 December. By now the enemy was rallying and counter-attacked, costing 22 Armoured Brigade 68 tanks.

Rommel had withdrawn to Marada, covering Agheila, but now he was receiving fresh tanks and had the benefit of better air support; it was the British who were now suffering from long supply lines. Although the Germans had withdrawn, Schmidt 'saw no signs of wilting morale among our rearguard troops. We stood and fought wherever there was high ground.'[15] Rommel's staff officers convinced him to make a spoiling attack, which he did, reentering Ajedabia on 22 January. This then turned into a full counter-attack that forced the Allies to withdraw until they were back on the Gazala line. In the three weeks of the spoiling attack, 13 Corps lost 1390 men, 72 tanks and 40 field guns, and the initiative was back with Rommel. On 27 January he told his wife that they were 'clearing up the battlefield, collecting up guns, armoured cars, tanks, rations and ammunition for our own needs'.[16] The original Allied plan, for another campaign, code-named *Acrobat,* to follow *Crusader* and press on into Tripolitania, was quietly shelved.

While Rommel was fully engaged in the west, there were still significant enemy forces on the frontier line, mainly at Bardia and Sollum/Halfaya, ordered to remain there in order to obstruct the British forces and disrupt the flow of supplies. Three South African Brigade, with the New Zealand Divisional Cavalry and an artillery battery, attacked Bardia on 16 December but did not succeed and lost 60 men. After a second attack on 31 December, however, the German garrison surrendered on 2 January.

The New Zealanders were keen to get into Bardia quickly, to release the many prisoners there. B Squadron of the Divisional Cavalry drove into the town that morning, found the POW camp and started distributing food to the emaciated captives. The Allied troops released 1171 prisoners, 650 of whom were New Zealanders, and captured 7982 of the enemy, including 1804 Germans. Among those released were several of Clem Paterson's former platoon mates. 'All had lost at least a stone weight in 8 weeks and showed it. They said the barrage was terrific (there were about 150 guns shelling the town before it was finally taken) and that they would rather be under German gunfire than their own!'[17]

Sollum was taken on 12 January, and on the 17th General Fedele de Giorgis surrendered the Halfaya garrison. The captives taken as a result brought the total number of enemy prisoners captured in the frontier actions to 13,842; the British casualties in these operations were fewer than 600. And so *Crusader* ended, 'in a minor anti-climax, though a welcome one'.[18]

The join-up of the Tobruk garrison and the
Eighth Army at Ed Duda. (DA-01668-F,
Alexander Turnbull Library)

General Johann Theodor von Ravenstein with a
British staff officer at Tobruk. (DA-02004-F,
Alexander Turnbull Library)

Gun pit at Sidi Rezegh airfield. Back row, left to right: C.A. ('Shorty') Rogers, Brian Cox, John Black. Front row: Laurie Daly, George Woolf, Bert Hambling. (Cox family)

The only members of No.1 Troop, C Squadron, New Zealand Divisional Cavalry to return from Sidi Rezegh: 'Shorty' Gollan, 'Robbie' Robinson, 'Curly' Leask, 'Mac' McRae, Harry Drury. (Robert Loughnan)

Robert (left) and Ian Loughnan. (Robert Loughnan)

Percy ('Titch') Titchener (left) and Stanley ('Shorty') Gollan. (Robert Loughnan)

John ('Jock') Staveley. (John Staveley)

Clarence ('Dick') Polglase and Zeta Gunn.
(Michelle Polglase)

Charles Costello. (Edith Costello)

Wounded prisoners of war alongside tents of the main dressing station at Sidi Rezegh. (J.S. Harper photograph, DA-08289-F, Alexander Turnbull Library)

Eric Heaps. (Heaps family)

Leslie McIver. (McIver family)

The author at the site of the Sidi Rezegh airfield, 2009. (Cox family)

Robin Cox and guide Mohsen by the mosque, Sidi Rezegh, 2007. (Cox family)

The blockhouse, Sidi Rezegh, 2009. (Cox family)

The mosque, Sidi Rezegh, 2009. (Cox family)

CHAPTER 14

Treating the Wounded

When the First Echelon arrived in Egypt medical facilities were quickly established and these expanded as further personnel arrived. As well as doctors, orderlies and other medical staff, the units included women from the New Zealand Army Nursing Service (NZANS), 602 of whom served overseas between 1939 and 1945.

For *Crusader,* casualty management was based around maintaining lines of communication to evacuate casualties for the two corps. The lines merged near Bir el Thalata, about 40 miles (65km) south of Sidi Barrani. A section of a field ambulance would be attached to, and under the command of, each brigade and the remainder of the field ambulances would be used as medical dressing stations (MDSs) as needed. There was a succession of medical aid centres: behind the fighting unit's regimental aid post (RAP) was usually an advanced dressing station (ADS), then a larger medical dressing station (MDS) followed by a bigger casualty clearing station (CCS). Last in the hierarchy was the field hospital. Ideally, MDSs would be no more than 25 miles (40km) apart so that casualties should not have to spend more than two and a half hours in ambulances without receiving dressings, medication, food, drink and other assistance. But the mobile campaign and roving enemy patrols meant this policy was short-lived.

The main medical establishment, 14 British CCS, was at Minqar el Zannan, 15 miles (24km) east of Bir el Thalata. It was close to the railhead; transport to Mersa Matruh and Alexandria could be by train, motor convoy or air. From Alexandria there were several hospitals available including a group in the Canal Zone and in Cairo; No.1 New Zealand General Hospital (NZGH) at Helwan and No.3 NZGH at Helmieh.

The closest New Zealand hospital to the battle area was 2 NZGH, a mobile hospital at Gerawla near Mersa Matruh.

In November New Zealand nurses moved from Helwan with the medical team; there were few comforts as it was just a tented hospital. And it was not without danger. After the hospital's opening ceremony the nurses heard what they thought was a plane misfiring. They 'rushed outside their tents to see what was happening ... when a masculine voice of authority shouted, "Tell those _____ girls to take cover! Jerry is machine gunning the station!" With more haste than dignity they did as they were bid, but it was many months before they could live down the incident.'[1]

As Victor Gregg, a rifleman with the 7 Armoured Division Support Group, wrote later, the battle of Sidi Rezegh was 'the bloodiest and the most frightening the battalion had yet experienced both in length and sheer brutality. Other battles would be just as bloody but they were shorter and interrupted by periods of rest, moments when the battle went off the boil. This was not the case at Sidi Rezegh.'[2] In the early phases several dressing stations were established, then moved as brigades were repositioned. From 23 November onwards they were very busy. On 24 November 6 Field Ambulance opened an MDS in a wadi some 7 miles (11km) east of Sidi Rezegh that was immediately inundated with wounded. On 25 November, when this MDS received 450 casualties – the next day the numbers 'had reached almost flood proportions'[3] – the fast-changing fortunes of the battle and the threat from enemy armour forced a decision to bring all the New Zealand medical units not otherwise deployed together in this wadi.

By the morning of the 28th there were 862 Italian, German, New Zealand, British and South African casualties in the now combined MDS, including 96 prisoners. These numbers placed great strain on resources and equipment, particularly tents, water and rations; some material salvaged from an abandoned German camp nearby helped to alleviate the situation. Having visited the MDS on the 28th, Freyberg proposed that the wounded should be evacuated to Tobruk as soon as practicable. Some of the 1300 wounded had already been evacuated to the east but this was now impossible because of the threat posed by German tanks. Two German medical officers and some orderlies released from a nearby POW camp worked well alongside the New Zealand staff.

On the afternoon of the 28th tanks from 22 Armoured Brigade, which had been held in reserve at the New Zealand Division HQ nearby, were drawn into a battle developing south of the MDS, leaving it, and the nearby POW cage, unprotected. At 5.15p.m. enemy armoured cars and lorried infantry from 15 Panzer Division came along the escarpment, captured the MDS and freed about 1200 prisoners. All the medical staff in the MDS became prisoners of war but were permitted to continue treating the wounded.

The enemy forces, now in control of the area, set up gun positions on the high ground surrounding the wadi, and opened fire on Sidi Rezegh and Belhamed. The Italians placed 14 field guns close to the dressing station's Red Cross flag, and 30 enemy tanks drew up near the Mobile Surgical Unit tents.

As the enemy fire intensified the British responded, and some shells fell around the hospital, the exploding shells and flying shrapnel causing more casualties in the MDS. The situation deteriorated further when a South African counter-attack got close to the MDS but was forced back. The fire increased and a fragment from one shell landed alongside an operating theatre and wounded a patient already on the operating table.

The medical staff worked under great difficulties. Not only did new casualties continue to arrive but the Italians showed little respect for the New Zealand staff or patients. There was little co-operation between the Germans and the Italians. When the New Zealanders attempted to pass Italian wounded to the German medical officers for treatment, they were sent back untreated, and the German medical orderlies generally avoided contact with the Italians. Relationships were better between the New Zealanders and the Germans whose commander, when the Germans withdrew on 30 November, left a letter instructing the Italians not to molest the patients or obstruct their care. This did not prevent the Italians looting and ransacking personal gear.

In the first two days of December German and Italian wounded were taken away, as were 14 medical officers and 182 other ranks, despite their protests about how this would affect the care of the wounded. The New Zealand medical officers were told they would be setting up a reception hospital in the back areas, but instead the entire medical staff was taken prisoner and transported by truck towards Derna and Benghazi.

In the confusion some lightly wounded casualties escaped. On the night of 2 December the commanding officer of 28 (Maori) Battalion, Lieutenant Colonel George Dittmer, escaped with 38 patients and staff and crossed into Egypt. Also in the MDS was Kippenberger, who had been wounded on 26 November at Belhamed. He and 23 others got away on 4 December. They found a captured British truck the Germans had left unattended, drove it out of the wadi and raced off into the desert. Two armoured cars stopped them but fortunately they were South

Africans. Freyberg received a 'very pleasant surprise when Kippenberger turned up' unexpectedly. He 'made him a Brigadier on the spot and sent him back to hospital [2 NZGH at Gerawla]'.[4] Both he and Dittmer were able to provide information about the situation at the MDS. Kippenberger later took over command of 5 Brigade in place of Hargest.

Despite Italian promises of supplies, by early December there had been no food deliveries and only 30 gallons (1351) of water was left for 860 patients and staff. Patients began to die from dehydration and others from the cold. On the night of the 5th, however, there was a lot of Italian activity, but by next morning they had departed. At 8a.m. troops from 7 Armoured Division appeared, trucks were immediately sent in and that afternoon convoys of patients and MDS personnel set off to the south. An ambulance convoy of the most serious cases followed at 6p.m. and by nightfall the wadi was deserted.

When 6 Brigade had moved west on 21 November, 6 Field Ambulance travelled with it to provide medical support. On 23 November 6 ADS was set up close to the brigade and, as doctor Captain Jock Staveley reported, they 'were absolutely swamped with patients. Mainly 25 Bn, some 24 Bn and a few 26 Bn.' Next day, 'at first light we started filling all available transport with casualties and considerable shelling developed. Mainly antitank stuff and we got most of it.' Then 'the convoy of 290 casualties reached 30 Corps just as it was being attacked by tanks and they all dispersed and they never formed up again. However all trucks and ambulances got back into Egypt.'[5]

On the 25th 6 ADS 'moved forward about 5 miles [8km] to a point just east of the blockhouse. Shelling was solid during the move and as soon as the brigade conference was over we prepared for the night attack.' Over following days the medics moved with 6 Brigade towards Sidi Rezegh, treating the casualties. There were shortages of supplies, including morphine, and 'a large number of red crosses for trucks going off with wounded would have saved a lot of casualties being shot up by tanks'.

By 28 November 6 ADS had 'casualties mounting up and no lines of communication'. Enemy attacks were intensifying and 'there was a great old tank battle to the east too. It was about a mile away but Jerry was stopped.' Then the medics had to move: 'we now had 100 patients and it meant carrying them with us ... I told wounded waiting loading on to the sixteen 3-tonners and the ambulances that they would have a hell of a journey but it was either that or staying behind and becoming POW. They gritted their teeth for the bumps.' They reached the new laager area 'at something like 4am, set up the Italian tent [they had acquired], got the serious casualties into it and then we all turned in'.

The ADS was now near Belhamed, with the battle for the corridor raging nearby. On the nights of 29 and 30 November approximately 600 wounded from 6 Brigade were evacuated through the corridor to Tobruk before an expected tank attack forced the ADS to shift further up the slope of Belhamed. On the 30th they had been 'subjected to heavy mortar bombing – no casualties in ADS although tents ripped a bit with the spray'. After a 'session with the Brigadier', Staveley discovered that they were 'for it the next day'. They waited there until they could contact the division, but were then told to stay where they were. Staveley had already been wounded: 'a tiny bit of shrap[nel]' in his right leg was 'causing some difficulties'.

At 7.15a.m. on 1 December, '35 German tanks came into view over a crest 250 yards away'. Caught between the artillery and the tanks, 'after fierce fighting and smoke screen protection for the tanks we were raked with MG fire and two of my men were killed'; six others were wounded. Staveley 'grabbed a Red Cross and made out to meet the supporting infantry and fortunately missed all the stuff flying about'. The remainder of the staff were captured; 'a Jerry officer put us all together and when we received all the POWs, mixed infantry and artillery, we started off on a two and a half mile [4km] trek to the mosque where there was a Jerry RAP'. He worked there all morning on 'our own wounded' and then returned to the 6 Brigade area. They collected more wounded 'but when we got back to the RAP all the crowd had been evacuated', eventually being sent to a POW camp at Benghazi.

At the RAP 'concentrated shelling began right on the mosque vicinity'. Later, from up on the escarpment, they 'watched Maryland bombers give the tanks below the Jerry HQ the works'. They then went to the German hospital at El Adem, 'a hell of a drive'. At the hospital Staveley worked with South African Lieutenant David Klass, trying 'to cover the British wounded in the various buildings. It was difficult.' Although it was a hospital, on 3 December they came under attack, 'a shell landed 10 feet [3m] away and knocked us both', wounding them badly. Later that night

the next lot came in the form of a 6 hour RAF attack. The bombing was appalling – a more concentrated nerve wracking blast I had not experienced. And the fighters strafed everything in the light of the flares they dropped ... I was then told that Klass had died on the table 10 minutes after the shell landed. The Jerries hated us by now and I was the only officer who had mixed with them, they let me know it.

The bombing continued, but gradually the Germans withdrew until 'by the 8th there were about a dozen Jerries left in the place'. The next day 'the last Jerry MO left with the little coffee house artist from Frankfurt, and by the night of the 9th we were completely on our own'. Staveley had been wounded in the shelling on 3 December; on the 10th he went into Tobruk where he 'had morphine and wounds dressed and had a grand sleep'. On the 12th he was 'taken down to wharf and by lifeboat out to *Somersetshire* and we sailed for Alex at 4pm'. Staveley, later promoted to major, was awarded the Military Cross 'for his work and devotion to duty with the ADS at Sidi Rezegh'.[6] After the war he had a very distinguished medical career and was awarded a KBE for his role as a pioneer in the field of blood transfusion.

Also evacuated into Tobruk was machine gunner Bill Andrew. His gun team were dug in above the mosque on 28 November when a direct hit from a mortar killed three of the team and badly wounded Andrew and another man. The next evening Andrew was moved into Tobruk hospital, and on 12 December he travelled to Alexandria on the same hospital ship as Staveley, then went by train to 3 NZGH at Helmieh. After two months in hospital, on 12 February he had 'last leave to Maadi and saw the boys' and shortly after went 'by train from Cairo to transit hospital near Suez'. On 18 February he boarded the hospital ship *Oranje* and after arriving in Sydney on 9 March was transferred to the *Matangi,* which berthed in Wellington on 15 March.[7]

The medical teams worked under very difficult conditions, and were frequently short of supplies, equipment, food and water. Nearly all of them were, at some time, overrun by the enemy; some men remained prisoners and others escaped. The Germans did, however, respect the Geneva Convention. Rommel himself visited a captured dressing station near Sidi Azeiz, and gave orders that the medical staff were to be left alone to carry on with their work. This included caring for German wounded; in fact one ward contained only Germans.

The medical units suffered significant casualties during the campaign. Ten were killed, 17 wounded and 202 taken prisoner; as the official records state 'as prisoners of war, 43.8% of the strength of the field medical units was lost to the New Zealand Division'. The estimated numbers of wounded treated were high; 740, 750 and 1010 for 4, 5 and 6 Field Ambulance respectively, and 160 for the Mobile Surgical Unit. This total of 2660 patients included Germans and Italians as well as New Zealanders (an estimated 1650), British and South Africans.[8]

Because the medical units had been consolidated into one MDS, that was the only place able to deal with surgical work adequately and when it was captured the division lost its surgical facilities and the ability to evacuate casualties. There were, however, still ADSs attached to 4 and 6 Brigades, and these were able to treat casualties and evacuate them into Tobruk. Five Brigade's ADS could evacuate casualties to the Indian CCS at Sidi Omar. Because the battle areas and immediate medical facilities were remote, and there were no clear lines of communication, the transfer to a hospital was potentially dangerous. All the hospitals were some distance away and could be reached only by a rough desert drive, or a risky trip by sea to Mersa Matruh or Alexandria.

After lying in his slit trench at Sidi Rezegh near 6 ADS, Robert Loughnan, with other wounded, was 'loaded on to 3-ton trucks, about eight or ten of us to each lying side by side across the deck, and the convoy set off for Tobruk. It was a dreadful trip. The drivers tried their best to give us a smooth ride but in the absence of any formed tracks there was no avoiding the lurching and swaying.' The convoy stopped at an ADS at Sidi Mahmoud, just outside Tobruk. With few staff available, Loughnan received little treatment there, but was eventually transferred into the hospital. Affected by the drugs he had been given, he was still

> not in full possession of all my mental functions at that time ... every so often we heard outside, three volleys of rifle-fire and the first time this happened I failed to realise this was over someone's grave but conceived the idea that a spy had been discovered and taken out and summarily shot. It did not just occur to me that this grisly task would not need three volleys, not at point blank range.

When a doctor and orderly came round to select walking wounded for evacuation by sea, Loughnan persuaded the doctor that he was well enough to be able to walk unsupported and 'half an hour later I lay at the Tobruk quayside fully clad, greatcoat and all, happily lapping up the meagre afternoon sun', awaiting a ship.[9] Also waiting there was General von Ravenstein, who had lived in relative comfort while a prisoner in Tobruk. He went for walks, attended church, drank whisky with the officer of the guard, discussed the war and Anglo-German relations with English officers and 'spent the night with the bedbugs in the cellar'.[10]

About 5p.m. on 5 December, the SS *Chakdina*, a 3033-ton vessel of the British India Steam Navigation Line, left Tobruk bound for Alexandria. As well as the crew of about 120, on board were 380 Allied wounded, including at least 123 New Zealanders, and approximately 100 German and Italian prisoners of war. On its first trip to Tobruk, the *Chakdina* had transported reinforcements from Alexandria, and since the regular hospital ship did not have enough room for all the casualties, some were put on the *Chakdina* with the prisoners. Among them were Loughnan and Ravenstein. Accompanying the *Chakdina* was the SS *Kirkland*, which had brought supplies of petrol. As these two ships left the Tobruk harbour, accompanied by HMS *Thorgrim*, a 300-ton Norwegian whaler that had been adapted for anti-submarine and minesweeping duties, they were joined by two escort destroyers, HMS *Eridge* and HMS *Farndale*. On board the *Thorgrim* was Ravenstein's previous escort, Robin Bell.

Off Bardia, shortly after 9 o'clock that evening, Italian torpedo bombers attacked the convoy and a torpedo hit the *Chakdina,* blowing its stern off. The ship sank in just five minutes. With many wounded and plaster cases on board, many men stood no chance. Loughnan, on a stretcher in the 'tweendecks when the torpedo hit, was soon in the water. As the aerial attacks continued, the *Farndale* and *Thorgrim* both moved in to try and pick up survivors. The *Kirkland* and *Eridge* sailed on.

Ravenstein was locked in his cabin when the torpedo struck; he pushed open a skylight, got out to the corridor and jumped into the water, where he spent about two hours clinging to a piece of wood before being pulled out by an English sailor and taken on board the *Thorgrim.* Robin Bell, after preventing the ship's engineer from trying to kill Ravenstein with a large spanner, provided him with some clothing and took him down to his bunk. As Bell concluded, 'fact is stranger than fiction at times'![11] The next day the *Thorgrim* and *Farndale* sailed along the

North African coastline under a Hurricane fighter patrol protection, and eventually the *Thorgrim* berthed in Mersa Matruh. Ravenstein, who had been well regarded by those who met him, was initially taken to Cairo, then sent to Pietermaritzburg in South Africa and finally to Canada. He was eventually repatriated to Germany in 1947.

Loughnan, caught in the water between a lifeboat and the *Farndale,* hooked his arm over a loop in a lifeline and hoped that someone could assist him to cross the wreckage beside the ship. However an Australian asked Loughnan for help, so he told him to climb over, but 'his last kick down on my shoulders forced me below the surface and the wreckage closed over my head'. Fortunately 'some strong hands whisked me up. Big tattooed ones they were, and they laid me down, oh so gently, in the bottom of the lifeboat, shivering and miserable and spewing.' Finally he caught the *Farndale* scrambling net, was hauled up by a sailor and 'found himself in the fo'c'sle where I lay on a locker for the rest of the trip to Alex, a proper cot-case and disinterested in anything at all'. He was admitted to 3 NZGH.

A year later, after the Alamein breakthrough, the division halted near Gambut and Loughnan and another C Squadron man returned to Sidi Rezegh to search out the graves of two of their mates. They quickly found them, in the little cemetery situated just below Sidi Rezegh. While searching, Loughnan realised, when he saw the shell damage on the mosque nearby, that he was close to where he had been wounded the previous year. He 'felt familiar with the little dun-coloured building up on the hill as seen from that particular angle – even the shell-hole through its dome'. When walking along he kicked an iron stake, which he immediately recognised as one from the marquee in which he had lain on a stretcher. 'Almost unerringly I went to a point at the edge of the line of graves and squatted down to glance up at the mosque. There could be no mistake. There I was at the head of the grave I had occupied for several hours a year ago.' It suddenly dawned on him 'why all the serious cases had been taken outside; why the "slitties" had to be in neat rows; why some were being dug, others filled in. Not many people can boast they have actually enjoyed lying in their own grave for some hours. I have.'[12]

The sinking of the *Chakdina* has received little official attention and merits only a paragraph in Murphy's campaign history. *New Zealand Medical Services in Middle East and Italy* devotes one page to the sinking, pointing out that the vessel was not a hospital ship. It observes that 'this was the only major misfortune in the evacuation of wounded in 2 New Zealand Expeditionary Force during the war, and the decision to use the *Chakdina* as a hospital ship, without markings, appears unjustifiable'.[13] The exact number of New Zealanders who died is uncertain, but it was at least 81. There is a striking similarity to the sinking of the troop transport *Marquette* on 23 October 1915, in which 32 New Zealand medical staff, including 10 nurses, were killed. Like the *Chakdina,* she was not marked as a hospital ship and was struck by a torpedo.

By the end of November 3 NZGH was busy with regular convoys of casualties from Libya. Many of the men were seriously ill when they arrived, some only with field dressings and with infected wounds. Surgical teams and nursing staff worked tirelessly to treat the men, who were frequently also suffering from nightmares. Being cared for by New Zealand nurses was a godsend; as their patients recuperated they helped them by writing their letters home, doing their shopping and carrying out other tasks. From time to time relationships developed between nurses and long-term patients and a number of future marriages had their beginnings in the hospital.

Private Clarence ('Dick') Polglase, a builder's labourer from Palmerston North, arrived in Egypt with the Fifth Reinforcements on 5 May 1941. Posted to 21 Battalion, after training he took part in the Libyan campaign, but his time in action was short-lived. Badly wounded at Sidi Rezegh, he was admitted to 2 NZGH at Gerawla until being transferred to 3 NZGH in Alexandria. Polglase spent the early months of 1942 in hospitals and convalescent centres, and was graded for light duties only. Eventually, in 1943, he was assessed as Grade 3 – fit for service in medical or administrative units – and attached to 2 NZGH, then at El Ballah near Kantara, on guard duties.

On 22 July 1943 the *Nieuw Amsterdam* left Wellington to return to Egypt carrying the Tenth Reinforcements, and among those on board were 20 NZANS sisters, including Zeta Gunn from Oamaru. It was the 'long awaited day'; with 'bands playing and everyone cheering, we set off on our grand adventure'. After arriving in Cairo on 18 August she was sent to 2 NZGH. While stationed there she met Dick Polglase, at a picnic by the canal on 26 September, after which they got together regularly for picnics, tennis and walks, as well as the round of social activities. On 4 January 1944 they both sailed to Italy, on different ships, and on 15 January Gunn wrote that they had 'announced engagement –

congratulations etc, thrilled and happy'. Although busy, they were able to see each other regularly throughout the year.

Gunn described 'the heart-wrenching wounds' she and the other nurses treated. Theirs was exhausting work in difficult conditions: 'sometimes we were so physically and emotionally tired that when we got off duty we wanted only to fall into bed and sleep.' But they were also 'expected to help troops socially and accept so many of the invitations to dances, dinners and parties. Not just for our own boys but to any units stationed nearby.' Even so, Gunn remembered her 'two and a half years of army life as the most rewarding and interesting time of my life. An experience that I will never forget.'

After more than four years overseas, Polglase returned to New Zealand, arriving on 8 April 1945. Gunn stayed a little longer, and returned on the final voyage of the hospital ship *Oranje,* which reached Wellington on 13 August 1945. It was a time for happy reunions: 'Dick arrived Saturday 10pm, home at last to safety, security, peace and love. Arrived Oamaru Monday evening – great family welcome. Round of greetings, journeys and preparations for the happy day of 23 October. Dick and I start our married life – happy and contented and no possible doubt of being "the one and only".'[14] For many of the men wounded or taken prisoner their Sidi Rezegh experiences were life changing; for a lucky few, like Polglase, those changes were very much for the better.

CHAPTER 15

For You the War is Over

Machine-gunner Randel Heron, caught in a hopeless situation above the Sidi Rezegh mosque, quickly realised that there was nothing he could do when a German officer said, 'For you the war is over.' As he wrote later, 'so ended my part in the shooting war, at 6.30a.m. on 26 November 1941.'[1]

Around one in every 10 New Zealanders who fought at Sidi Rezegh was taken prisoner, and most would spend the next three and a half years in POW camps, initially in Italy. In September 1943, when Italy capitulated, the Germans took over the camps, and the prisoners, except those who managed to escape during the transition, were transported to Germany. The period of captivity was hard; food was short and conditions often primitive and uncomfortable, and some of the men endured extraordinary events.

Heron's experience was typical. After their positions were overrun by German tanks, the New Zealanders were searched and taken into captivity with only the clothes they were wearing. They were transported by truck or forced into a long march to a staging compound, often just a crude wire cage with no facilities at the back of the enemy lines. To their dismay, the prisoners came under Italian control because of an agreement between Hitler and Mussolini 'that all prisoners taken by German forces in North Africa must be handed over to the Italians'.[2] Heron and his section were penned in for the night with ground sheets their only shelter from heavy rain; 'very few of us had blankets or greatcoats. Fortunately I had been wearing my greatcoat when captured.' They received no food or drink and the following day were 'herded like cattle on to huge Lancia trucks, each hauling a trailer, and transported to Benghazi via Derna, a hair-raising trip'. They were given a small tin of meat, which they later realised was horse.[3]

By 5 December Benghazi, the main prisoner collection centre, held some 6000 troops from Britain, Australia, India, New Zealand and South Africa. As Heron recalled, 'Benghazi was a nightmare! Limited food, very little water, and sanitary arrangements, which were primitive in the extreme. Many men suffered from dysentery as a result of the filthy conditions under which we were forced to live. Shelter from the cold nights was minimal.'[4]

Other prisoners were taken to Bardia. After 5 Brigade HQ was overrun Brigadier Hargest and some other officers were driven there, but later that evening the men 'arrived in various stages of exhaustion, having walked the eighteen miles [29km] from Sidi Azeiz, carrying as much of their kit as they could manage'.[5] Conditions were poor. Officers had a shed to live in, but other ranks were kept in a stony compound next to the coast with only a wall for protection until they rigged up some primitive shelters using old blankets, stones and corrugated iron. After being greeted by the German commander, Hargest was soon handed over to the

Italians who ran the compound. After an uncomfortable cold, wet night, at noon the next day Hargest was finally able to talk to the commandant, 'a talkative, gesticulating, useless Italian if ever there was one'. He asked to be taken to see where the men were kept, 'and when we arrived a dreadful sight confronted us. The little compound had now nearly nine hundred prisoners, for whom there was little more than standing room. They had had neither food nor water, and those who had walked the eighteen miles were suffering acutely.' The Italians eventually delivered some bread, tinned meat and salty water.

For latrines 'small, inadequate holes had been dug in one corner. These had filled up and overflowed across the terribly congested yard.' Hargest visited the mosque that the Germans were using as a hospital and saw that 'the conditions were appalling'. He arranged for New Zealand medical orderlies to assist and 'by the next day when I was allowed in things were infinitely better'. He inspected an Italian hospital and 'received a pleasant surprise' as it was 'large and airy and reasonably clean'.

The officers, although better housed, lacked eating and drinking utensils and Hargest found the sight of 70 British officers scavenging in a refuse dump for anything that could hold liquid or be used as a spoon very depressing, 'I think we touched bottom in misery that afternoon.'[6] To lift morale, the padre started holding evening church services and this led to a programme of talks. Most of the men in the compound remained there until Bardia fell on 2 January 1942, though some officers were evacuated by submarine either to Benghazi or direct to Italy, and 60 sick men departed for Italy in a German hospital ship.

In early December 1941 the first draft of prisoners left Benghazi by ship, and others followed. Some went first to Tripoli, and others direct to Italy, in cargo or passenger ships, or occasionally Italian warships. Most of the prisoners in the early shiploads were destined for Naples and then transferred to a camp at Capua. Later contingents went to Brindisi, Taranto or Bari, and by early

1942 most of the New Zealand prisoners had been transferred to southern Italy.

On 3 December the Italians drove Hargest and some other officers down to the harbour where 'we saw the long, low lines of a submarine'. The captain of the submarine, the *Ammiraglio [Admiral] Millo* welcomed them aboard: 'as you see, you cannot get away from the ship, so please let me do all I can to make you happy.' The captain, Hargest recalled, 'was predisposed to us from the beginning, having married a New Zealand girl while out in China on service, the daughter of a master mariner from Auckland'. For her the war was a nightmare, torn with two anxieties – 'for her father, who was the master of an ocean-going vessel, and for her husband who, besides the risks attendant on his calling, might well be the instrument of her father's death'. After they set out, the captain said, 'I expect you would like to hear the BBC.' When Hargest said he would, the Italian replied '"So would I...", and we had the BBC forthwith'.

After three nights and two full days the submarine entered Benghazi

Harbour. When Hargest left the submarine, the captain asked for his wife's address 'and said that his wife would write to her people in Auckland asking them to forward news of me to my home. Soon he went off and I never saw him again. Later at Sulmona I was given to understand by the Italians that his submarine had been lost, together with all its complement and twenty-two British officer prisoners of war.'

Shortly afterwards Hargest was taken aboard a small torpedo boat that was to escort a large steamer, carrying British prisoners to Italy. He had a good look at the steamer but could not see any prisoners 'and concluded that they were all battened down below decks'. At dinner that night one of the officers turned on the radio, and 'their faces froze into tenseness' as the news came through that 'the Japanese onslaught on Pearl Harbor had been announced, and the Americans and the Axis powers were at war. The prospect filled them with gloom.' Hargest also felt 'utterly helpless', knowing New Zealand would now be very vulnerable.[7]

On 8 December two brothers from Nelson, Charles and Eric Costello of 26 Battalion, also left Benghazi in far less comfortable circumstances. Captured at Sidi Rezegh on 30 November, they were transported to Benghazi and were among the 2000-strong contingent that boarded the 6000-ton cargo steamer Hargest had seen.

The Italians called the ship *Sebastiano Venier* (also *Sebastiano Veniero*) but another name, *Jason,* was visible under the paint. She had been built in Italy and sold to a Dutch company that named her the *Jason.* During the delivery, however, Italy declared war and refused to hand over the vessel, which was taken over by a Venetian shipping line and renamed *Sebastiano Veniero.* The Allies preferred the original name, and to them she remained the *Jason* (confusingly sometimes also called *Jantzen*). She had been the only ship in a supply convoy of five to survive air and naval attacks, sailing alone into Benghazi Harbour at the beginning of December 1941.

As the prisoners were loaded into the vessel's holds and the hatches were battened down, the sight of the crew members, with anxious faces and their boots already strung around their necks in case they needed to abandon ship, did little to ease their worries. Soon the ship set sail to cross the Mediterranean, a dangerous voyage with British ships and aircraft doing their best to attack shipping and deny Rommel the supplies he needed.

The following afternoon, Lieutenant Commander E.F. Pizey, captain of the British submarine HMS *Porpoise,* spotted the *Jason* just off Cape Methoni, near Pilos on the south-west coast of the Greek Peloponnese. With the periscope raised higher than usual in the rough seas, the submarine fired four torpedoes at the *Jason,* where lookouts, seeing the periscope, immediately raised the alarm. The captain decided to abandon ship, even before the fatal third torpedo hit, striking one of the forward holds. Around 500 men, mainly prisoners, were killed. Some men were able to get to the deck but the captain and some of the crew had already taken to the lifeboats, leaving the prisoners to their fate.

Looking on, horrified, from his torpedo boat was Hargest, who heard the explosion and rushed to the deck. He could see the steamer going down and 'the crew were already abandoning her and taking to the boats', there was 'no sign of the prisoners. They must have been still battened down. I was horror-stricken. We were still circling about dropping depth charges.' He rushed to the captain of his vessel, 'railing against the despicable cowardice of the crew in deserting two thousand men to certain death. I urged him to stop dropping depth charges and to compel the crew to return to the ship.' They ceased depth charging, then 'sailed close up to the boats and ordered the crew to return. To my relief they went and the ship headed for land.'[8]

On board the ship, now bow down, was a German naval engineer who sent all the men to the stern, to help raise the bow. After doing what he could to help the injured, he took 'a large spanner and a Luger automatic' and persuaded the ship's engineers to start the engines. The ship slowly headed to the nearby coast, where a massive surge lifted her onto a reef, firmly aground but still some 50m from shore.[9] Some men were able to get away in boats and rafts, but most had to either swim or slide down an improvised lifeline. The next day the weather improved and those still on board were transferred by lifeboat or by stretchers slung on the ropes. Once on shore they were kept in cold, wet and cramped conditions. Forty-five New Zealand soldiers were killed in the *Jason* tragedy, almost all of them from 4 and 6 Brigades captured around Sidi Rezegh and Belhamed.

Charles Costello had decided to stay on the ship until the weather had settled: some men had been flung off the lifeline as it whipped up and down when the ship was buffeted. He then 'got off boat by rope. Wet through, taken into shed, no eats, no dry clothes. Stand up all night, cold as hell.' On the following day they received a small snack and 'then marched 7 1/2 miles (12km) to [Pilos] Castle, put in cells, 36 in ours. No blankets yet, cold as blazes.' Two days later they were 'issued with one blanket and mess tin in morning. Hot meal at night, first for 30 hours.' They were later issued with greatcoats.

The conditions were appalling: the weather was freezing and meals were erratic. After a short stay in a camp at Akhaia christened 'Dysentery Acre', because of an outbreak of the illness, the men were taken to Patras on 31 December. Costello recorded 'no meal for 45 hours'. The lack of food, ill-health and boredom continued for weeks; by 27 January he was 'very moody lately, getting sick of this place'. In February groups started moving to Italy, which for the Costello brothers meant Campo 75 at Bari. Before Charles Costello left, he had 'just heard folks [in New Zealand] have been notified, much rejoicing'. In 1943 they were transported to Stalag VIIIA at Görlitz, in Germany.[10]

After doing what he could to urge his captain to help the *Jason,* Hargest continued on his journey to Italy. After arriving at Messina, he was transferred to Campo PG 78 at Sulmona, in the hills 100 miles [160km] east of Rome; a few days later an exhausted Brigadier

Miles also arrived. After four months, both Hargest and Miles were transferred to Campo PG 12, on a hill above Florence. There they met several senior British officers, including Generals Neame and O'Connor.

On 28 March six men, including Hargest and Miles, escaped. The two New Zealanders planned to travel by train until they were close enough to the Swiss border to be able to cross on foot. They successfully evaded detection, crossed into Switzerland and then separated. The French Resistance helped Miles to travel to Spain but on 20 October 1943, exhausted and depressed, he committed suicide at Figueras, north of Barcelona. Hargest also made it to Spain and then went to England. He was later appointed New Zealand observer for the invasion of France. After previously being wounded, Hargest was killed by shellfire on 12 August 1944.

Captain Charles Gatenby travelled directly to Italy in the cramped torpedo chamber of a submarine. Selection for the voyage had been stressful; the men did not know before boarding that the submarine held only six prisoners. 'Before boarding when their names were called out in no particular order they had been under the belief they were being taken out to be shot.'[11] After disembarking at Port Taranto, Gatenby was sent to Campo 85 at Tuturano. In January 1942 he was transferred to Campo PG 38 (Poppi) in the Arno Valley. Poppi, a stone villa perched on a steep hillside, was intended to be a camp for New Zealand junior officers. It was extremely cold during the winter, but the lack of food was the men's biggest problem. Eventually 'salvation came in the form of Red Cross food parcels'. When the men heard of their arrival they 'could hardly believe the announcement, for it meant that our rapidly growing fears of starvation were removed'.[12]

Gatenby was later transferred to Campo PG 47 near Modena, where the men were relatively well fed, the camp was comfortable and there were plenty of leisure activities available. On 13 August 1943 he was taken to a civilian hospital in Carpi, about 9 miles (14.5km) from Modena, for an operation; shortly afterwards the Germans took over the hospital. 'I don't think they were as good captors as the Italians; they weren't quite used to it.'

While recovering from his operation, he noticed that one of the guards, a German corporal, was not very vigilant. When the Italian orderlies wheeled out crates of rubbish, he would 'pretend to put his bayonet in it, but never actually poke it in, and thus save cleaning it afterwards'. One day, when this guard was on duty, Gatenby persuaded an orderly to put him in a crate and he was wheeled to the gate. 'Then there was the crucial moment. As long as no officer was about, I felt sure I wouldn't feel this bayonet. But I sweated somewhat, some few seconds of mental agony in that box.' He was in luck, and soon he was dumped in the rubbish pit and he 'waited there till dark. I headed towards the foothills and mountains to the south.'

For about a month Gatenby walked south into the Apennines, hoping to hide until he made contact with the Allied army. Friendly Italians helped him with food and shelter, until one day he met another escaper, Englishman Major Leslie Young. They joined forces and continued walking, crossing some steep, rocky mountains as the weather turned colder until, helped by the locals, they camped up in a mountain village called Corvaro, north-east of Rome. There they spent Christmas, resting up in a shepherd's hut waiting for Young, who had fallen ill, to recover.

One day, they were visited by an Italian, Count Carlo Tevini, who 'claimed he was a British agent and had with him a girl called Silvia Elfer, again claiming to be a British agent. They were in great danger from the Fascist Gestapo, who were apparently tracking them down. It was imperative, according to Carlo, that they get through to the British lines as quickly as possible.' Tevini said he knew a pass through the mountains. Gatenby 'was finally persuaded' to be the leader of the group and decision-maker, and 'away we went, towards this gleaming white snow of the mountain pass'. Eventually, in intense cold, they made their way through the pass, 'overlooking Anzio on the other side'.

Gatenby made a reconnaissance and, after talking to Italian villagers, found that the Germans had five divisions containing Anzio and his group would have to cross some minefields to join the Americans. On the night of 4 February 'it was pitch dark when we set off, overcast, slight rain, frozen mud and snow'. They 'got along quite well at first' and crawled the way through a minefield, Gatenby leading 'with the others hanging on to my ankle, each in turn. We got through.'

With time running out and still 2 or 3 miles (3.2–5km) to go they decided to walk, 'when suddenly a machine gun opened up. The Count stopped a burst. He fell coughing and spluttering, trying to say something. I crawled over and felt him over. Both my hands were covered in blood. He was bleeding badly from the chest and unable to say anything. I thought, "for certain, Carlo will die".' Gatenby crawled back to Elfer, who wanted to stay with Tevini, but the Germans were now shooting and throwing grenades so Gatenby grabbed her and they 'ran like fury, fell into an irrigation ditch, stayed there till the noise and tumult had died down'. Elfer was 'sobbing and crying', and Gatenby threatened to shoot her if she did not shut up. 'I didn't mean it, of course, but that's how I felt at the time, nerves somewhat shattered by that small experience.'

They crossed another minefield then machine guns opened up on both sides and 'next thing the Yanks start firing with their machine guns, both sides frightened that the other is going to make some punitive attack'. They continued crawling. 'I think I'm quite safe when suddenly I'm turned over on to my back; a bullet has caught me in the left arm. I hear a queer, odd gurgling noise behind me.' He crawled back and found that Elfer had been hit. 'I said to her "are you alright, Silvia?" She said "I'm hit in the throat." I said "can you crawl? You've got to crawl, it's not far to go now, where those machine guns are, you're safe." She said she'd try.'

When they got closer to the machine guns Gatenby yelled out at the top of his voice, '"hold your fire! Englishmen!" No good saying New Zealander, most people never knew where New Zealand was.' The Americans told him to 'advance with your hands up. I could only hold one arm up. The other was numb and bleeding like a pig. I did advance, into the arms of an American patrol of their front line.'

Nearly six months after his escape, on 7 February 1944, Gatenby crossed the Allied lines at Anzio, having walked well over 400 miles (640km). He had difficulty persuading the Americans who he and Elfer were, because he 'was dressed in rags like an Italian peasant, hadn't shaved for weeks, filthy and lousy, and they swore no-one could get through their minefields'. Finally Gatenby was able to speak with a battalion commander who asked who the New Zealand divisional commander was. 'He knew him; we were duly rushed to hospital. I still didn't know where Les Young was. Unfortunately Silvia died. A brave girl if ever there was one. I was put on a tank landing craft and taken to a hospital ship and down to Naples.'[13] From there he went to 2 NZGH at Caserta, where he was interrogated and was able to provide the Allies with valuable information. He was later awarded the MBE (Military Division) for distinguished service in the field.

In June 1944, when Gatenby was managing the New Zealand Forces Club in Rome, he ran into Tevini one day in the street. He could hardly believe his eyes. Tevini had been captured by the Gestapo, who had nursed him back to health, only to torture him to get information about his partisan connections. Tevini was from a powerful Italian family, and through Vatican intervention he was still alive when the Allies marched into Rome. Young also survived and was repatriated shortly afterwards.

Randel Heron's departure from Benghazi meant 'a 24-hour dash across the Med, in the bilges, standing in smelly water; that ended at Brindisi, from where we were taken to a transit camp at Tuturano'. They were 'accommodated in bivouac tents made of three Italian groundsheets laced together end-to-end, making a kind of tunnel. We "slept" nine to a tent, head to foot. The "bedding" was straw plus two blankets, each about four feet [1.2m] square and made of some kind of fibre.' The food was very basic, mainly bread, macaroni or rice. Heron spent Christmas 1941 in that camp, in bleak and snowy conditions.

In early February 1942, along with most of the New Zealand prisoners, Heron was 'transported by train' and 'on arrival we set out on foot, in pouring rain, to walk several miles, most of which appeared to be uphill, to a prison camp set in a small valley'. This was Campo PG 52, in the hills north of the Italian Riviera, 10 miles (16km) from Chiavari.[14] The camp had about 40 rough, draughty huts with no heating and poor lighting. The eventual arrival of Red Cross parcels helped to alleviate the initial food shortages.

Heron was later sent to Campo PG 57, near Udine in north-east Italy. Although the men had wooden huts, shortages of fuel and blankets made the winters hard. Water was plentiful, and Red Cross parcels of food and clothing supplemented the Italian rations and supplies. The men established educational classes and a library, played music and played sport on the large open area used for parades.

Artilleryman Ian Loughnan went first to a hospital at Derna before being transferred to a hospital ship, and 'we sailed off to Italy'. On the ship, to his surprise, 'an Italian priest came in, and asked me my name and wrote it down. I learnt much later that my name was handed in to the Vatican Radio and was broadcast within two days of them receiving it.' His name was 'picked up from that Vatican radio broadcast by someone in New Zealand and they contacted my parents', weeks before the official news was delivered.[15]

Loughnan eventually also found himself in Campo 57, where he attended Mass daily and sang in the choir. He got on well with the Italian camp chaplain, and when the latter started to arrange for the construction of a chapel, Loughnan and other men helped to build it. (It was at Campo 57 that the New Zealander resolved to become a priest himself after the war.) Several months later, just before the chapel was ready to open, they heard news 'that

Mussolini had fled, and that Italy was without a government'. While some men decided to make a break for it, Loughnan and some others decided to 'wait until the first Mass was said the following morning, and then run for it'. But 'as we came out of the chapel we found that German soldiers had surrounded the camp and were pointing machine guns at us! They "invited" us to go to the Fatherland with them. We accepted, but hardly graciously.' Then it was off to Stalag VIIIA in Görlitz.[16]

According to Heron, the men in Campo 57 were told that they would be taken to Trieste and picked up by the Royal Navy, but to their horror, they 'found the next morning that the camp was surrounded by German tanks'. They were loaded into cattle trucks, and after a very cramped train trip, with primitive facilities, finally arrived at Stalag XVIIIC at Markt Pongau. A week later they were off again – 'four days and four nights being rattled around in a cattle truck, with limited opportunity to sit or sleep, not to be recommended as a way of touring the Austrian Tyrol or Germany' – until they arrived at their new camp, Stalag VIIIA. Although not 'pleasant', it was to be home for Heron, Loughnan and the Costello brothers until February 1945, when life for these POWs turned into a nightmare.

By January 1945, with the Russian army advancing westwards, the German authorities decided to evacuate POW camps in their path, to delay the liberation of the prisoners. Over the first few months of 1945, tens of thousands of prisoners were forced to march westwards, across Poland, Czechoslovakia and Germany. This forced march came to be known under various names, but to Heron, it was simply 'The Long Walk'.

On 14 February the first group of prisoners and staff of Stalag VIIIA set out; Heron was in the last group to leave. Under guard and heavily laden, they started walking away from the advancing Russians, quickly discarding anything not considered essential. 'The first day was a nightmare, over twenty miles [32km] through snow and slush, ending up in a farmyard where I slept, in the open, under a plough.' With only the odd day off, they walked through all sorts of weather and terrain, and 'most times we had to spend the night in the open'. Food was sparse, supplemented by anything that could be raided from farmyards, and as a special treat on 23 April 'a Red Cross truck was allowed through the German lines and for my 31st birthday, I, along with the rest of the group, received a food parcel'.

One day, in the town of Duderstadt, they stopped at a factory. 'When we walked up the snow-lined track leading to the building we became aware of a number of dead bodies lying beside the roadway, a sight which did not actually do much to cheer us up.' Inside the factory had slatted floors and 'as many of the men incarcerated there were suffering from dysentery, it was hazardous to be located on one of the lower floors'. There were other hazards too, as the RAF was machine-gunning German troops, and the POWs 'were on the receiving end of such attacks on more than one occasion, and in particular on the early evening of 22nd April'. That night 'one of the three barns we had just occupied was hit and set on fire. We had met up with a group of RAF men that day and ironically it was their barn that was hit. Three men were killed.'

Finally, 'after approximately ten weeks and some 400 miles [640km] since leaving Stalag VIIIA, we met up with British troops. At 10a.m. on 2nd May 1945, British tanks rolled into the hamlet where we had been spending the night in a farmyard. I was in the process of having a wash down when a shout went up, announcing the arrival of the British troops.' It was time to celebrate: 'the rest of the day was spent in relieving the farmer of one of his pigs to be cooked and eaten and treating the German guard to a dunking in the farmer's midden.' For an obnoxious guard this 'was an appropriate punishment, rather than that suggested by a Dutch soldier accompanying the British troops, which was to take him around the corner where, we were led to believe, the guard would have been "bumped off".'

Commandeered German lorries transported them 'the few miles to

Luneberg Heath, where General Montgomery was to receive the German surrender a few days later'. On 4 May 'a rickety old Dakota' flew them back to Hertfordshire, where they were 'escorted individually by a member of the WRAF [Women's Royal Air Force] and taken to a hangar converted into a mess hall, and fed'. Having endured three years and 158 days in captivity after being confronted by that tank commander at Sidi Rezegh, for Heron the war really was over.[17]

Loughnan also endured the long trek across Germany and shortly afterwards he returned to New Zealand. He fulfilled his wish to become a Dominican priest and was ordained on 15 December 1951, 10 years and two weeks after he was wounded at Sidi Rezegh; he spent over 25 years in the Pacific Islands as a missionary. Then, in 1993, he received a letter explaining that the 'local Italian people were in the process of restoring the Chapel we had built in Campo 57'. On 3 September that year, former artilleryman Ian Loughnan, now Father Ambrose Loughnan OP,[18] spoke at the Mass to celebrate the rebuilding of the chapel that he had helped to erect. It was, he said 'only the second time that Mass had been said here'; the first Mass, exactly 50 years earlier, had been the one he had attended immediately before his capture. It was 'a great joy' for Loughnan 'to say this Mass for peace and as an act of reconciliation for many of us'.[19]

CHAPTER 16
Counting the Cost of Crusader

General Auchinleck, in his report on the campaign, concluded that *Crusader* 'was a success, but rather slower, more costly and less complete than I had hoped'.[1] Although the victory was not comprehensive, Rommel had been pushed back to where he had started nine months earlier, Cyrenaica with its valuable airfields had been regained, Tobruk had been relieved and the Allies had won some much-needed time. If the campaign had not succeeded, Rommel's 1942 offensive could have started a lot earlier and much closer to Egypt. By mid-February he was back at Gazala, still 120 miles (193km) from the border, and in the summer of 1942 military equipment that would be critical for the Allies' success, including the vital Sherman tanks, began to arrive in North Africa. In this context Churchill's statement, 'it may almost be said,

Before Alamein we never had a victory. After Alamein we never had a defeat', perhaps understates the significance of the Eighth Army's achievement in *Crusader.*[2]

The battle had not gone as planned, and the New Zealanders found themselves at its forefront during the critical days from 23 November until 1 December. Freyberg had anticipated that the New Zealanders might be called to march on Tobruk, with 6 Brigade poised to move on the vital Sidi Rezegh ridge when the call came. The time and attention paid to training the troops for fitness and for mobility in the desert and in night attacks had proved vital as the campaign evolved. For New Zealand's 4 and 6 Brigades, together with the supporting British armour and attached troops, this 'had been a memorable campaign', and their performance had been crucial.[3] Although they were unable to hold Sidi Rezegh and Belhamed they had inflicted such losses on Rommel's forces that he was forced to withdraw shortly afterwards.

As Major General William Gentry wrote later, when the New Zealand Division entered *Crusader* it was 'at the peak of its fighting form'. Although it became more skilful 'especially in the higher ranks, and was probably more effective', it is doubtful that 'it ever fought again with the same fury and determination as it did in that short and confused campaign'.[4] The victory, however, was less than decisive, and 'few doubted that Rommel would come again', although he was not invincible.[5]

Auchinleck acknowledged that, although the Allies 'enjoyed full air support', their 'experience with tanks was less happy'. Training time had been short, and 'to learn to handle tanks cost us dear, particularly when we found that ours were no match for the German tanks and that our own anti-tank guns were greatly inferior to the German'.[6] For Alf Blacklin, the British tanks were good, but 'they spoil the thing by sticking a stupid little two-pounder in the turret. Result – Jerry's cruisers and heavies have a 6-pounder or 75mm and knocks hell out of ours before they can close in to an effective range.'[7]

The anti-tank gunners faced a similar predicament. With the same 2-pounder Blacklin's team found that 'anti-tank work is a suicides' game, you only stand an even chance with light tanks – the heavy ones stand off just out of effective range of your guns and let go at you with a 6-pounder or a 75mm gun'.[8] He recalled seeing, while on patrol, the Panzers approach 'to 700 yards, ignored the 2-pounders and picked off the 25's one by one, then he started on the 2-pdrs and shot them up. Admitted the tanks outnumbered them but although the 25's got some of the tanks most of the 2-pdrs got off 80-90 rounds and couldn't claim one.' He commented after *Crusader,* 'it was the 25pdrs that saved us and is still saving us'.[9] The British 6-pounder anti-tank gun was not introduced until 1942.

After the disastrous opening encounter, 30 Corps was unable, in Auchinleck's words, 'to impede the enemy's return or to intervene effectively when his tanks attacked the

New Zealand Division'. Despite their gallantry, 'our armoured troops were worsted in almost every encounter with the enemy tanks, not only because they were comparatively inexperienced but also because the enemy tanks mounted guns of greater range'.[10] Gentry's view was that the British 'error lay in under-estimating the effect of the superior gun power and over-estimating the effect of numbers'.[11] Whereas the 88mm anti-tank gun was used very effectively in *Battleaxe,* it was 'highly probable' that the 50mm anti-tank gun caused most of the damage in *Crusader.*[12] Once the Germans had picked their ground and dug in with anti-tank weapons deployed, they were very difficult to shift.

The Germans, who were very effective at concentrating their forces, considered that the British erred initially by setting their forces on divergent courses: they should, according to Lieutenant General Fritz Bayerlein, have 'first concentrated on Sidi Rezegh and then thrust forward in echelon formation'. Even better would have been to go straight for Acroma, which would have also cut off supplies. It was not necessary to tie up two divisions in the border area and because of this 'the decisive blow was thus struck by only a fraction of the total force engaged in the offensive'. The British never succeeded in operating 'with a concentration of ... forces at the decisive point'. This was a 'fundamental mistake', as was the 'unwieldy and rigidly methodical technique of command', which did not lend itself easily to adapting to changes of fortune as the battle progressed.[13]

Brigadier (subsequently Major General) Barrowclough wrote in 1950 that 'a more acceptable plan for the relief of Tobruk and the destruction of 15 and 21 Panzer Divisions, would have been to have moved the whole 8 Army (less 4 Indian Division) direct to the area about Sidi Rezegh'. From there they could have faced outwards and 'commanded the whole of the desert to the south of Tobruk and completely cut off Rommel's supply'. As he admitted, this was 'of course being wise after the event'.[14]

The British practice of splitting their armoured brigades, and planning to fight the campaign with 'detached brigade groups', weakened their attacking ability and reduced the effectiveness of the artillery.[15] The fast-moving, widespread campaign meant that mobility at which the New Zealanders excelled, especially at night, and bringing up reserves was vital. Maintaining supplies became a major factor for all the forces but especially for the Germans and Italians with their long lines of communication and shipping losses; as the campaign lengthened the pressure on them became almost insurmountable. The ability to recover and repair equipment, in particular tanks and vehicles, then bring them back into action was also critical. It was something at which the Germans proved to be very adept.

There were other tactical problems too. The British standard of armoured leadership needed improvement and their tank tactics 'were inferior to those of the Germans because we had failed adequately to coordinate the action of tanks, infantry and artillery on the battlefield'.[16] The New Zealand Division suffered through the lack of training with the British tanks. In the attack on Point 175 on 23 November, the I-tanks' advance was not co-ordinated with the infantry, who suffered heavy casualties, and the Valentines were badly hit by enemy anti-tank guns. Regrettably, some of these mistakes would be repeated in 1942, at considerable cost to the New Zealanders.

Freyberg considered there were lessons for the New Zealand Division to learn. In his January 1942 report he noted first the vital importance of 'the will to win'. Fundamental to this were 'physical fitness of all ranks' and 'proficiency and confidence in the use of weapons'. The use of surprise 'is still the outstanding factor in achieving success'.[17] He especially identified the enemy's superiority in handling tanks and their co-ordination of tanks, artillery, anti-tank guns and infantry.[18] The division was 'very inexperienced' in tank warfare; 'tanks and infantry should train together'.[19] He believed the campaign had shown that the concept of 'armour "in support" of infantry had proved to be a myth'.[20] Throughout *Crusader* control of armour caused tension between the infantry wanting armoured support and the armour being sent on fruitless missions to support infantry from attacks that never came.

Freyberg's strong opposition to splitting divisions into brigade groups brought into sharp focus the differences between him and Auchinleck. In his diary on 22 November 1941 he recalled a conversation 'with Army Cmd when he referred to this being "a Bde Gp War". I asked him since when? The war in Africa has been against Italians until this year. Against the Boche consider the striking power and manoeuvrability of a Division is necessary to give weight and effect to attack.'[21] Freyberg's draft report included adverse comments about 'the dangerous practice of committing our small force piecemeal' and also to the ineffectiveness of brigade groups.[22] Auchinleck reviewed the draft and ordered the deletion of these comments.[23] This reinforced in Freyberg's mind 'that the only way to safeguard the interests of New Zealand and of the Division was to get the Division away from Desert Command'.[24]

Freyberg described the first phase of *Crusader* as 'a battle to destroy the German elements in Libya'. He felt it was 'fair to claim that the part played by the Division to date has destroyed a large portion of the German force, together with a great deal of equipment and material, and it will prove a great contribution in the main Libyan campaign'.[25] Later, however, he looked more critically at *Crusader,* and concluded that at Tobruk and subsequently at Gazala the enemy 'should have been caught like a rat in a trap'.[26]

The fast-moving campaign, with many separate battles occurring simultaneously, put command structures under pressure. The British were not helped by the remoteness of the army commander, who sometimes had inadequate information about the state of the battle, and difficulties in communication between the two corps commanders and the commander of the

Tobruk garrison. This resulted in the absence of clear direction from 13 Corps on the night of 30 November. Barrowclough felt that the division should fall back to the Tobruk perimeter and Freyberg sent Miles into Tobruk to seek 'further orders' from Godwin-Austen.[27]

But decisions 'that the corridor must be held' continued to be made when the only reason for maintaining it seemed to be as an evacuation route for the men who had been wounded trying to keep it open.[28] Inglis later wrote that he 'felt that it was foolish to stay strung out for miles along the so-called corridor'.[29] As Murphy concluded in the official history, with no decision made, and little chance of either the South Africans appearing or help arriving from the British armour, there was only 'certainty that dawn would disclose a sea of troubles'.[30] As it did.

Crusader was very much a soldiers' battle, in which tactical mistakes were made by both sides. Desert warfare was a new experience for most of the New Zealanders, including the officers and

NCOs, and the intensity of this campaign quickly exposed any shortcomings. The British armoured brigade group dispersal and the inability to concentrate these forces resulted in the loss of the early encounter. Rommel's 'dash to the frontier' handed the initiative to the New Zealanders at Sidi Rezegh for a few critical days, and also put his supply situation under stress. And brigade group tactics meant that the New Zealand Division was without the use of its third brigade at a critical time when attempting to link with the Tobruk garrison.

It was the troops on the ground who suffered the repercussions of these decisions, and they fought with great determination. When the New Zealanders started their march on Tobruk on 23 November, Freyberg saw it as the division's most important action of the war. It was a decisive move, a demonstration of leadership and aggression. 'If we had not done so,' he often said, 'the battle of Alamein would have been fought a year earlier – and without the Sherman tank'. In Italy, when confronting a dangerous situation at the River Senio, he commented that 'it's not as difficult as the one which faced us at Sidi Rezegh on 23 November. Nothing the Division has faced since then was as dangerous as that. We cracked that one – and we will crack this.'[31]

The campaign had been costly for both sides. British casualties totalled 17,700: 2900 killed, 7300 wounded and 7500 missing (mainly POWs). German and Italian overall casualties were higher at 38,300: 2300 killed, 6100 wounded and 29,900 missing.[32] And the victory had come at a high price to New Zealand.

On 3 December 1941 Freyberg wrote to Fraser advising that 4 and 6 Brigades had withdrawn, and warning him that 'the fighting has been severe and our losses are heavy'.[33] Auchinleck sent his own message: 'these brigades fought magnificently and inflicted very heavy losses on the enemy, but I fear their own losses have also been severe.'[34] On 9 December Churchill also wrote to the New Zealand prime minister, saying that he 'was deeply grieved about the severe losses your heroic Division has suffered in the forefront of the battle.'[35]

By the end of the campaign New Zealand had suffered 4620 casualties: 671 were killed and 208 died of wounds. The number of wounded totalled 1699 and a further 2042 were prisoners of war, including 201 wounded and five who died of wounds while captives.[36] In addition to these casualties, 202 died on active service, including deaths through sickness and accident. 'This was a greater loss than that of any other Eighth Army division. It was 1000 more than the New Zealand casualties in Crete, nearly double those in Greece and three times the figure for the Orsogna or Cassino battles in Italy.'[37] About half of those who were killed or died of wounds were with 6 Brigade. In 25 Battalion 120 men were killed, mostly in the attack on Point 175. There were 101 killed in 24 Battalion, 89 in 26 Battalion and 83 in 21 Battalion. Some of the regiments of the Divisional Artillery were also badly hit, particularly 5 Field Regiment (49 killed), 6 Field Regiment (55) and 7 Anti-Tank (49). The heavy casualties meant 'there were few communities in New Zealand untouched' and the impacts were long-lasting.[38]

In Northland, two brothers from a family of 11, Louis Matthew ('Lou') and Eugene Charles ('Charlie') Nelley, were farming in partnership before they enlisted. They had been in the Territorials before the war and, as good mates, joined up together. As part of 24 Battalion they travelled overseas and on Lou's 24th birthday they were in action when their company was called in to support 25 Battalion at Point 175. Both men were in action until Charlie was wounded; Lou had to leave his brother behind and it was the last he saw of him. What happened to him is uncertain: according to different accounts he either died of his wounds or was killed when the ship he was on was bombed. He is recorded as killed in action on 27 November, aged 27. Lou was later captured when 24 Battalion was overrun; he was taken to Benghazi, then shipped to Italy. However 'when the Italians capitulated and as our guard ran off we were again at large'. He was a 'POW for 21 months including 8 weeks at large behind the German lines' before he 'contacted Indian troops on 7 November 1943'.[39]

The family had already lost another son, Joseph, who died of wounds in Crete on 28 May 1941. A fourth brother, Walter ('Wally'), had been with the Engineers in Greece, but the army sent him home to manage the family farm, as the boys' father had died since the four sons had departed. And a fifth son, Ted, volunteered later in the war, was wounded at Cassino and again, badly, near Florence. He eventually recovered and returned to New Zealand.

After Crete, 27-year-old Charlie wrote back to his sister, Laura, explaining that 'as yet we have been unable to locate Joe'. He described his brother's time in action and what had happened when he was wounded. Charlie warned that 'his chances of returning are not very promising', and he wanted to 'prepare you for a greater shock if there is one coming though I pray to God there is not; I would rather go myself any day than see anything happen to Joe'. But if he had been 'unfortunate enough to meet his death at the age of nineteen we know he has done so doing a good job well, and as its in the course of his duty that he would have it no other way. We can feel justly proud of him.'[40] Not knowing just what had happened to Charlie hit his mother very hard; for the rest of her life she lived in hope that he would return.

A Soldier's Thoughts of New Zealand

Back from the noisy firing line,
With little to do, but fill in time
While awaiting orders, we oft times find
Our thoughts fly to New Zealand.

For though we enlisted, and left our all
In answer to our country's call,
If we live we live, if we fall we fall
Who would not die for New Zealand?

Land of hills and plains and trees,
Rivers, lakes and rolling seas,
Sunshine and flowers, birds and bees:

Our homeland – our New Zealand.

Land of glaciers and thermal springs,
Deep ravines where echo rings,
Where all day long the bellbird sings;
Land of our birth – New Zealand.

We think of you in this far off land
With the scorching sun and shifting sand,
Of your winding streams and forest grand:
Maoriland – New Zealand.

We will welcome the day when our task is done,
When victory is ours, the Allies have won,
When the world is rid of the Nazi Hun,
And we're free to return to New Zealand.

With glee we will sing, and shout aloud
When we sight above your misty shroud

*The snow-capped peaks of the
'Long White Cloud':
Ao-te-aroa – New Zealand.*

E.C. (Charlie) Nelley
26 August 1941

Another Northlander who joined C Company of 24 Battalion was Frank Wintle from Tara, Mangawai. A butcher and a regular rugby player, he enlisted on 10 July 1940 and in December headed overseas. Shortly after arriving in Egypt he was with 24 Battalion in the Greek campaign before returning to Egypt and later heading west for *Crusader.* On 25 November he was one of the 24 Battalion men killed when his platoon was caught in heavy fire during the advance from Point 175 to the blockhouse. To add to what must have been a great blow to his family, his cousin James Carter, also from Northland and with 24 Battalion, was killed on the same day. As well as being recorded on official memorials, Frank Wintle is remembered with memorial gates to 'Frank Wintle & Comrades' at St Michael's Church,

Hakaru, and also on the roll of honour inside the church.

Four lads from provincial South Island joined 27 (Machine Gun) Battalion. Thomas Horne attended Timaru Boys' High School, where he excelled at swimming and athletics before leaving school at 14 to become a shepherd. He joined up soon after the war started; according to his family, he had always wanted to be a soldier and was excited at the prospect of serving his country. Eric Heaps attended Nelson College where he was a talented artist, a good cricketer and an outstanding boxer. After leaving school he worked for his accountant father, for Shell Oil and on a family tobacco farm. He enjoyed camping, swimming and skiing. One day, when his mother took some of the family into Nelson, Heaps went off on his own and the next time they saw him he was in uniform, having joined up with some of his Nelson mates. In Invercargill Alton Lee attended Southland Technical College, then joined his father and brother in partnership running Lee Bros, a general store at Thornbury, between Riverton and Invercargill. He was an excellent sportsman, playing rugby, cricket, badminton and tennis. When war broke out, Alton Lee was one of the first in the district to volunteer. Leslie ('Les') McIver, the second of 11 children, was born in 1906 at Mt Somers in South Canterbury. His only surviving sibling, his sister Violet, recalls that he was 'short of stature and a character, like his father, but he was also quiet and unassuming'.[41] He worked with his brothers around Mid Canterbury as a musterer and farmhand; on his enlistment documentation his occupation is shown as labourer.

At Sidi Rezegh, Horne, Heaps and Lee took part in the attack on Point 175 on 23 November. Phil Hammond was with Horne until he took cover behind the back wheel of their truck after they came under fire, but he was killed shortly after. Alton Lee was shot between the eyes that afternoon; Randel Heron remembered seeing his body as they advanced over the escarpment: 'his tin helmet had a hole in it. I probably thought at the time, what a useless piece of equipment.'[42]

Heaps and McIver both died of wounds some days later. Heaps's brother Noel was also in Eric's platoon, and John Black recalled that when Heaps was wounded on the morning of 26 November, when they were isolated and under fire after a night advance, Noel 'had to pull out with the platoon, leaving Eric behind. Eric received another wound that day which unfortunately proved fatal.' He died on 30 November.[43] McIver died of wounds on the same day. His family understands that 'soldiers at the front line were asked who would ride the motor bike through enemy territory to deliver a message, and Les immediately put his hand up. It was during this ride that he was picked off.'[44]

All the families were deeply affected by their losses. Ninety-one-year-old Hugh Heaps, Eric's brother, 'heard of Eric's death just before he was to play cricket in a game between New Plymouth Boys' High School and Nelson College', and his father still made him play. Eric's uncle, 'who worked on the cables, had to keep it to himself until his death was confirmed, and he was very upset at the news'.[45] An obituary for Alton Lee, which appeared in the local paper, reported that he had been buried by his mates the day after he was killed. According to Leslie McIver's sister, Violet Williams, 'the Postmaster from Mayfield was the one who turned up at the family home at Anama to break the sad news that Les had died of wounds received a day or so before his death. The Post Office would receive the news by telegraph and the protocol was that such news should be conveyed in person.'[46]

Thomas Horne had left for overseas shortly after marrying Hughena Don on 23 November 1940, and the family 'are not sure whether he even knew his new wife was pregnant when he left for war'.[47] A son, also named Thomas, was born, and he and his mother lived with Horne's sister, Sarah, in Timaru. Horne was killed on his first wedding anniversary, and the son he never knew died young of infantile paralysis (poliomyelitis).

The men who did not return are remembered throughout New Zealand in schools, on community war memorials, and especially, within their families. McIver's nephew, Graeme McIver, remembers walking with his mother to see the wreaths beside the roll of honour at Papanui in Christchurch. One wreath was from McIver's older brother, Charlie. He was active within the RSA, and 'kept up this way of honouring his closest sibling for a number of years'.[48]

The return of men to New Zealand in July 1943 on furlough must have heightened the emotion for families that had suffered loss. The Nelson returned men received a civic welcome at the cathedral steps, where Mayor E.R. Neale expressed the city's thanks. He was, however, very sensitive to the gaps in their ranks, reminding the crowd that 'lest we forget, I feel sure that everyone present would wish even in the joy of your home-coming and at this historic spot where so many men have been farewelled and welcomed home in two wars, that we should remember and honour those who will never come back'.[49]

EPILOGUE

Return to Sidi Rezegh

The first short trip Robin and I made to Sidi Rezegh, in April 2007, gave us only a fleeting introduction to the battlefield. With our guides, we drove from Tobruk, taking the rutted Bypass Road from El Adem until we were almost at the escarpment by Belhamed; we could see gun pits beside the road as we passed over the slight rise of Ed Duda. We then backtracked, travelling along a shallow valley until Mousa pointed and said, 'There is Sidi Rezegh'. On the edge of the nearby ridge was the mosque. We spent some time walking around the area, the scene of the last desperate attack before the ridge was taken, and looking towards the Trigh Capuzzo, with the northern escarpment beyond. It was moving, and at the same time slightly unreal, to think that we were right at the centre of where the battle had been fought, so close to where my father had been. On our second trip, in September 2009, after we had visited the war cemeteries and sites related to the battles for Tobruk, Mousa took us straight to Sidi Rezegh. There we had lunch inside the mosque, rather similar to Ravenstein's 'slightly bizarre desert picnic': bread, cheese, tuna and olives. We then continued eastwards along the rough track on the plateau in the direction of the airfield to the blockhouse. Both the mosque and the blockhouse look just as they were in 1941, although the shell hole in the mosque's dome has been repaired, and the effect of the New Zealand shelling on the blockhouse is still clearly evident.

Along the track we could see sangars, gun pits, barbed wire and occasional pieces of shrapnel, although all the major debris of the battle had been cleared long ago. Of more concern were the many landmines scattered randomly across the landscape. From time to time we stopped to walk around, carefully, and take photos, especially of the area where my father was during the last days of the campaign, on the edge of the airfield –

the scene of the gun team photo taken nearly 70 years before.

The landscape is featureless and unchanged, we saw it just as it was when the battle was fought,

> a land of bare stones and drifting sand, of escarpments and defiles, of low ridges and shallow depressions; a roadless land where trucks were driven on a compass bearing, where armoured vehicles fought whirling battles in the dust and smoke, and infantry were pawns on a thousand-square-mile chessboard; a generals' paradise of parry and thrust where formations had no front or rear or flank and where sudden reversals of fortune could lose a battle after it had been won.[1]

From the blockhouse we took a detour around the southern rim of the Rugbet en-Nbeidat, a wide, rather shallow wadi, until we were able to cross over and turn north, before stopping. It was now late on this autumn afternoon and we were very close to Point 175; almost, I felt, where the start line for the attack would have been. By now the sun was dropping quickly towards the horizon and Mousa was anxious to get away before dark. But I was keen to see as much of this key area as I could and continued to walk around the escarpment, looking at the sangars and pieces of shrapnel still lying on the ground. In the still, clear air of dusk there was a good view of the many wadis cut into the face of the escarpment. Towards the west the blockhouse stood out prominently. The Trigh Capuzzo crossed the flat below with the northern escarpment beyond, while away to the west were Belhamed and Ed Duda. It was easy to see why this had been such an important feature and the battles to occupy it so hard fought. As darkness fell we returned to Tobruk, passing by Zaafran on the way.

Travelling over the battlefield brought home just how demanding a challenge the New Zealand troops had faced. The area is very exposed with minimal cover, the ground rock hard with only a thin layer of sand. The maps are misleading, their contour lines not really showing how shallow the wadis are and how low the hills.

Because the land is so flat, even an extra 2 or 3 metres of height meant a great deal in terms of visibility. Experienced troops who had time to select and prepare their defensive positions well were at a considerable advantage.

For the men attacking continually by day and by night, the extreme fighting at close range, with the bayonet in the face of tank attack, small arms, machine gun and artillery fire, must have been daunting. These men were not the SAS but ordinary New Zealanders: bank clerks, mill hands, labourers, accountants, farmers, civil servants, salesmen and schoolmasters. They were, indeed, ordinary men doing extraordinary things.

This was a messy victory, but an important one. In a battle that was to have been determined largely by an armoured encounter, the New Zealanders, through sheer determination, had played a major part in the final outcome; their versatility and ability to cope with unexpected setbacks had been an important factor. As one New Zealander said succinctly,

'Jerry was mucked about and we were mucked about, but we were more used to it!'[2]

After the division had taken time to regroup, including spending three months in Syria, in June 1942 the New Zealanders were recalled urgently to Egypt as Rommel's army advanced swiftly into Egypt. They fought in the desert to the south and west of El Alamein – the First Battle of Alamein – and again suffered heavy casualties. There were also changes in Middle East command, with General Sir Harold A l e x a n d e r   a p p o i n t e d Commander-in-Chief, Middle East Forces and Lieutenant General Bernard Montgomery appointed General Officer Commanding the Eighth Army in August 1942.

Freyberg met Montgomery shortly afterwards and told him of his 'great anxiety in the past with higher commanders who have had a mania for breaking up military organisation'. He expressed his views about how the New Zealand Division should be deployed: he 'was determined not to take part in the Battle of Alamein unless I was given an undertaking that we would fight as a Division'. He was 'given the assurance', and on 3 October 1942 he cabled Fraser to express his 'confidence in the new set-up for the Battle of Alamein because they had reverted to Divisional organisation'.[3]

On 23 October 1942 the Second Battle of Alamein began and over the ensuing months the division, again part of the Eighth Army, pursued the enemy across North Africa. They crossed the border into Libya again on 11 November, two days later the Eighth Army took Tobruk and Benghazi fell on 20 November. By now the long-suffering people of Cyrenaica had endured their land being traversed six times: by Graziani's Italian army, followed in turn by armies under the leadership of Wavell, Rommel, Auchinleck, Rommel again and finally Montgomery. As a result of these battles the names of some previously insignificant places were indelibly written into New Zealand history.

Shortly after the war in North Africa ended in May 1943, some 6000 New Zealand troops, including my father, returned home on furlough. They arrived in Wellington on 12 July 1943, more than three years since most of them had left 'for the great adventure'. The *Evening Post* editorial that day praised 'the old campaigners' who 'have won imperishable renown for themselves and their country, for the New Zealand Division is known all over the world as one of the finest band of soldiers who ever fought in a good cause'.[4]

There were other plaudits for the New Zealanders. As Churchill himself wrote, 'all the accounts I have received pay the highest tribute to their brilliant work.'[5] Auchinleck also praised the New Zealanders for 'the finest fighting he'd ever known'.[6] And the New Zealanders under Freyberg, according to news correspondent Alan Moorehead, were simply 'the finest infantry division in the Middle East'.[7]

There was also respect from their enemy. Describing the Battle of Alamein, Heinz Werner Schmidt wrote that 'the New Zealanders – excellent troops, stern in defence, ready in attack, and most intelligent – were also in the line, despite the repeated and costly battles in the desert where they had been so long'.[8] The November battle of *Crusader* 'was won largely by the New Zealanders'.[9] And Rommel endorsed Schmidt's opinion: he regarded the New Zealand Division as 'among the elite of the British Army'.[10]

For some, including my father, the return to New Zealand meant the end of their service. Brian Cox was awarded a number of medals, including the Africa Star, but when they arrived, attached was a hand-written note stating that he 'was not entitled to Clasp to the Africa Star as claimed'. My father had applied for the Eighth Army Clasp, to be attached to the Africa Star, a campaign medal awarded to anyone who had served at least one day between 10 June 1940 and 12 May 1943. However, the clasp was awarded only to 'active' members between 23 October 1942 and 12 May 1943 and my father was deemed ineligible because he was evacuated, owing to illness, before 23 October. He was only one of thousands of New Zealand soldiers who were ineligible for the clasp for various reasons, including those who were taken prisoner before that date.

This ineligibility was a sore point for many who served in the Eighth Army in *Crusader* and the First Battle of Alamein, as it gave the impression that the Eighth Army came into existence only after Montgomery took over. Auchinleck tried to have this anomaly corrected in 1944, without success, and was still trying to have the situation rectified as late as 1961. As he explained to then Secretary of State for Defence, John Profumo, there was 'a distinct feeling' that events in the desert before Montgomery had been 'deliberately ignored and deprecated mainly for political reasons connected chiefly with the Prime Minister's [Churchill's] prestige and the need to display him as the architect of victory'.[11]

Although the New Zealanders had performed well, this was a victory for the whole Eighth Army and all the forces had played a significant part. The New Zealand Field Censorship Section, in examining letters written in Baggush after the campaign, reported that the troops were 'generous in praise of the British troops, especially of the tank units and the Royal Air Force'. The censor was able to report that 'there can be no question of NZEF morale being anything but of the highest order'.[12] Freyberg wrote 'the test for troops is whether they can take it and fight back. For the first time in this war the odds were about even and we had a chance to "fight back". We know now that we can both "take it" and "fight back". Nobody, I hope, doubted it.'[13]

At the pivotal point in the *Crusader* campaign, after the armoured assault had failed, the New Zealand Division immediately began the move west. The fighting over successive days and nights to achieve the link-up with the troops of the Tobruk garrison, who fought with great determination to take and hold their positions, was hard and costly but significant in achieving the ultimate success. Godwin-Austen summed it up: 'the story of this campaign is simple. Freyberg and the New Zealanders broke the Afrika Korps but in doing so destroyed themselves.'[14]

Although my father and many others were not entitled to wear the Eighth Army Clasp, they had achieved an important victory. This campaign saw 'some of the finest infantry assaults in the annals of the British Army'. These included the attack of the Black Watch on 'Tiger' and, for the New Zealand Division, 'the hard fight for Point 175, and the last relentless night attack on the Mosque'. These actions 'showed what men could do with little more than the weapons they could carry. They deserve to be remembered.'[15]

As we drove back from the battle site in the early evening I reflected that this was the start of our return trip; travelling via Benghazi, Tripoli and London, we would be home in a week. I had been especially pleased that we could visit the escarpment near Point 175, and the edge of the airfield, as these were two places on the battlefield where I knew for certain that my father had been. After he left Sidi Rezegh it would be a little over 18 months before he would be back in New Zealand, and by then the name of El Alamein would have replaced Sidi Rezegh in the news reports. This campaign, so significant in New Zealand's military history and so devastating for the families of the men who died, was already becoming the forgotten battle of the desert war.

NOTES

Introduction

[1]   W.E. Murphy, *Official History of New Zealand in the Second World War 1939–1945: The Relief of Tobruk,* Historical Publications Branch, Department of Internal Affairs, Wellington, 1961, Appendix 1.

[2]   Olivia Manning, *The Danger Tree,* Volume 1 of *The Levant Trilogy,* Penguin Books Ltd, London, 1982 reprint, p.54.

Chapter 1: The First Libyan Campaign

[1]   W.A. Glue & D.J.C. Pringle, *Official History of New Zealand in the Second World War 1939–1945: 20 Battalion and Armoured Regiment,* Historical Publications Branch, Department of Internal Affairs, Wellington, 1957, p.23.

[2]   C.A. Borman, *Official History of New Zealand in the Second World War 1939–1945: Divisional Signals,* Historical Publications Branch, Department of Internal Affairs, Wellington, 1954, p.47.

[3]   Barrie Pitt, *The Crucible of War. Western Desert 1941,* Jonathan Cape, London, 1980, p.54.

[4]   Jonathan Dimbleby, *Destiny in the Desert,* Profile Books, London, 2012, p.37.

[5]   Jim Henderson, *Official History of New Zealand in the Second World War 1939–1945: 4th and 6th Reserve Mechanical Transport Companies,* Historical Publications Branch, Department of Internal Affairs, Wellington, 1954, p.30.

[6]   Ibid., p.32.

[7]   Pitt, *Crucible,* p.106.

[8]   Henderson, *Official History,* p.36.

[9]   W. Andrew, personal diary.

[10]   W.G. McClymont, *Official History of New Zealand in the Second World War 1939–1945: To Greece,* Historical Publications Branch, Department of Internal Affairs, Wellington, 1959, p.70.

[11]   Brigadier George Clifton, *The Happy Hunted,* Cassell & Co., London, 1952, pp.36, 45.

[12]   Ibid., pp.46, 48.

[13]   McClymont, *Official History,* p.69.

[14]   Henderson, *Official History,* p.45.

[15]   McClymont, *Official History,* pp.72–73.

[16]   Correlli Barnett, *The Desert Generals,* Cassell, London, 1999, p.64.

Chapter 2: Tobruk

[1]   Jonathan Dimbleby, *Destiny in the Desert,* Profile Books, London, 2012, pp.58–59.

[2]   B.H. Liddell Hart (ed.), *The Rommel Papers,* Arrow Books, London, 1984, p.111.

[3]   Chester Wilmot, *Tobruk 1941,* Penguin Group (Australia), Camberwell, 2007, pp.105, 100.

[4]   Ibid., p.117.

[5]   Liddell Hart, *Rommel Papers,* p.123.

[6]   Ibid., p.128.

[7]   Ibid., p.146.
[8]   W.E. Murphy, *Official History of New Zealand in the Second World War 1939–1945: The Relief of Tobruk,* Historical Publications Branch, Department of Internal Affairs, Wellington, 1961, p.9.
[9]   Ibid., p.10.
[10]   Alan Moorehead, *African Trilogy,* Four Square Books, London, 1959, p.172.
[11]   Letter, J.A. Blacklin to M. Fearnside, 22 December 1941.
[12]   Heinz Werner Schmidt, *With Rommel in the Desert,* George G. Harrap & Co. Ltd, London, 1951, p.92.

Chapter 3: The Plan for Crusader

[1]   W.E. Murphy, *Official History of New Zealand in the Second World War 1939–1945: The Relief of Tobruk,* Historical Publications Branch, Department of Internal Affairs, Wellington, 1961 p.1.

[2]   Ibid., p.5.

[3]   Ibid.

[4]   *Official History of New Zealand in the Second World War 1939–1945: Documents Relating to New Zealand's Participation in the Second World War 1939–45: Volume II,* Historical Publications Branch, Department of Internal Affairs, Wellington, 1951, 95 – General Freyberg to the Minister of Defence, 13 September 1941.

[5]   Lieutenant General Sir Bernard Freyberg VC, comments: Second Libyan Campaign, 1941 – November–December. Volume 1 – Planning and Training. WAII11/1 Correspondence concerning the Libyan Campaign, Feb 1949 – Jul 1950.

[6]   *Documents* 96 – The Prime Minister of New Zealand to General Freyberg, 16 September 1941.

[7]   *Documents* 98 – General Freyberg to the Prime Minister, 19 September 1941.

[8]   Correlli Barnett, *The Desert Generals,* Cassell, London, 1999, p.83.

[9]   Murphy, *Official History,* p.43.

[10]   Barnett, *Desert Generals,* p.88.

[11]   Murphy, *Official History,* p.108.

[12]   *Operations in the Middle East from 1st November 1941 to 15th August 1942.* Despatch submitted to the Secretary of State for War on 27th January 1943, by General Sir Claude J.E. Auchinleck, G.C.I.E., C.B., C.S.I., D.S.O., O.B.E., A.D.C., Commander in Chief, the Middle East Forces. Published as a supplement to the *London Gazette* of Tuesday, 13 January 1948, Number 38177, p.311.

[13]   Murphy, *Official History,* p.39.

[14]   Ibid.

[15]   General Freyberg's comments WAII11/1.

[16]   Ibid.

[17]   J.A.I. Agar-Hamilton and L.C.F. Turner, *The Sidi Rezeg Battles 1941,* Oxford University Press, Cape Town, 1957, p.66.

[18]   Barnett, *Desert Generals,* p.90.

[19]   Barrie Pitt, *The Crucible of War. Western Desert 1941,* Jonathan Cape, London, 1980, p.346.

[20]   Murphy, *Official History,* p.40.

[21]   General Freyberg's comments WAII11/1.

[22]   Paul Freyberg, *Bernard Freyberg, VC: soldier of two nations,* Hodder & Stoughton, London, 1991, p.344.

[23]   *Documents* 102 – General Freyberg to the Minister of Defence, 9 October 1941.

[24]   Ibid.

[25]   *Documents* 103 – The Prime Minister of New Zealand to the Prime Minister of the United Kingdom, 13 October 1941.

[26]   *Documents* 105 – The Prime Minister of the United Kingdom to the Prime Minister of New Zealand, 24 October 1941.

[27]   Inglis to Kippenberger, letter, 25 January 1952. WAII11/1 Correspondence concerning the Libyan Campaign, Feb 1949 – Jul 1950.

[28]   Letter, J.A. Blacklin to M. Fearnside, 4 March 1942.

[29]	R.J.M. Loughnan, 'The Memoirs of R.J.M. Loughnan', unpublished.

[30]	Letter, Blacklin to Fearnside, 18 April 1942. 31 Auchinleck, *Operations,* p.333.

Chapter 4: The Great Approach March

[1]	Martyn Uren, *Kiwi Saga,* Collins, Auckland, 1943, p.149.

[2]	W.E. Murphy, *Official History of New Zealand in the Second World War 1939–1945: The Relief of Tobruk,* Historical Publications Branch, Department of Internal Affairs, Wellington, 1961, p.29.

[3]	Uren, *Kiwi Saga* pp.151–52.

[4]	J.A.B. Crawford. 'Hargest, James', from the Dictionary of New Zealand Biography. Te Ara – the Encyclopedia of New Zealand, updated 8-Oct-2013 URL: http://www.TeAra.govt.nz/mi/biographies/4h16/hargest-james

[5]	Letter, C.L.S. Paterson to family, 11 January 1942.

[6]   W. Andrew, personal diary, 13 November 1941.

[7]   J.F. Cody, *Official History of New Zealand in the Second World War 1939–1945: 28 (Maori) Battalion,* Historical Publications Branch, Department of Internal Affairs, Wellington, 1956, p.141.

[8]   Uren, *Kiwi Saga,* p.152.

[9]   Major General Sir Howard Kippenberger, *Infantry Brigadier,* Oxford University Press, London, 1949, p.81.

[10]   Freyberg Diary, 13 November 1941, WAII8/5/44 GOC Diary – 3 September 1941 – 2 September 1942.

[11]   Libyan Campaign – 'Crusader', July–November 1941, Conference notes. WAII8/3/18.

[12]   Ibid.

[13]   Libyan Campaign, Special Order of the Day, General Sir A. Cunningham, 17 November 1941, WAII8/3/18.

[14]   Jonathan Dimbleby, *Destiny in the Desert,* Profile Books, London, 2012, p.138.

[15] Sir John Staveley, Medical Officer, 6 Field Ambulance, unpublished diary, 18 November 1941.

[16] Freyberg Diary, 15 November 1941, WAII8/5/44.

[17] Paterson letter.

[18] Geoffrey Cox, *A Tale of Two Battles: A personal memoir of Crete and the Western Desert 1941,* Kimber, London, p.151.

[19] Letter, Captain Charles Gatenby to Mrs Eugenie Gatenby, 16 November 1941.

[20] Angus Ross, *Official History of New Zealand in the Second World War 1939–1945: 23 Battalion,* Historical Publications Branch, Department of Internal Affairs, Wellington, 1959, p.100.

[21] Letter, Lieutenant General A. Godwin-Austen to Brigadier H. Latham, 22 September 1950, Crusader Campaign 1941, correspondence files 21 Battalion, also 6 Brigade, 23, 24, 25, 26, 27, 28 Battalions, WAII3/5/21.

[22] Paterson letter.

[23] Major Robert Crisp, *Brazen Chariots,* W.W. Norton & Company, New York, 2005, p.23.
[24] Freyberg Diary, 18 November 1941, WAII8/5/44.
[25] Kippenberger, *Infantry Brigadier,* pp.84–85.
[26] Ibid., p.81.

Chapter 5: The Battle of the Armour

[1] Libyan Campaign – General Officer Commanding's printed report WAII8/3/19, p.5.
[2] Freyberg Diary, 19 November 1941, WAII8/5/44, GOC Diary – 3 September 1941 – 2 September 1942.
[3] Ibid.
[4] Letter, C.L.S. Paterson to family, 11 January 1942.
[5] *Evening Post,* 20 November 1941, p.10.
[6] *Press,* 21 November 1941, p.7.
[7] *Press,* 22 November 1941, p.9.
[8] Major General I.S.O. Playfair, *The Mediterranean and Middle*

East Volume III (September 1941 to September 1942) British Fortunes reach their Lowest Ebb, Her Majesty's Stationery Office, London, 1960, p.39.

[9] Ibid., p.40.

[10] Correlli Barnett, *The Desert Generals,* Cassell, London, 1999, p.97.

[11] GOC's report, p.5, WAII8/3/19.

[12] Freyberg Diary, 20 November 1941, WAII8/5/44.

[13] Ibid.

[14] GOC's report, pp.5–6, WAII8/3/19.

[15] Freyberg Diary, 20 November 1941, WAII8/5/44.

[16] Ibid., 21 November 1941.

[17] W.E. Murphy, *Official History of New Zealand in the Second World War 1939–1945: The Relief of Tobruk,* Historical Publications Branch, Department of Internal Affairs, Wellington, 1961, p.100.

[18] Ibid.

[19] Letter, J.A. Blacklin to M. Fearnside, 22 December 1941.

[20] Murphy, *Official History,* p.117.

[21] GOC's report, p.6, WAII8/3/19.
[22] James Hargest, *Farewell Campo 12,* Whitcombe & Tombs Ltd, Wellington, 1945, p.13.
[23] Paterson letter.
[24] GOC's report, p.7, WAII8/3/19.
[25] Murphy, *Official History,* p.100.
[26] Headquarters 6 New Zealand Infantry Brigade WD, 21 November 1941, WAII1/1659/DA58/1/14, War Diary 1 November – 30 November 1941, Volume 1 Appendix.
[27] Frazer D. Norton, *Official History of New Zealand in the Second World War 1939–1945: 26 Battalion,* Historical Publications Branch, Department of Internal Affairs, Wellington, 1952, p.82.
[28] Murphy, *Official History,* p.124.
[29] GOC's report, pp.7–8, WAII8/3/19.
[30] Alan Moorehead, *African Trilogy,* Four Square Books, London, 1959, p.183.
[31] Letter, J.A. Blacklin to M. Fearnside, 4 March 1942.

[32] *Operations in the Middle East from 1st November 1941 to 15th August 1942.* Despatch submitted to the Secretary of State for War on 27th January 1943, by General Sir Claude J.E. Auchinleck, G.C.I.E., C.B., C.S.I., D.S.O., O.B.E., A.D.C., Commander in Chief, the Middle East Forces. Published as a supplement to the *London Gazette* of Tuesday, 13 January 1948, Number 38177, p.312.

[33] B.H. Liddell Hart (ed.), *The Rommel Papers,* Arrow Books, London, 1984, p.159.

[34] Murphy, *Official History,* pp.106–08.

[35] Playfair, *Mediterranean,* p.48.

[36] *Press,* 25 November 1941, p.7.

[37] GOC's report, p.8, WAII8/3/19.

[38] Freyberg Diary, 22 November 1941, WAII8/5/44.

[39] GOC's report, p.8, WAII8/3/19.

[40] Ibid.

[41] Murphy, *Official History,* p.136.

[42] GOC's report, p.9, WAII8/3/19.

[43] Libyan Campaign – 'Crusader', July–November 1941, Order to

6 NZ INF BDE from NZ DIV, 22 November 1941, WAII8/3/18.

[44] Freyberg Diary, 22 November 1941, WAII8/5/44.

[45] Libyan Campaign, Message from General Freyberg to Commander, 13 Corps, 22 November 1941, WAII8/3/18.

[46] 6 New Zealand Infantry Brigade – WD 22 November 1941, WAII1/1659/DA58/1/14, War Diary 1 November – 30 November 1941, Volume 1 Appendix.

[47] GOC's report, p.11, WAII8/3/19.

Chapter 6: Totensonntag: The Sunday of the Dead

[1] Libyan Campaign – General Officer Commanding's printed report WAII8/3/19, pp.11–12.

[2] E.K. Tomlinson to Murphy, letter, 13 May 1951, WAII3/5/20 Crusader campaign 1941, correspondence files M–Z.

[3]   J.R.B. Heron, unpublished manuscript.

[4]   G.J. NcNaught to Murphy, letters 29 June 1950 and 12 July 1950, WAII3/4/19 Crusader campaign 1941, correspondence files F-Mac.

[5]   H.S. Wilson, undated report, WAII3/5/20 Crusader campaign 1941, correspondence files M–Z.

[6]   W.E. Murphy, *Official History of New Zealand in the Second World War 1939–1945, Episodes and Studies Volume 2: Point 175 – The Battle of Sunday of the Dead,* Historical Publications Branch, Department of Internal Affairs, Wellington, 1950, p.3.

[7]   Ibid., p.7.

[8]   Headquarters 6 New Zealand Infantry Brigade WD 23 November 1941, WAII1/1659/DA58/1/14, War Diary, 1 November – 30 November 1941, Volume 1 Appendix.

[9]   McNaught letters, WAII3/4/19.

[10]   Murphy, *Official History (Point 175),* p.14.

[11]   T.P. Winter to Murphy, letter 18 March 1953, WAII3/5/20 Crusader campaign 1941, correspondence files M–Z.

[12]   H.S. Wilson report WAII3/5/20.

[13]   Ibid.

[14]   2 NZEF War History Branch – 2 Libyan Campaign – Planning and Preparation – Part 2, Chapters 7 to 11. WAII1/249, DA401.24/2/1.

[15]   3 Company 27 (Machine Gun) Battalion, WD 23 November 1941, WAII1/1663 DA66/1/23 War Diary 13 November to 5 December 1941.

[16]   P.L. Hammond, unpublished manuscript.

[17]   J.A. Black, unpublished manuscript.

[18]   E.K. Tomlinson to Murphy, letter, WAII3/5/20.

[19]   W.E. Murphy, *Official History of New Zealand in the Second World War 1939–1945: The Relief of Tobruk,* Historical Publications Branch, Department of Internal Affairs, Wellington, 1961, p.189.

[20] B.V. Cox to Robin Kay, record of conversation, WAII1/168/DA60/20/2, 2NZEF – 27 Machine Gun Battalion – Inward Correspondence – Appendix – Regarding Photographs – Regarding Maps.

[21] Hammond, unpublished manuscript.

[22] Lieutenant General Sir Edward Puttick, *Official History of New Zealand in the Second World War 1939–1945: 25 Battalion,* Historical Publications Branch, Department of Internal Affairs, Wellington, 1960, p.134.

[23] Murphy, *Official History (Point 175),* p.30.

[24] Murphy, *Official History (Tobruk),* pp.191–92.

[25] Ibid., p.194.

[26] Puttick, *Official History,* p.134.

[27] Murphy, *Official History (Point 175),* p.29.

[28] Murphy, *Official History (Tobruk),* p.194.

[29] Black, unpublished manuscript.

[30] Murphy, *Official History (Point 175),* p.2.

[31]   Major General I.S.O. Playfair, *The Mediterranean and Middle East Volume III (September 1941 to September 1942) British Fortunes reach their Lowest Ebb,* Her Majesty's Stationery Office, London, 1960, p.50.

[32]   Heinz Werner Schmidt, *With Rommel in the Desert,* George G. Harrap & Co. Ltd, London, 1951, p.108.

[33]   B.H. Liddell Hart (ed.), *The Rommel Papers,* Arrow Books, London, 1984, pp.161–62.

[34]   E.H. Smith, *Official History of New Zealand in the Second World War 1939–1945, Episodes and Studies: Guns Against Tanks: L Troop, 33rd Battery, 7th New Zealand Anti-Tank Regiment in Libya, 23 November 1941,* Historical Publications Branch, Department of Internal Affairs, Wellington, 1948, p.8.

[35]   Frazer D. Norton, *Official History of New Zealand in the Second World War 1939–1945:*

26 Battalion, Historical Publications Branch, Department of Internal Affairs, Wellington, 1952, p.90.

[36] 6 New Zealand Infantry Brigade WD 23 November 1941, WAII1/1659/DA58/1/14, War Diary 1 November – 30 November 1941, Volume 1 Appendix.

[37] J.A.I. Agar-Hamilton and L.C.F. Turner, *The Sidi Rezeg Battles 1941,* Oxford University Press, Cape Town, 1957, p.273.

[38] Ibid., p.275.

[39] 6 New Zealand Infantry Brigade WD 23 November 1941, WAII1/1659/DA58/1/14, War Diary 1 November – 30 November 1941, Volume 1 Appendix.

[40] Liddell Hart, *Rommel Papers,* p.162.

Chapter 7: The Division Moves West

[1]   Libyan Campaign – General Officer Commanding's printed report WAII8/3/19, p.10.

[2]   Libyan Campaign – 'Crusader', July–November 1941, Letter from General Godwin-Austen to General Freyberg, 23 November 1941, WAII8/3/18.

[3]   Ibid.

[4]   Major General I.S.O. Playfair, *The Mediterranean and Middle East Volume III (September 1941 to September 1942) British Fortunes reach their Lowest Ebb,* Her Majesty's Stationery Office, London, 1960, p.52.

[5]   Libyan Campaign, Letter from General Godwin-Austen to General Freyberg, 23 November 1941, WAII8/3/18.

[6]   Michael Carver, *Tobruk,* B.T. Batsford Ltd, London, 1964, p.102.

[7]   GOC's Report, p.11, WAII8/3/19.

[8] Paul Freyberg, *Bernard Freyberg, VC: soldier of two nations,* Hodder & Stoughton, London, 1991, p.344.

[9] *Evening Post,* 28 November 1941, p.5.

[10] GOC's Report, p.12, WAII8/3/19.

[11] *Official History of New Zealand in the Second World War 1939–1945: Documents Relating to New Zealand's Participation in the Second World War 1939–45: Volume II,* Historical Publications Branch, Department of Internal Affairs, Wellington, 1951, Document 120, p.92.

[12] Correlli Barnett, *The Desert Generals,* Cassell, London, 1999, p.111.

[13] Libyan Campaign, Letter from General Godwin-Austen to General Freyberg, 23 November 1941, WAII8/3/18.

[14] Brigadier H.B. Latham to Major General H.K. Kippenberger, letter, 26 September 1950, WAII3/5/21, Crusader Campaign 1941, correspondence files 21

Battalion, also 6 Brigade, 23, 24, 25, 26, 27, 28 Battalions.

[15]   Barnett, *Desert Generals,* p.112.

[16]   Libyan Campaign, Message from General Auchinleck to General Cunningham, WAII8/3/18.

[17]   Barnett, *Desert Generals,* p.117.

[18]   Major General Sir Howard Kippenberger, *Infantry Brigadier,* Oxford University Press, London, 1949, p.92.

[19]   Ibid.

[20]   W.E. Murphy, *Official History of New Zealand in the Second World War 1939–1945: The Relief of Tobruk,* Historical Publications Branch, Department of Internal Affairs, Wellington, 1961, p.224.

[21]   Ibid., pp.224–25.

[22]   Frazer D. Norton, *Official History of New Zealand in the Second World War 1939–1945: 26 Battalion,* Historical Publications Branch, Department of Internal Affairs, Wellington, 1952, p.92.

[23]   *Auckland Star,* 26 November 1941, p.7.

[24]   *Evening Post,* 26 November 1941, p.7.

[25]   Geoffrey Cox, *A Tale of Two Battles: A personal memoir of Crete and the Western Desert 1941,* Kimber, London, 1987, pp.167–68.

[26]   Freyberg Diary, 24 November 1941, WAII8/5/44, GOC Diary – 3 September 1941 – 2 September 1942.

[27]   Kippenberger, *Infantry Brigadier,* p.94.

[28]   Letter, C.L.S. Paterson to family, 11 January 1942.

[29]   Murphy, *Official History,* p.236.

[30]   L.M. Nelley to Murphy, letter 13 May 1951, WAII3/5/20, Crusader campaign 1941, correspondence files M–Z.

[31]   Martyn Uren, *Kiwi Saga,* Collins, Auckland, 1943, p.165.

[32]   Murphy, *Official History,* p.242.

[33]   *Press,* 28 November 1941, p.7.

Chapter 8: The Attacks on Sidi Rezegh and Belhamed

[1]	Libyan Campaign – 'Crusader', July–November 1941, Letter from General Godwin-Austen to General Freyberg, 25 November 1941, WAII8/3/18.

[2]	W.E. Murphy, *Official History of New Zealand in the Second World War 1939–1945: The Relief of Tobruk,* Historical Publications Branch, Department of Internal Affairs, Wellington, 1961, p.249.

[3]	Headquarters 6 New Zealand Infantry Brigade WD, 25 November 1941, WAII1/1659/DA58/1/14, War Diary, 1 November – 30 November 1941, Volume 1 Appendix.

[4]	Murphy, *Official History,* p.251.

[5]	Major General Sir Howard Kippenberger, *Infantry Brigadier,* Oxford University Press, London, 1949, p.95.

[6]   W.D. Dawson, *Official History of New Zealand in the Second World War 1939–1945: 18 Battalion and Armoured Regiment,* Historical Publications Branch, Department of Internal Affairs, Wellington, 1961, p.198.

[7]   Ibid., p.199.

[8]   Murphy, *Official History,* p.254.

[9]   Freyberg Diary, 26 November 1941, WAII8/5/44, GOC Diary – 3 September 1941–2 September 1942.

[10]   Dawson, *Official History,* p.200.

[11]   Murphy, *Official History,* p.273.

[12]   Headquarters 6 New Zealand Infantry Brigade WD 26 November 1941, WAII1/1659/DA58/1/14, War Diary 1 November – 30 November 1941, Volume 1 Appendix.

[13]   Murphy, *Official History,* p.263.

[14]   6 New Zealand Infantry Brigade WD 26 November 1941, WAII1/1659/DA58/1/14, War Diary 1 November – 30 November 1941, Volume 1 Appendix.

[15] Freyberg Diary, 26 November 1941, WAII8/5/44.

[16] Libyan Campaign – General Officer Commanding's printed report, WAII8/3/19, p.15.

[17] Frazer D. Norton, *Official History of New Zealand in the Second World War 1939–1945: 26 Battalion,* Historical Publications Branch, Department of Internal Affairs, Wellington, 1952, p.102.

[18] 2 NZEF – War History Branch – 2 Libyan Campaign – Chapter 23, 26 November 1941, WAII1/253, DA401.24/2/7.

[19] Email, J.R.B. Heron to author, May 2009.

[20] J.A. Black, unpublished manuscript.

[21] 6 New Zealand Infantry Brigade WD 26 November 1941, WAII1/1659/DA58/1/14, War Diary 1 November – 30 November 1941, Volume 1 Appendix.

[22] Freyberg Diary, 26 November 1941, WAII8/5/44.

[23] Ibid.

[24] Brigadier L.W. Inglis, Narrative of Second Libyan Campaign, 26 November 1941, p.13, WAII11/1, correspondence concerning the Libyan campaign, February 1949 – July 1950.

[25] Letter, C.L.S. Paterson to family, 11 January 1942.

[26] Ibid.

[27] Inglis Narrative 26 November 1941, p.14, WAII11/1.

[28] *Evening Post,* 28 November 1941, p.5.

[29] Ibid., 29 November 1941, p.9.

[30] Ibid., 2 December 1941, p.8.

[31] 6 New Zealand Infantry Brigade WD 26 November 1941, WAII1/1659/DA58/1/14, War Diary 1 November – 30 November 1941, Volume 1 Appendix.

[32] Murphy, *Official History,* p.286.

[33] 6 New Zealand Infantry Brigade WD 26 November 1941, WAII1/1659/DA58/1/14, War Diary 1 November – 30 November 1941, Volume 1 Appendix.

[34] Charles Gatenby, unpublished manuscript.

[35] M.A. Cameron to Murphy, letter, 21 October 1949, WAII3/4/18, Crusader Campaign 1941, correspondence files A–E.

[36] Gatenby, unpublished manuscript.

[37] Cameron letter, WAII3/4/18.

[38] Murphy, *Official History*, pp.289–91.

[39] L.M. Nelley to Murphy, letter, 12 May 1951, WAII3/5/20, Crusader Campaign 1941, correspondence files M–Z. Eugene Charles (Charlie) Nelley of 24 Battalion, was 27 when he was killed. Another brother, Joseph Rudland Nelley, had died on Crete on 28 May.

[40] E.K. Tomlinson to Murphy, letter, 13 May 1951, WAII3/5/20, Crusader Campaign 1941, correspondence files M-Z.

[41] 6 New Zealand Infantry Brigade WD 26 November 1941, WAII1/1659/DA58/1/14, War Diary 1 November 1941–30

November 1941, Volume 1 Appendix.

Chapter 9: Rommel's Dash to the Frontier

[1]   B.H. Liddell Hart (ed.), *The Rommel Papers,* Arrow Books, London, 1984, p.163.

[2]   Geoffrey Cox, *A Tale of Two Battles: A personal memoir of Crete and the Western Desert 1941,* Kimber, London, 1987, pp.166–67.

[3]   W.E. Murphy, *Official History of New Zealand in the Second World War 1939–1945: The Relief of Tobruk,* Historical Publications Branch, Department of Internal Affairs, Wellington, 1961, p.208.

[4]   Rowland Ryder, *Ravenstein. Portrait of a German General,* Hamish Hamilton, London, 1978, pp.74–75.

[5]   Heinz Werner Schmidt, *With Rommel in the Desert,* George G. Harrap & Co. Ltd, London, 1951, pp.112–14.

[6]   Major Robert Crisp, *Brazen Chariots*, W.W. Norton & Company, New York, 2005, pp.101–03.

[7]   James Hargest, *Farewell Campo 12*, Whitcombe & Tombs Ltd, Wellington, 1945, p.15.

[8]   Murphy, *Official History*, p.317.

[9]   Libyan Campaign – 'Crusader', July–November 1941, Letter from Brigadier Hargest to General Freyberg, 25 November 1941, WAII8/3/18.

[10]   Hargest, *Farewell*, p.15.

[11]   J.F. Cody, *Official History of New Zealand in the Second World War 1939–1945: 28 (Maori) Battalion*, Historical Publications Branch, Department of Internal Affairs, Wellington, 1956, p.151.

[12]   Jim Henderson, *Official History of New Zealand in the Second World War 1939–1945: 22 Battalion*, Historical Publications Branch, Department of Internal Affairs, Wellington, 1958, p.112.

[13]   Murphy, *Official History*, pp.332–33.

[14]   Murphy, *Official History,* pp.337–38.

[15]   Account by Bombardier M. Niven of P4, of the overrunning of the 5 Brigade HQ at Sidi Azeiz on 27 November 1941, WAII11/1, correspondence concerning the Libyan campaign, February 1949 – July 1950.

[16]   Murphy, *Official History,* p.339.

[17]   Hargest, *Farewell,* pp.22–23.

[18]   Murphy, *Official History,* p.340.

[19]   Angus Ross, *Official History of New Zealand in the Second World War 1939–1945: 23 Battalion,* Historical Publications Branch, Department of Internal Affairs, Wellington, 1959, pp.119–20.

[20]   Murphy, *Official History,* p.331.

[21]   *Operations in the Middle East from 1st November 1941 to 15th August 1942.* Despatch submitted to the Secretary of State for War on 27th January 1943, by General Sir Claude J.E. Auchinleck, G.C.I.E., C.B., C.S.I., D.S.O., O.B.E., A.D.C.,

Commander in Chief, the Middle East Forces. Published as a supplement to the *London Gazette* of Tuesday, 13th January, 1948, Number 38177, pp.339–40.

Chapter 10: Rommel Returns to Sidi Rezegh

[1] W.D. Dawson, *Official History of New Zealand in the Second World War 1939–1945: 18 Battalion and Armoured Regiment,* Historical Publications Branch, Department of Internal Affairs, Wellington, 1961, p.205.

[2] Letter, C.L.S. Paterson to family, 11 January 1942.

[3] Letter, J.A. Blacklin to M. Fearnside, 22 December 1941.

[4] Libyan Campaign – General Officer Commanding's printed report, WAII8/3/19, p.16.

[5] Geoffrey Cox, *A Tale of Two Battles: A personal memoir of Crete and the Western Desert 1941,* Kimber, London, 1987, p.180.

[6]   *Operations in the Middle East from 1st November 1941 to 15th August 1942.* Despatch submitted to the Secretary of State for War on 27th January 1943, by General Sir Claude J.E. Auchinleck, G.C.I.E., C.B., C.S.I., D.S.O., O.B.E., A.D.C., Commander in Chief, the Middle East Forces. Published as a supplement to the *London Gazette* of Tuesday, 13 January, 1948, Number 38177, p.340.

[7]   Heinz Werner Schmidt, *With Rommel in the Desert,* George G. Harrap & Co. Ltd, London, 1951, p.118.

[8]   Brigadier L.W. Inglis, Narrative of Second Libyan Campaign, 28 November 1941, p.20, WAII11/1, correspondence concerning the Libyan campaign, February 1949 – July 1950.

[9]   Headquarters 6 New Zealand Infantry Brigade WD 28 November 1941, WAII1/1659/DA58/1/14, War Diary 1 November – 30

November 1941, Volume 1 Appendix.

[10] Freyberg Diary, 28 November 1941, WAII8/5/44, GOC Diary – 3 September 1941 – 2 September 1942.

[11] *Press,* 29 November 1941, p.9.

[12] GOC's Report, p.17, WAII8/3/19.

[13] 6 New Zealand Infantry Brigade WD 28 November 1941, WAII1/1659/DA58/1/14, War Diary 1 November – 30 November 1941, Volume 1 Appendix.

[14] Rowland Ryder, *Ravenstein. Portrait of a German General,* Hamish Hamilton, London, 1978, p.89.

[15] J.F. Cody, *Official History of New Zealand in the Second World War 1939–1945: 21 Battalion,* Historical Publications Branch, Department of Internal Affairs, Wellington, 1953. Appendix 1, Capture of Major General von Ravenstein, 29 November 1941, p.3.

[16]   Geoffrey Cox, *A Tale of Two Battles: A personal memoir of Crete and the Western Desert 1941,* Kimber, London, 1987, p.184.

[17]   Inglis Narrative 29 November 1941, p.25, WAII11/1.

[18]   Ryder, *Ravenstein,* p.94.

[19]   This and following quotes, R.J.M. Loughnan, 'The Memoirs of R.J.M. Loughnan', unpublished.

[20]   Major General I.S.O. Playfair, *The Mediterranean and Middle East Volume III (September 1941 to September 1942) British Fortunes reach their Lowest Ebb,* Her Majesty's Stationery Office, London, 1960, p.64.

[21]   Freyberg Diary, 28 November 1941, WAII8/5/44.

[22]   GOC's Report, p.17, WAII8/3/19.

[23]   J.A.I. Agar-Hamilton and L.C.F. Turner, *The Sidi Rezeg Battles 1941,* Oxford University Press, Cape Town, 1957, p.370.

Chapter 11: Mounting Pressure on 4 and 6 Brigades

[1]   W.D. Dawson, *Official History of New Zealand in the Second World War 1939–1945: 18 Battalion and Armoured Regiment,* Historical Publications Branch, Department of Internal Affairs, Wellington, 1961, p.212.
[2]   Ibid., p.213.
[3]   Lt G.H. Fearnside, *Bayonets Abroad: A History Of The 2/13th Battalion AIF In The Second World War,* John Burridge Military Antiques, Swanbourne, Western Australia, 1993, pp.146–48.
[4]   Ibid., p.151.
[5]   Letter, J.A. Blacklin to M. Fearnside, 22 December 1941.
[6]   Brigadier L.W. Inglis, Narrative of Second Libyan Campaign, 29 November 1941, p.26, WAII11/1, correspondence concerning the Libyan campaign, February 1949 – July 1950.
[7]   Ibid.

[8]   Major General I.S.O. Playfair, *The Mediterranean and Middle East Volume III (September 1941 to September 1942) British Fortunes reach their Lowest Ebb,* Her Majesty's Stationery Office, London, 1960, p.66.

[9]   J.A.I. Agar-Hamilton and L.C.F. Turner, *The Sidi Rezeg Battles 1941,* Oxford University Press, Cape Town, 1957, p.382.

[10]   Inglis Narrative 29 November 1941, pp.22–3, WAII11/1.

[11]   Freyberg Diary, 29 November 1941, WAII8/5/44, GOC Diary – 3 September 1941 – 2 September 1942.

[12]   Libyan Campaign – General Officer Commanding's printed report, WAII8/3/19, p.19.

[13]   Geoffrey Cox, *A Tale of Two Battles: A personal memoir of Crete and the Western Desert 1941,* Kimber, London, 1987, p.187.

[14]   Ibid.

[15]   Freyberg Diary 30 November 1941, WAII8/5/44.

[16] L.M. Nelley to Murphy, letter, 12 May 1951, WAII3/5/20, Crusader campaign 1941, correspondence files M–Z.

[17] R.M. Burdon, *Official History of New Zealand in the Second World War 1939–1945: 24 Battalion*, Historical Publications Branch, Department of Internal Affairs, Wellington, 1954, p.87.

[18] Official Archivist, 2 NZEF. *Return to the Attack – The New Zealand Division in Libya*, Army Board, Wellington, 1944, p.34.

[19] Interview with Captain Charles Gatenby, MBE, 26 Infantry Battalion. Recorded by Radio New Zealand, ID 37407 Sound Archives Nga Taonga Korero.

[20] Letter, C. Gatenby to E. Gatenby, 1942.

[21] Dawson, *Official History,* p.214.

[22] Headquarters 6 New Zealand Infantry Brigade, WD 30 November 1941, WAII1/1659/DA58/1/14, War Diary, 1 November – 30 November 1941, Volume 1, Appendix.

[23]   Freyberg Diary, 30 November 1941, WAII8/5/44.
[24]   Ibid.
[25]   W.E. Murphy, *Official History of New Zealand in the Second World War 1939–1945: The Relief of Tobruk,* Historical Publications Branch, Department of Internal Affairs, Wellington, 1961, p.426.
[26]   Glyn Harper, *Kippenberger, An Inspired New Zealand Commander,* HarperCollins, Auckland, 1997, p.122.
[27]   Playfair, *Mediterranean,* p.67.
[28]   6 New Zealand Infantry Brigade WD
[30]   November 1941, WAII1/1659/DA58/1/14, War Diary, 1 November – 30 November 1941, Volume 1, Appendix.
[29]   Agar-Hamilton and Turner, *Sidi Rezeg,* pp.391–94.
[30]   Ibid., p.404.
[31]   J.A. Black, unpublished manuscript.
[32]   *Press,* 2 December 1941, p.7.
[33]   *Press,* 3 December 1941, p.7.

[34]   3 Company 27 (Machine Gun) Battalion, WD 30 November 1941, WAII1/1663 DA66/1/23 War Diary, 13 November to 5 December 1941.

[35]   6 New Zealand Infantry Brigade WD 30 November 1941, WAII1/1659/DA58/1/14, War Diary, 1 November – 30 November 1941, Volume 1, Appendix.

Chapter 12: 4 and 6 Brigades Withdraw

[1]   Headquarters 6 New Zealand Infantry Brigade WD 1 December 1941, WAII1/1659/DA58/1/14 War Diary, 1 November – 30 November 1941, Volume 1, Appendix, p.19.

[2]   Libyan Campaign – General Officer Commanding's printed report, WAII8/3/19, p.20.

[3]   Freyberg Diary, 1 December 1941, WAII8/5/44, GOC Diary – 3 September 1941 – 2 September 1942.

[4]   J.A.I. Agar-Hamilton and L.C.F. Turner, *The Sidi Rezeg Battles 1941,* Oxford University Press, Cape Town, 1957, p.405.

[5]   W.D. Dawson, *Official History of New Zealand in the Second World War 1939–1945: 18 Battalion and Armoured Regiment,* Historical Publications Branch, Department of Internal Affairs, Wellington, 1961, p.215.

[6]   Brigadier L.W. Inglis, Narrative of Second Libyan Campaign, 1 December 1941, pp.28-9, WAII11/1, correspondence concerning the Libyan campaign, February 1949 – July 1950.

[7]   Ibid., p.29.

[8]   Major General Sir Howard Kippenberger, *Infantry Brigadier,* Oxford University Press, London, 1949, pp.103–11.

[9]   Inglis Narrative, p.42, WAII11/1.

[10]   Father Ambrose Loughnan OP, *Full Circle to God,* Loughley Books, Rangiora, 2000, p.3.

[11]   Brigadier Miles to Major General Puttick, letter, 21 April 1942, WAII11/1, correspondence

concerning the Libyan campaign, February 1948 – July 1950.

[12] Alan Henderson, David Green, Peter Cooke, *The Gunners. A History Of New Zealand Artillery,* Raupo Books, North Shore, 2008, p.235.

[13] W.E. Murphy, *Official History of New Zealand in the Second World War 1939–1945: The Relief of Tobruk,* Historical Publications Branch, Department of Internal Affairs, Wellington, 1961, p.441.

[14] GOC's Report, p.20, WAII8/3/19.

[15] Murphy, *Official History,* p.444.

[16] Freyberg Diary, 1 December 1941, WAII8/5/44.

[17] *Evening Post,* 5 December 1941, p.5.

[18] Ibid., 8 December 1941, p.7.

[19] Bombardier F. Martyn, *Middle East Guns,* privately published, 1943, p.10.

[20] Major General I.S.O. Playfair, *The Mediterranean and Middle East Volume III (September*

1941 to September 1942) British Fortunes reach their Lowest Ebb, Her Majesty's Stationery Office, London, 1960, p.68.

[21] Headquarters 6 New Zealand Infantry Brigade WD 1 December 1941, WAII1/1659/DA58/1/14, War Diary 1 November – 30 November 1941, Volume 1, Appendix.

[22] Murphy, *Official History,* p.451.

[23] Major General H.E. Barrowclough; Memorandum relating to the events in 6 NZ Bde Area on the morning of the 1st December 1941, 9 October 1950, WAII3/5/21, Crusader campaign 1941, correspondence files 21 Battalion, also 6 Brigade, 23 24, 25, 26, 27, 28 Battalions.

[24] Copy of a letter dated 27th March (1955) from Lt Colonel H.D. Drew, OBE, MC, to Major General I.S.O. Playfair, WAII11/1, correspondence concerning the Libyan

campaign, February 1949 – July 1950.

[25] Brigadier A. Gatehouse to W.E. Murphy, letter, 27 September 1960, WAII3/4/19, Crusader campaign 1941, correspondence files, F–Mac.

[26] Barrie Pitt, *The Crucible of War: Western Desert 1941,* Jonathan Cape, London, 1980, p.448.

[27] Barrowclough Memorandum, 9 October 1950, WAII3/5/21.

[28] Freyberg Diary, 1 December 1941, WAII8/5/44.

[29] Lieutenant General Sir Bernard Freyberg VC, comments: Second Libyan Campaign, 1941 – November–December. Volume 1 – Planning and Training. WAII11/1, Correspondence concerning the Libyan Campaign, February 1949 – July 1950.

[30] Murphy, *Official History,* p.455.

[31] Gatehouse letter, 27 September 1960, WAII3/4/19.

[32] Murphy, *Official History,* p.453.

[33] Ibid., p.455.

[34] Pitt, *Crucible,* p.449.

[35] Inglis Narrative, 1 December 1941, p.34, WAII11/1.

[36] C.A. Borman, *Official History of New Zealand in the Second World War 1939–1945: Divisional Signals,* Historical Publications Branch, Department of Internal Affairs, Wellington, 1954, p.202.

[37] GOC's Report, p.21, WAII8/3/19.

[38] 3 Company 27 (Machine Gun) Battalion, WD 1 December 1941, WAII1/1663 DA66/1/23 War Diary, 13 November to 5 December 1941.

[39] P.L. Hammond, unpublished manuscript.

[40] Inglis Narrative, p.32, WAII11/1.

[41] Freyberg Diary, 1 December 1941, WAII8/5/44.

[42] GOC's report, p.21, WAII8/3/19.

[43] Agar-Hamilton and Turner, *Sidi Rezeg,* p.415.

[44] Ibid.

[45] *Operations in the Middle East from 1st November 1941 to*

15th August 1942. Despatch submitted to the Secretary of State for War on 27th January 1943, by General Sir Claude J.E. Auchinleck, G.C.I.E., C.B., C.S.I., D.S.O., O.B.E., A.D.C., Commander in Chief, the Middle East Forces. Published as a supplement to the *London Gazette* of Tuesday, 13th January, 1948, Number 38177, pp.313, 341.

[46] Freyberg Diary, 2 December 1941, WAII8/5/44.

[47] *Press,* 5 December 1941, p.7.

[48] GOC's report, p.21, WAII8/3/19.

[49] Hammond, unpublished manuscript.

[50] Frazer D. Norton, *Official History of New Zealand in the Second World War 1939–1945: 26 Battalion,* Historical Publications Branch, Department of Internal Affairs, Wellington, 1952, p.129.

[51] Lieutenant General Sir Edward Puttick, *Official History of New Zealand in the Second World*

War 1939–1945: 25 Battalion, Historical Publications Branch, Department of Internal Affairs, Wellington, 1960, p.158.

[52]   GOC's report, p.21, WAII8/3/19.

Chapter 13: Wrapping up the Campaign

[1]   *Auckland Star,* 6 December 1941, p.7.

[2]   Letter, C.L.S. Paterson to family, 11 January 1942.

[3]   *Operations in the Middle East from 1st November 1941 to 15th August 1942.* Despatch submitted to the Secretary of State for War on 27th January 1943, by General Sir Claude J.E. Auchinleck, G.C.I.E., C.B., C.S.I., D.S.O., O.B.E., A.D.C., Commander in Chief, the Middle East Forces. Published as a supplement to the *London Gazette* of Tuesday, 13th January, 1948, Number 38177, p.341.

[4]   W.E. Murphy, *Official History of New Zealand in the Second World War 1939–1945: The Relief of Tobruk,* Historical Publications Branch, Department of Internal Affairs, Wellington, 1961, p.472–73.

[5]   W.D. Dawson, *Official History of New Zealand in the Second World War 1939–1945: 18 Battalion and Armoured Regiment,* Historical Publications Branch, Department of Internal Affairs, Wellington, 1961, pp.220–23.

[6]   Ibid., p.227.

[7]   Ibid., pp.227–30.

[8]   J.F. Cody, *Official History of New Zealand in the Second World War 1939–1945: 28 (Maori) Battalion,* Historical Publications Branch, Department of Internal Affairs, Wellington, 1956, p.156.

[9]   Libyan Campaign – General Officer Commanding's printed report, WAII8/3/19 p.23.

[10]   Angus Ross, *Official History of New Zealand in the Second World War 1939–1945: 23*

Battalion, Historical Publications Branch, Department of Internal Affairs, Wellington, 1959, p.125.

[11]   B.H. Liddell Hart (ed.), *The Rommel Papers,* Arrow Books, London, 1984, p.173.

[12]   Paterson letter, 11 January 1942.

[13]   Cody, *Official History,* p.176.

[14]   Ross, *Official History,* pp.130–31.

[15]   Heinz Werner Schmidt, *With Rommel in the Desert,* George G. Harrap & Co. Ltd, London, 1951, p.122.

[16]   Liddell Hart, *Rommel Papers,* p.182.

[17]   Paterson letter, 11 January 1942.

[18]   Murphy, *Official History,* p.515.

Chapter 14: Treating the Wounded

[1]   J.B. McKinney, *Official History of New Zealand in the Second World War 1939–1945: Medical Units of 2 NZEF in Middle East and Italy,* Historical Publications

Branch, Department of Internal Affairs, Wellington, 1952, p.157.

[2]   Victor Gregg, *Rifleman: A Front Line Life,* Bloomsbury Publishing Plc, London, 2011, p.68.

[3]   McKinney, *Official History,* p.163.

[4]   Freyberg Diary, 6 December 1941, WAII8/5/44, GOC Diary – 3 September 1941 – 2 September 1942.

[5]   This and following quotes, Sir John Staveley, personal diary.

[6]   2 NZEF – War History Branch – 2 NZ Division – Chronological Narrative – Crusader Campaign, 1 December 1941, para 191, WAII1/284 DA401.

[7]   W. Andrew, personal diary.

[8]   Colonel T.D.M. Stout, *Official History of New Zealand in the Second World War 1939–1945: New Zealand Medical Services in the Middle East and Italy,* Historical Publications Branch, Department of Internal Affairs, Wellington, p.283.

[9]   R.J.M. Loughnan, 'The Memoirs of R.J.M. Loughnan', unpublished.

[10]   Rowland Ryder *Ravenstein. Portrait of a German General,* Hamish Hamilton, London, 1978, pp.98–99.
[11]   Ibid., p.104.
[12]   Loughnan, *Memoirs.*
[13]   Stout, *Official History,* p.264.
[14]   Zeta Gunn, personal diary.

Chapter 15: For You the War is Over

[1]   J.R.B. Heron, unpublished manuscript.
[2]   Spence Edge and Jim Henderson, *No Honour, No Glory,* William Collins, Auckland, 1983, p.22.
[3]   Heron manuscript.
[4]   Ibid.
[5]   James Hargest, *Farewell Campo 12,* Whitcombe & Tombs Ltd, Wellington, 1945, p.29.
[6]   Ibid., pp.30–32.
[7]   Ibid., pp.37–50.
[8]   Hargest, *Farewell Campo 12,* p.51.
[9]   Edge and Henderson, *No Honour, No Glory,* pp.69-79.

[10] Charles Costello, unpublished diary.

[11] Email, Marise Perry to author, 20 January 2013.

[12] J.D. Gerard, *Unwilling Guests*, A.H. & A.W. Reed, Wellington, 1945, p.59.

[13] Interview with Captain Charles Gatenby, MBE, 26 Infantry Battalion. Recorded by Radio New Zealand, ID 37407 Sound Archives Nga Taonga Korero.

[14] Heron manuscript.

[15] Father Ambrose Loughnan OP, *Full Circle to God*, Loughley Books, Rangiora, 2000, p.4.

[16] Ibid., p.15.

[17] Heron manuscript.

[18] The 'OP' after Loughnan's name stands for Ordinis Praedicatorum – Latin for Order of Preachers.

[19] Loughnan, *Full Circle*, The Prologue.

Chapter 16: Counting the Cost of Crusader

[1]   *Operations in the Middle East from 1st November 1941 to 15th August 1942.* Despatch submitted to the Secretary of State for War on 27th January 1943, by General Sir Claude J.E. Auchinleck, G.C.I.E., C.B., C.S.I., D.S.O., O.B.E., A.D.C., Commander in Chief, the Middle East Forces. Published as a supplement to the *London Gazette* of Tuesday, 13th January, 1948, Number 38177, page 309.

[2]   Winston S. Churchill, *The Second World War (Volume 4, The Hinge of Fate),* Cassell, London, 1951, p.603.

[3]   D.W. Sinclair, *Official History of New Zealand in the Second World War 1939–1945: 19 Battalion and Armoured Regiment,* Historical Publications Branch, Department of Internal Affairs, Wellington, 1954, p.226.

[4]   W.E. Murphy, *Official History of New Zealand in the Second World War 1939–1945: The Relief of Tobruk,* Historical Publications Branch, Department of Internal Affairs, Wellington, 1961, p.521.

[5]   Sinclair, *Official History,* p.227.

[6]   Auchinleck, *Operations,* p.310.

[7]   Letter, J.A. Blacklin to M. Fearnside, 20 June 1942.

[8]   Letter, Blacklin to Fearnside, 26 March 1942.

[9]   Letter, Blacklin to Fearnside, 20 June 1942.

[10]   Auchinleck, *Operations,* p.312.

[11]   W. Gentry to H.K. Kippenberger, letter, 16 June 1950, WAII11/1 correspondence concerning the Libyan campaign, February 1949 – July 1950.

[12]   Major General I.S.O. Playfair, *The Mediterranean and Middle East Volume III (September 1941 to September 1942) British Fortunes reach their Lowest Ebb,* Her Majesty's

Stationery Office, London, 1960, p.28.

[13] Lieutenant General Fritz Bayerlein in B.H. Liddell Hart (ed.), *The Rommel Papers,* Arrow Books, London, 1984, p.184.

[14] Major General H.E. Barrowclough, Memorandum on the plan of attack by 8 Army November–December 1941, 9 October 1950, WAII3/5/21, Crusader campaign 1941 correspondence files, 21 Battalion also 6 Brigade, 23, 24, 25, 26, 27, 28 Battalions.

[15] Murphy, *Official History,* p.40.

[16] Auchinleck, *Operations,* p.315.

[17] Libyan Campaign – General Officer Commanding's printed report, WAII8/3/19, p.26.

[18] Ibid., p.1.

[19] Ibid., p.28.

[20] Lieutenant Colonel J.L. Scoullar, *Official History of New Zealand in the Second World War 1939–1945: Battle for Egypt: The Summer of 1942,* Historical Publications Branch, Department

of Internal Affairs, Wellington, 1955, p.4.

[21] Freyberg Diary, 22 November 1941, WAII8/5/44, GOC Diary – September 1941 – 2 September 1942.

[22] Unexpurgated Copy of Report on Crusader, Libya, WAII8/11/E.

[23] Correspondence dealing with Report 'New Zealand Division in Cyrenaica', WAII8/3/20, Libyan campaign, Commander in Chief's alterations to printed report.

[24] Scoullar, *Official History*, p.5.

[25] *NZ Official History of New Zealand in the Second World War 1939–1945: Documents Relating to New Zealand's Participation in the Second World War 1939–45: Volume II,* Historical Publications Branch, Department of Internal Affairs, Wellington, 1951, 111 – General Freyberg to the Prime Minister, 7 December 1941.

[26] Murphy, *Official History,* p.519.

[27]   Ibid., pp.422–27.

[28]   GOC's Report, p.20, WAII8/3/19.

[29]   L.M. Inglis to H.K. Kippenberger, letter, 22 January 1952, WAII11/1 correspondence concerning the Libyan campaign, February 1949 – July 1950.

[30]   Murphy, *Official History,* p.428.

[31]   Geoffrey Cox, *A Tale of Two Battles: A personal memoir of Crete and the Western Desert 1941,* Kimber, London, 1987, pp.197–98.

[32]   Murphy, *Official History,* Appendix 1.

[33]   *Documents* 109 – General Freyberg to the Prime Minister, 3 December 1941.

[34]   *Documents* 108 – General Auchinleck to the Chief of General Staff (Wellington) 3 December 1941.

[35]   *Document* 113 – The Prime Minister of the United Kingdom to the Prime Minister of New Zealand, 9 December 1941.

[36] *Documents* 111 – General Freyberg to the Prime Minister, 7 December 1941.

[37] Murphy, *Official History,* p.521.

[38] Ibid.

[39] L.M. Nelley to Murphy, letter, 12 May 1951, Crusader campaign 1941, correspondence files M–Z, WAII3/5/20.

[40] Letter, Charles Nelley to Laura Nelley, 1941.

[41] Graeme McIver, unpublished manuscript, 11 September 2013.

[42] Email, J.R.B. Heron to author, 15 May 2009.

[43] J.A. Black unpublished manuscript.

[44] McIver manuscript.

[45] Email, Geoffrey Heaps to author, 13 October 2013.

[46] McIver manuscript.

[47] Email, Nathania Kenny to author, 18 September 2013.

[48] McIver manuscript.

[49] *Nelson Evening Mail,* 21 July 1943.

Epilogue: Return to Sidi Rezegh

[1]   J.F. Cody, *Official History of New Zealand in the Second World War 1939–1945: 28 (Maori) Battalion,* Historical Publications Branch, Department of Internal Affairs, Wellington, 1956, p.140.

[2]   D.W. Sinclair, *Official History of New Zealand in the Second World War 1939–1945: 19 Battalion and Armoured Regiment,* Historical Publications Branch, Department of Internal Affairs, Wellington, 1954, p.230.

[3]   Lt Gen Sir B.C. Freyberg to Maj Gen H.K. Kippenberger, letter 5 November 1947, WAII11/1 correspondence concerning the Libyan campaign, February 1949 – July 1950.

[4]   *Evening Post,* 12 July 1943, p.4.

[5]   *NZ Official History of New Zealand in the Second World War 1939–1945: Documents Relating to New Zealand's Participation in the Second World*

War 1939–45: Volume II, Historical Publications Branch, Department of Internal Affairs, Wellington, 1951, 113 – The Prime Minister of the United Kingdom to the Prime Minister of New Zealand, 9 December 1941.

[6]   Glyn Harper, *Kippenberger, An Inspired New Zealand Commander,* HarperCollins, Auckland, 1997, p.128.

[7]   Alan Moorehead, *African Trilogy,* Four Square Books, London, 1959, p.188.

[8]   Heinz Werner Schmidt, *With Rommel in the Desert,* George G. Harrap & Co. Ltd, London, 1951, p.163.

[9]   Ibid., p.114.

[10]   B.H. Liddell Hart (ed.), *The Rommel Papers,* Arrow Books, London, 1984, p.240.

[11]   Stephen Bungay, *Alamein,* Aurum Press Ltd, London, 2002, pp.217–18.

[12]   Lieutenant Colonel J.L. Scoullar, *Official History of New Zealand in the Second World War*

1939–1945: Battle for Egypt: The Summer of 1942, Historical Publications Branch, Department of Internal Affairs, Wellington, 1955, pp.2–3.

[13] Libyan Campaign – General Officer Commanding's printed report, WAII8/3/19, p.2.

[14] Brigadier H.B. Latham to Major General Sir Howard Kippenberger, letter, 26 September 1950, WAII3/5/21, Crusader campaign 1941 correspondence files, 21 Battalion also 6 Brigade, 23, 24, 25, 26, 27, 28 Battalions.

[15] Murphy, *Official History*, p.521.

BIBLIOGRAPHY

Archives New Zealand (Wellington Head Office)

Libyan Campaign – 'Crusader', July–November 1941: ID R16700553, ADQZ 18906, WAII8/3/18

Unexpurgated Copy of Report on Crusader, Libya: ID R16700627, ADQZ 18906, WAII8/11/E

Libyan Campaign – General Officer Commanding's printed report: ID R16700552, ADQZ 18906, WAII8/3/19

Libyan Campaign – Commander in Chief's alterations to printed report: ID R16700551, ADQZ 18906, WAII8/3/20

General Officer Commanding Diary – 3 September 1941 – 2 September 1942: ID R16700545, ADQZ 18906, WAII8/5/44

Correspondence concerning the Libyan Campaign, Feb 1949 – Jul 1950: ID R12681219, ADQZ 18908, WAII11/1

Correspondence of Major General H Kippenberger: ID R12681220, ADQZ 18908, WAII11/2

Crusader Campaign 1941, correspondence files A–E: ID R16801370, ADQZ 18902, WAII3/4/18

Crusader Campaign 1941, correspondence files F–Mac: ID R16801371, ADQZ 18902, WAII3/4/19

Crusader Campaign 1941, correspondence files M–Z: ID R16801372, ADQZ 18902, WAII3/5/20

Crusader Campaign 1941, correspondence files 21 Battalion, also 6 Brigade, 23, 24, 25, 26, 27, 28 Battalions: ID R16801373, ADQZ 18902, WAII3/5/21

Crusader campaign 1941 correspondence files: ID R16801374, ADQZ 18902, WAII3/20/22

Middle East, Libya 1941, a letter from Brigadier H. Latham to General B.C. Freyberg: ID R20591228, ADQZ 18899, WAII2/1/1

Headquarters 6 New Zealand Infantry Brigade – War Diary, 1 November 1941 – 30 November 1941, Volume 1: ID R23517676, ADQZ 18886, WAII1/1659 DA58/1/14

27 (Machine Gun) Battalion War Diary November 1941, 3 Company: ID R23517715, ADQZ 18886, WAII1/1663 DA66/1/23

Headquarters 2 New Zealand Division, General Staff – War Diary, 1 November 1941 – 6 December 1941 (Appendix 8 messages): ID R23517359, ADQZ 18886, WAII1/1630 DA21.1/1/23

2NZE Headquarters NZ Division (G Branch) – Inward Correspondence – 27 Machine Gun Battalion – Libya 1941: ID R20108386, ADQZ 18886, WAII1/114 DA27/2

2NZEF – 27 Machine Gun Battalion – Inward Correspondence – Appendix – Regarding Photographs – Regarding Maps: ID R20109104, ADQZ 18886, WAII1/168 DA60/20/2

2NZEF – 24 Battalion – Account of Part Played at Sidi Rezegh – Written to contradict the impression that the 26 NZ Battalion had played a chief role – S.J. Hedge, C. Laurie, M.A. Hill: ID R20109032, ADQZ 18886, WAII1/163 DA60/10/1

2NZEF – Africa Star and Eighth Army clasp: ID R20107498, ADQZ 18886, WAII1/10 DA1/9/A29/2

New Zealand War Histories, NZ Divisional Campaign Narrative – Second Libyan Campaign, November–December 1941, Chapters 1 to 6: ID R23517296, ADQZ 18886, WAII1/1615 DA401.23/1

2 NZEF – War History Branch – 2 Libyan Campaign – Planning and Preparation – Part 2, Chapters 7 to 11: ID R20109810, ADQZ 18886, WAII1/249 DA401.24/2/1

2 NZEF – War History Branch – 2 Libyan Campaign – Chapter 22: ID R20109821, ADQZ 18886, WAII1/253 DA401.24/2/6

2 NZEF – War History Branch – 2 Libyan Campaign – Chapters 23–24: ID R20109823, ADQZ 18886, WAII1/253 DA401.24/2/7

2 NZEF – War History Branch – 2 Libyan Campaign – Chapter 28: ID R20109837, ADQZ 18886, WAII1/257 DA401.24/2/9

2 NZEF – War History Branch – 2 NZ Division – Chronological Narrative – Crusader Campaign: ID R20109916, ADQZ 18886, WAII1/284 DA401

United Kingdom War Cabinet Historical Section Official War Narratives – WWII – Section 1, Chapter G – General Auchinleck's Offensive and the Relief of Tobruk – Phase 3 – The Relief of Tobruk by Brigadier G.F. Ellenberger (1/12/1941–10/12/1941): ID R933860, ABFK/W3799/3 DA512.24/1/3

United Kingdom War Cabinet Historical Section Official War Narratives – WWII – Section 1, Chapter G – General Auchinleck's Offensive and the Relief of Tobruk – Phase 3 – The Relief of Tobruk by Brigadier G.F. Ellenberger (1/12/1941–10/12/1941): ID R933946, ABFK/W3799/12 DA512.24/1/3

United Kingdom War Cabinet Historical Section Official War Narratives – WWII – Section 1, Chapter G – General Auchinleck's Offensive and the Relief of Tobruk – Phase 8 – Operations on Egyptian Frontier and Phase 9 – Summing Up – by Brigadier G.F. Ellenberger (17/12/1941–17/1/1942): ID R933862, ABFK/W3799/3 DA512.24/1/5

Primary sources

Transcripts, diaries, personal correspondence and photographs from the following men or their families:
W. Andrew: 1941 diary, photographs.

J.A. Black: Interviews and correspondence (April 2006 – June 2008), transcript of personal reminiscences.

J.A. Blacklin: Personal letters of 950053 Gunner Joseph Alfred Blacklin, 432 Battery 149th Anti-Tank Regiment, Royal Horse Artillery, photographs.

C.J. Costello: 1941–42 diary, personal records, photographs, emails and interviews with family member 2013–14.

B.V. Cox: 1940 diary, personal records, photographs.

C. Gatenby: Personal correspondence, transcript of personal reminiscences, photographs, emails and interviews with family members, 2013–14.

Z.J. Gunn: Diaries, personal records, photographs.

P.L. Hammond: Interviews (May 2006 – June 2012), personal records, transcript of personal reminiscences, photographs.

E.W.E. Heaps: Correspondence and photographs from family members, 2013.

J.R.B. Heron: Correspondence (2008–11), transcript of personal reminiscences, photographs.

T.R. Horne: Correspondence from family member, 2013.

A.W. Lee: Correspondence from family member, 2013.

R.J.M. Loughnan: Transcript of personal reminiscences, interviews with family member, photographs.

L.J. McIver: Correspondence and photographs from family members, 2013.

L.M. and E.C. Nelley: Correspondence, papers, personal letters and photographs from family members, 2014.

C.L.S. Paterson: 1942 personal correspondence, interview with family member, photographs.

E.C. Polglase: Personal records, photographs, interview with family member.

Sir John Staveley: 1941 diary, photographs.

F. Wintle: Correspondence with family member, 2014.

Reports

Operations in the Middle East from 1st November 1941 to 15th August 1942. Despatch submitted to the Secretary of State for War on 27th January 1943, by General Sir Claude J.E. Auchinleck, G.C.I.E., C.B., C.S.I., D.S.O., O.B.E., A.D.C., Commander in Chief, the Middle East Forces. Published as a supplement to The London Gazette of Tuesday, 13th January, 1948, Number 38177, page 309.

Australia in the War of 1939–1945. Series 1 – Army. Volume III – Tobruk and El Alamein (1st edn, 1966). Author Maughan, Barton

Sound Recordings

Interview with Captain Charles Gatenby, MBE, 26 Infantry Battalion. Recorded by Radio New Zealand, ID 37407 Sound Archives Nga Taonga Korero.

Interview with Sir Geoffrey Sandford Cox. Imperial War Museum interview 13 August 2004, IWM Catalogue number 26937.

Books

(All volumes in the *Official History of New Zealand in the Second World War 1939–1945* are now also available at www.nzetc.victoria.ac.nz.)

Agar-Hamilton, J.A.I. and L.C.F. Turner. *The Sidi Rezeg Battles 1941,* Oxford University Press, Cape Town, 1957.

Allison, E.S. *Kiwi at Large,* Robert Hale Ltd, London, 1961.

Barber, Laurie. *War Memorial. A Chronology Of New Zealand and World War II,* Heinemann Reed, Auckland, 1989.

Barnett, Correlli. *The Desert Generals,* Cassell, London, 1999.

Beevor, Antony. *The Second World War,* Weidenfeld & Nicolson, London, 2012.

Bierman, John and Colin Smith. *Alamein – War without hate,* Viking, London, 2002.

Borman, C.A., *Official History of New Zealand in the Second World War 1939–1945: Divisional Signals,* Historical Publications Branch, Department of Internal Affairs, Wellington, 1954.

Bryant, Arthur. *The Turn of the Tide. Based on the War Diaries of Field Marshal of Viscount Alanbrooke,* The Reprint Society, England, 1958.

Bungay, Stephen. *Alamein,* Aurum Press Ltd, London, 2002.

Burdon, R.M., *Official History of New Zealand in the Second World War 1939–1945: 24 Battalion,* Historical Publications Branch, Department of Internal Affairs, Wellington, 1953.

Carver, Michael. *Tobruk,* B.T. Batsford Ltd, London, 1964.

Churchill, Winston S. *The Second World War (Volume 4, The Hinge of Fate),* Cassell, London, 1951.

Churchill, Winston S. *Never Give In! The Best of Winston Churchill's Speeches,* Pimlico, London, 2003.

Clifton, Brigadier George. *The Happy Hunted,* Cassell & Co., London, 1952.

Cody, J.F. *Official History of New Zealand in the Second World War 1939–1945: 21 Battalion,* Historical Publications Branch, Department of Internal Affairs, Wellington, 1953.

Cody, J.F. *Official History of New Zealand in the Second World War 1939–1945: 28 (Maori) Battalion,* Historical Publications Branch, Department of Internal Affairs, Wellington, 1956.

Cox, Geoffrey. *A Tale of Two Battles: A personal memoir of Crete and the Western Desert 1941,* Kimber, London, 1987.

Crisp, Major Robert. *Brazen Chariots,* W.W. Norton & Company, New York, 2005.

Davin, Dan. *For the Rest of Their Lives,* Ivor Nicholson & Watson, London, 1947.

Davin, D.M. *Official History of New Zealand in the Second World War 1939–1945: Crete,* Historical Publications Branch, Department of Internal Affairs, Wellington, 1953.

Dawson, W.D. *Official History of New Zealand in the Second World War 1939–1945: 18 Battalion and Armoured*

Regiment, Historical Publications Branch, Department of Internal Affairs, Wellington, 1961.

The Dictionary of New Zealand Biography, Volume Four, 1921–1940, Auckland University Press and the Department of Internal Affairs, Auckland, 1998.

Dimbleby, Jonathan. *Destiny in the Desert,* Profile Books, London, 2012.

Edge, Spence and Jim Henderson. *No Honour No Glory,* William Collins, Auckland, 1983.

Fearnside, Lt G.H. *Bayonets Abroad: A History Of The 2/13th Battalion AIF in the Second World War,* John Burridge Military Antiques, Swanbourne, Western Australia, 1993.

Fitzsimons, Peter. *Tobruk,* HarperCollins, Sydney, 2006.

Ford, Ken. *Operation Crusader 1941 – Rommel in Retreat,* Osprey Publishing, Oxford, 2010.

Freyberg, Paul. *Bernard Freyberg, VC: soldier of two nations,* Hodder & Stoughton, London, 1991.

Gardiner, Noel. *Freyberg's Circus,* Ray Richards & William Collins, Auckland, 1981.

Gerard, J.D. *Unwilling Guests,* A.H. & A.W. Reed, Wellington, 1945.

Glue, W.A. and D.J.C. Pringle. *Official History of New Zealand in the Second World War 1939–1945: 20 Battalion and Armoured Regiment,* Historical Publications Branch, Department of Internal Affairs, Wellington, 1957.

Gregg, Victor. *Rifleman: A Front Line Life,* Bloomsbury Publishing Plc, London, 2011.

Hargest, James. *Farewell Campo 12,* Whitcombe & Tombs Limited, Wellington, 1945.

Harper, Glyn. *Kippenberger, An Inspired New Zealand Commander,* HarperCollins, Auckland, 1997.

Harper, Glyn and Colin Richardson. *In the Face of the Enemy – The complete history of the Victoria Cross and New Zealand,* HarperCollins, Auckland, 2006.

Hastings, Max. *All Hell Let Loose,* HarperPress, London, 2011.

Helm, A.S. *Fights and Furloughs in the Middle East,* Whitcombe & Tombs, Christchurch, 1944.

Henderson, Alan, David Green and Peter Cooke. *The Gunners. A History Of New Zealand Artillery,* Raupo, North Shore, 2008.

Henderson, Jim. *Official History of New Zealand in the Second World War 1939–1945: 22 Battalion,* Historical Publications Branch, Department of Internal Affairs, Wellington, 1958.

Henderson, Jim. *Official History of New Zealand in the Second World War 1939–1945: 4th and 6th Reserve Mechanical Transport Companies,* Historical Publications Branch,

Department of Internal Affairs, Wellington, 1954.

Henderson, Jim. *Gunner Inglorious,* Whitcombe & Tombs, Christchurch, reprint, 1974.

Hensley, Gerald. *Beyond the Battlefield – New Zealand and its Allies 1939-45,* Viking; published by the Penguin Group, Auckland, 2009.

Hutching, Megan. *The Desert Road – New Zealanders Remember the North African Campaign,* HarperCollins, Auckland, 2005.

Hutching, Megan. *Inside Stories – New Zealand Prisoners of War Remember,* HarperCollins, Auckland, 2002.

Jackson, Francis. *Passage to Tobruk,* Raupo Books, Wellington, 1943.

Judd, Brendon. *The Desert Railway,* The Railway Book Committee, Auckland, 2003.

Kay, Robin. *Official History of New Zealand in the Second World War 1939–1945: 27 (Machine Gun) Battalion,* Historical Publications Branch, Department of Internal Affairs, Wellington, 1958.

Kershaw, Robert. *Tank Men – The Human Story of Tanks at War,* Hodder & Stoughton, London, 2009.

Kippenberger, Major General Sir Howard. *Infantry Brigadier,* Oxford University Press, London, 1949.

Liddell Hart, B.H. (ed.) *The Rommel Papers,* Arrow Books, London, 1984.

Loughnan, Father Ambrose, OP. *Full Circle to God,* Loughley Books, Rangiora, 2000.

Loughnan, R.J.M. *Official History of New Zealand in the Second World War 1939–1945: Divisional Cavalry,* Historical Publications Branch, Department of Internal Affairs, Wellington, 1963.

Lyman, Robert. *The Longest Siege. Tobruk. The Battle That Saved North Africa*, Pan Books, London, 2010.

McClymont, W.G. *Official History of New Zealand in the Second World War 1939–1945: To Greece,* Historical Publications Branch, Department of Internal Affairs, Wellington, 1959.

McEwan, Watty. *The Salamander's Brood,* Fraser Books, Masterton, 2007.

MacGibbon, John. *Struan's War – Battlegrounds, recreation and sightseeing in North Africa 1941–1944, in the photographs and diaries on New Zealand Division Gunner Struan MacGibbon,* Ngaio Press, Wellington, 2001.

McGibbon, Ian. *Kiwi Sappers,* Reed Publishing, Auckland, 2002.

McGill, David. *P.O.W. The Untold Stories of New Zealanders as Prisoners of War,* Mills Publications, Lower Hutt, 1987.

McKee, Alexander. *El Alamein. Ultra and the Three Battles,* Souvenir Press, London, 1991.

McKinney, J.B. *Official History of New Zealand in the Second World War 1939–1945: Medical Units of 2 NZEF in Middle East and Italy,* Historical Publications Branch, Department of Internal Affairs, Wellington, 1952.

McLean, Denis. *Howard Kippenberger Dauntless Spirit. A life of an outstanding New Zealand leader,* Random House, Auckland, 2008.

Macksey, Kenneth. *Military Errors of World War Two,* Cassell & Co, London, 1998.

Manning, Olivia. *The Levant Trilogy,* Penguin Books Limited, Harmondsworth, England, 1982.

Martyn, Bombardier F. *Middle East Guns,* Privately published, 1943.

Mason, W. Wynne. *Official History of New Zealand in the Second World War*

1939–1945, Prisoners of War, Historical Publications Branch, Department of Internal Affairs, Wellington, 1954.

Moorehead, Alan. *African Trilogy,* Four Square Books, London, 1959.

Murphy, W.E. *Official History of New Zealand in the Second World War 1939–1945, Episodes and Studies Volume 2: Point 175 – The Battle of Sunday of the Dead,* Historical Publications Branch, Department of Internal Affairs, Wellington, 1950.

Murphy, W.E. *Official History of New Zealand in the Second World War 1939–1945: The Relief of Tobruk,* Historical Publications Branch, Department of Internal Affairs, Wellington, 1961.

Neillands, Robin. *Eighth Army – from the Western Desert to the Alps 1939–1945,* John Murray, London, 2004.

Norton, Frazer D. *Official History of New Zealand in the Second World War*

1939–1945: 26 Battalion, Historical Publications Branch, Department of Internal Affairs, Wellington, 1952.

Official Archivist, 2 NZEF. *Return to the Attack – The New Zealand Division in Libya,* Army Board, Wellington, 1944.

Official History of New Zealand in the Second World War 1939–1945: Documents Relating to New Zealand's Participation in the Second World War 1939–45: Volume II, Historical Publications Branch, Department of Internal Affairs, Wellington, 1951.

Pallud, Jean-Paul. *The Desert War Then And Now,* After the Battle, Old Harlow, Essex, England, 2012.

Paton, Harold. *Private Paton's Pictures – Behind the lines with Kiwi soldiers in North Africa 1941–1943,* Penguin Books, Auckland, 2003.

Pitt, Barrie. *The Crucible of War. Western Desert 1941,* Jonathan Cape, London, 1980.

Playfair, Major General I.S.O. *The Mediterranean and Middle East Volume III (September 1941 to September 1942) British Fortunes reach their Lowest Ebb,* Her Majesty's Stationery Office, London, 1960.

Puttick, Lieutenant General Sir Edward. *Official History of New Zealand in the Second World War 1939–1945: 25 Battalion,* Historical Publications Branch, Department of Internal Affairs, Wellington, 1960.

Ross, Angus. *Official History of New Zealand in the Second World War 1939–1945: 23 Battalion,* Historical Publications Branch, Department of Internal Affairs, Wellington, 1959.

Ryder, Rowland. *Ravenstein. Portrait of a German General,* Hamish Hamilton, London, 1978.

Schmidt, Heinz Werner. *With Rommel in the Desert,* George G. Harrap & Co. Ltd, London, 1951.

Scoullar, Lieutenant Colonel J.L., *Official History of New Zealand in the Second World War 1939–1945: Battle for Egypt: The Summer of 1942*, Historical Publications History Branch, Department of Internal Affairs, Wellington, 1955.

Shackleton, Michael. *Desert Surgeons – New Zealand's Mobile Surgical Unit in World War II*, Ngaio Press, Wellington, 2011.

Sinclair, D.W. *Official History of New Zealand in the Second World War 1939–1945: 19 Battalion and Armoured Regiment*, Historical Publications Branch, Department of Internal Affairs, Wellington, 1954.

Smith, E.H. *Official History of New Zealand in the Second World War 1939–1945, Episodes and Studies: Guns Against Tanks: L Troop, 33rd Battery, 7th New Zealand Anti-Tank Regiment in Libya, 23 November 1941*, Historical Publications Branch, Department of Internal Affairs, Wellington, 1948.

Smith, Roger. *Up the Blue: a Kiwi private's view of the Second World War,* Ngaio Press, Wellington, 2000.

Stevens, Major General, W.G. *Official History of New Zealand in the Second World War 1939–1945: Problems of 2 NZEF,* Historical Publications Branch, Department of Internal Affairs, Wellington, 1958.

Stevens, Major General W.G. *Freyberg, V.C. The Man,* A.H. & A.W. Reed, Wellington, 1965.

Stout, Colonel T.D.M. *Official History of New Zealand in the Second World War 1939–1945: New Zealand Medical Services in the Middle East and Italy,* Historical Publications Branch, Department of Internal Affairs, Wellington, 1956.

Thompson, Martyn. *On Active Service,* Longman, Auckland, 1999.

Thompson, Martyn. *Our War – The grim digs – New Zealand Soldiers in North*

Africa 1940–1943, Penguin, Auckland, 2005.

Uren, Martyn. *Kiwi Saga,* Collins, Auckland, 1943.

War Office (by the Ministry of Information). *The Eighth Army September 1941 to January 1943,* His Majesty's Stationery Office, London, 1944.

Wilmot, Chester. *Tobruk 1941,* Penguin Group (Australia), Camberwell, 2007.

Wood, F.L.W. *Official History of New Zealand in the Second World War 1939–1945: Political and External Affairs,* Historical Publications Branch, Department of Internal Affairs, Wellington, 1958.

Wright, Matthew. *Desert Duel – New Zealand's North African War 1940–1943,* Reed, Auckland, 2002.

Wright, Matthew. *Freyberg's War: the man, the legend and reality,* Penguin, Auckland, 2005.

Newspapers

Auckland Star, paperspast.natlib.govt.nz

Christchurch Star-Sun, Archives from Christchurch City Libraries

Evening Post, paperspast.natlib.govt.nz

Nelson Evening Mail, Archives from the Isel Museum, Nelson

Press, Archives from Christchurch City Libraries

Back Cover Material

Sidi Rezegh, fought during Operation Crusader in Libya over November and December 1941, has been described as 'the forgotten battle of the Desert War'. The Eighth Army's objective in *Crusader* was to retake Cyrenaica, the eastern region of Libya, and ultimately drive the Italians and Germans out of North Africa. The campaign was partially successful, and did achieve the badly needed relief of Tobruk, where Australian and other Allied troops had been trapped.

The New Zealand Division played a major role in *Crusader,* a campaign that was important in ultimately achieving British victory in North Africa. Despite this, it is a battle that has largely been neglected by historians, failing to receive as much attention as Crete, El Alamein or Cassino. Yet more New Zealand soldiers were killed or taken prisoner during *Crusader* than in any other campaign fought by 'the Div' during the war.

Peter Cox, whose father fought at Sidi Rezegh with 27 (Machine Gun) Battalion, draws on his experience of twice visiting the battlefield to tell the story of this complex and costly campaign. He sets the scene for the fighting in Libya, describes the unforgiving and inhospitable desert landscape, follows the stages of the action itself and recounts the often moving and heroic stories of the soldiers who fought there. Many never returned home.

This is both a clearly told and very accessible account of a significant New Zealand contribution to the Second World War and a tribute to the thousands of servicemen who took part in the punishing battle of Sidi Rezegh. **PETER COX** told the story of his father Brian's wartime service in his first book, *Good Luck to All the Lads* (2008), and was then motivated to write this more complete account of the battle (see also www.sidirezegh.com). Peter was born and educated in Nelson, and now works as a company director in Christchurch. He is married with two adult children.

A

Abyssinia, *4*

Acrobat campaign, *333*

Acroma, *325, 326, 409*

Agar, Lieutenant Colonel, *306*

Agheila, *333*

Ajedabia, *23, 333*

Akhaia, *386*

Alamein, battles of, *370, 404, 414*

Al-burdi,
  see Bardia
  (Al-burdi),

Alexandria, *11, 28, 350, 363, 365, 368, 372*

Allen, Lieutenant Colonel John, *248*

Andrew, Bill, *11, 13, 82, 84, 363*

Andrew, Lieutenant Colonel Leslie, *323*

anti-tank weapons, *52, 54, 107, 406, 409*

Auchinleck, General Sir Claude, *30, 32, 44, 47, 52, 62, 71, 86, 171, 175, 236, 311, 317, 404, 406, 412*

Australian Army:
Australian Imperial Force, *32, 35, 74*
  Divisions,
  6 Division, *21, 25*
  9 Division, *25*
  Brigade, *21, 23*
  17 Brigade, *21, 23*
  19 Brigade, *11, 13, 21, 23*

Axis forces, *38, 50, 52, 62, 286*
  see also German army; Italian army,

B

Baggush, *4, 5, 74, 76, 84, 313, 320, 323, 329, 333*

Bardia (Al-burdi), *2, 11, 13, 18, 21, 28, 54, 79, 86, 109, 111, 114, 118, 121, 164,*

166, 169, 225, 228, 233, 236, 315, 323, 325, 331, 333, 335

  prisoners of war, 378, 381

Bardia–Tobruk Road, 109, 118, 121, 323, 325

Barrowclough, Brigadier (later Major General) Harold, 82, 111, 179, 409

  Point 175, 125, 128, 133, 136, 141, 143, 146, 177, 248

  Sidi Rezegh, 121, 141, 169, 177, 199, 201, 204, 212, 217, 218, 248, 272, 277, 299, 301, 304, 409

  Tobruk corridor, 246, 248, 414

Bastico, General Ettore, 38, 71

Battle of the Salient, Tobruk, 28

Battleaxe operation, 30, 52, 60, 62, 406

Bayerlein, Lieutenant General Fritz, 409

Beda Fomm, 13, 18

Belhamed, 62, 66, 69

  6 Advance Dressing Station, 357, 360, 363

  6 Brigade transport moved close to, 277, 280, 282

  attacks and loss of, 190, 191, 194, 199, 201, 204, 207, 238, 243, 246, 253, 255, 265, 267, 272, 277, 280, 289, 292, 294, 296, 299, 313, 315, 323, 355, 404, 406

  prisoners of war, 386

Bell, Robin, 251, 253, 255, 368

Benghazi, 13, 18, 23, 32, 333, 355, 360, 376, 378, 381, 383, 420

Bergonzoli, General Annibale, 13

Bir el Chleta, 121, 169, 175, 272

Bir el-Gubi, 102

Bir el-Hariga, 111

Bir el Thalata, 89, 350

Bir en-Naghia, 331

Bir Idwan, 84

Bir Stella, 76

Black, John, 136, 141, 201, 204, 282, 284, 424, 426

Blacklin, Gunner J.A.('Alf'), 35, 66, 69, 107, 114, 240, 267, 406

Blamey, General Sir Thomas, 32, 74

Bonifant, Major Ian, 272, 280, 282

Bötcher, General Karl, 240

Brega, 2

Brevity operation, 30

Brink, Major General George, 58

Britain: Defence Committee, 18
  interest in Libya, 2, 4
  strategy of liberating Europe through Middle East, 32

British Army: anti-tank weapons, 52

co-operation with Royal Air Force, 47

Middle East Command (Middle East Forces), 4, 5, 30, 74, 86

Ninth Army, 71

signals intelligence (SIGINT), 9, 18, 23, 236

tank numbers, 52, 54, 62, 118, 171

Tiger convoy of tanks and Hurricane fighters, 28

see also Royal Air Force (RAF); Royal Navy,

British Army, Eighth Army, 47, 50, 52, 54, 58, 60, 74, 95, 100, 102, 109, 111, 118, 171, 225, 263, 313, 333, 404, 409

Corps: 13 Corps (Infantry), 21, 25, 50, 52, 54, 58, 62, 84, 97, 102, 104, 107, 114, 118, 164, 171, 199, 201, 220, 222, 236, 238,

240, 243, 282, 296, 304, 306, 333, 414 (see also Western Desert Force), 13 Corps Headquarters, 228, 260, 263, 272, 275, 280, 289 13 Corps Reserve, 325, 326 30 Corps (Armoured), 50, 52, 54, 58, 60, 79, 102, 104, 107, 109, 111, 114, 123, 148, 164, 169, 171, 177, 222, 265, 280, 304, 320, 325, 357 corps structure, 50 Western Desert Force, 4, 9, 11, 13, 21 (see also 13 Corps), Divisions, 1 Armoured Division, 60, 317 7 Armoured Division, 11, 21, 28, 30, 50, 52, 60, 95, 118, 121, 166, 222, 243, 289, 329, 357

70 Infantry Division, 11, 21, 28, 30, 35, 50, 107, 325 Brigades, 54, 60 22 Guards Brigade, 50, 60, 222, 333 Armoured Brigades, 54, 409, 414 4 Armoured Brigade, 52, 54, 60, 94, 97, 102, 104, 114, 118, 164, 171, 225, 243, 269, 272, 282, 289, 299, 301, 313 7 Armoured Brigade, 52, 60, 97, 102, 104, 107, 114, 118, 164, 181 22 Armoured Brigade, 35, 52, 60, 97, 102, 104, 114, 118, 143, 164, 243, 269, 272, 282, 289, 299, 301, 333, 352, 355 Support Group (7 Armoured Division), 60, 97, 104, 114, 118, 121, 263, 269, 352

Army Tank Brigades: 1 Army Tank Brigade, *50, 111, 311*
32 Army Tank Brigade, *35, 52, 209*
Infantry Brigades: 14 Infantry Brigade, *35*
16 Infantry Brigade, *35*
23 Infantry Brigade, *35*
Battery, *35*
2 Black Watch, *107*
Border Regiment, *320*
1 Essex, *194, 217, 267, 315, 320*
8 Hussars, *128*
1 Royal Fusiliers, *11*
Royal Tank Regiments:, *107*
5 Royal Tank, *301*
8 Royal Tank, *111, 128, 133, 141*
44 Royal Tank, *111, 181, 207, 292*

Royal Horse Artillery, *35*
Royal Engineers, *217*
Medical: 14 British CCS, *350*
Browne, Sergeant J.M., *4, 5*
Buq Buq, *4, 11*
Burrows, Lieutenant Colonel Frederick A. ('Bull), *267, 317*

C
Cairo, *71*
Cameron, Maurice, *214*
Campbell, Brigadier Jock, *114*
Canada, *76*
Capel, Private George, *201*
Capuzzo, *13, 28, 50, 66, 109, 121, 166, 220, 228, 235, 323, 333*
Carmuset er-Reghem, *331*
Carter, James, *424*

casualties: Australia 23,

British, *16, 30, 107, 186, 194, 333, 335, 401, 416*

German, *28, 30, 139, 186, 209, 235, 243, 325, 335, 416*

Italian, *218, 335, 416*

South African, *143*

see also medical facilities and treatment of wounded,

casualties, New Zealand: first Libyan campaign, *5, 16*

Greece and Crete, *43, 416*

casualties, New Zealand: Operation Crusader, *186, 212, 333, 360, 363, 365, 388, 416*

5 Brigade, *230, 233, 235*

6 Brigade, *139, 141, 146, 148, 386, 416*

18 Battalion, *181*

19 Battalion, *207*

20 Battalion, *181, 184, 238, 292*

21 Battalion, *114, 248, 306, 416*

22 Battalion, *111, 333*

23 Battalion, *326, 333*

24 Battalion, *177, 181, 184, 214, 217, 275, 416*

25 Battalion, *139, 141, 181, 416*

26 Battalion, *143, 146, 184, 214, 217, 277*

27 (Machine Gun) Battalion, *141*

28 (Maori) Battalion, *166, 323, 325, 329, 331*

Chakdina sinking, *372*

Divisional Artillery, *294, 296, 416*

Divisional Cavalry, *258, 260*

Jason sinking, *386*

medical units, *363, 365*

see also prisoners
of war – New
Zealand,
Chakdina, torpedo
hit, *368, 370, 372*
Churchill, Sir
Winston, *5, 9, 18, 28, 30,
32, 47, 62, 86, 404*
Clifton, Lieutenant
Colonel George, *13,
76, 265*
Cockburn, Brigadier
Scott, *301*
Compass operation,
9, 11, 13, 16, 18, 21, 25
Costello, Charles
and Eric, *383, 386, 399*
Cox, Captain
Geoffrey, *89, 179, 222,
243, 251, 253*
Cox, Sergeant
Brian, *133, 136, 282, 284*
Cramer, General, *233*
Crete, *43, 44, 47, 74, 76, 79,
82, 84, 420*
Crisp, Captain
Robert, *225*
Crusader campaign:
achievements, *404*

advance of 4 and
6 New Zealand
Brigades, *16, 18, 21,
23, 25, 28*
November, *164, 166,
169, 171, 175, 177, 179, 181,
184, 186*
approach march,
82, 84, 86, 89, 91, 94, 95
armoured
offensive, *97, 100,
102, 104, 107, 109, 111, 114,
118, 121*
counting the cost,
*404, 406, 409, 412, 414, 416,
420, 421, 424, 426*
maps, *62, 114, 286, 326*
medical facilities
and treatment of
wounded, *350, 352,
355, 357, 360, 363, 365, 368,
370, 372, 374*
New Zealand
Division
withdrawal, *289, 292,
294, 296, 299, 301, 304, 306,
308, 311, 313*
overview, *32, 35, 38,
40*

planning, *43, 44, 47, 50, 52, 54, 58, 60, 62, 66, 69, 71*

preparation, *74, 76, 79, 82*

tactical problems, *406, 409, 412, 414*

wrap up, *315, 317, 320, 323, 325, 326, 329, 331, 333, 335*

see also names of military units, personnel, battles and places,

Crüwell, Lieutenant General Ludwig, *38, 102, 104, 220, 225*

Cunningham, Lieutenant General Sir Alan, *47, 50, 52, 54, 58, 60, 79, 86, 102, 104, 107, 118, 166, 171, 175*

Cyrenaica, *2, 4, 13, 21, 32, 38, 47, 52, 62, 331, 404*

D

Daly, Lieutenant Tom, *133, 141*

Derna, *13, 355, 376, 396*

Desert Airforce, *255*

desert warfare training, *5, 47, 74, 76, 79, 82, 84, 86, 404*

Diamond, Private Leonard, *326, 329*

Dittmer, Lieutenant Colonel George, *166, 355, 357*

Drew, Lieutenant Colonel H.D., *301, 304*

E

Easter Battle, Tobruk, *23, 25, 28*

Ed Duda, *50, 62, 66, 164, 181, 190, 191, 194, 196, 199, 204, 207, 209, 217, 238, 240, 243, 251, 267, 272, 275, 296, 311, 313, 315, 317, 320, 323*

Egypt, *4*

British defence, *4, 5, 28, 38, 164*

medical facilities, *350, 357, 363, 365, 372*

New Zealand Division in, *43, 74, 313, 325, 329, 350, 355, 357*

Rommel's frontier raid, *220, 222, 225, 228, 230, 233, 235, 236, 414*

El Adem, *222, 267, 315, 325, 333, 360*

El Agheila, *23*

El Beida, *94*

Elfer, Silvia, *391*

Enigma (Ultra) intelligence material, *9, 18, 23, 28, 38, 71, 331*

F

Farndale, *368, 370*

Farrell, 'Saint', *136*

Fellers, Colonel Bonner, *71*

Fezzan, *2*

Fort Capuzzo, see Capuzzo,

Fort Pilastrino, *23*

Fraser, Peter, *43, 44, 47, 62, 74, 100*

Freyberg, Major General Bernard, *13, 16, 43, 44, 47, 54, 58, 60, 62, 84, 325, 404, 414*

and advance of 4 and 6 New Zealand Brigades, *16, 18, 21, 23, 25, 28*

November, *166, 169, 171, 177, 179, 414, 416*

and approach march, *89*

and armoured offensive, *97, 102, 104, 109, 111, 114, 118, 121*

and attacks on Sidi Rezegh and Belhamed, *66, 69, 190, 194, 196, 201, 204, 207, 269, 272, 280, 282, 289, 296*

briefing of officers, *82, 86*

and Kippenberger, *357*

leadership, *44*

opposition to splitting divisions into brigade groups, *54, 60, 169, 412*

planning, *62, 69, 79, 164*

and Ravenstein's capture, *251, 253*

and Rommel's raid on Egyptian frontier, *225, 240*
and Rommel's return to Sidi Rezegh, *243, 246, 253, 263*
and Totensonntag (Sunday of the Dead), *121*
training, *9, 44, 47, 74, 76, 79*
and treatment of wounded, *352*
views on Crusader campaign, *412, 414*
and withdrawal of NZ Division, *296, 301, 304, 306, 308, 311, 313*

G

Gabr Saleh, *58, 60, 100, 102*
Galloway, Brigadier Alexander, *171*
Gambara, General Gastone, *38*

Gambut, *38, 79, 100, 111, 123, 166, 169, 228*
Gariboldi, General Italo, *23*
Gasr el Arid, *121*
Gatehouse, Brigadier Alec, *54, 299, 301, 304*
Gatenby, Captain Charles, *89, 91, 214, 277, 388, 391, 393, 396*
Gatenby, Eugenie, *91*
Gazala area, *325, 326, 329, 331, 333, 404, 414*
Gentry, Lieutenant Colonel (later Major General) William, *82, 296, 406*
Gerawla, *352*
German army:
anti-tank weapons, *52, 54*
Battle of the Salient, Tobruk, *28*
Easter Battle, Tobruk, *23, 25, 28*
High Command, *4, 23, 40*

medical officers, *352, 355*

mixed forces in divisions, *50, 52, 54*

Signal Exchange, *109*

strength, *52*

supplies, *38, 40, 175, 331, 333, 383, 409, 414*

tank numbers, *52, 54, 62, 71, 118, 171*

German army formations:
Deutsches Afrika Korps (DAK), *23, 38, 60, 102, 123, 125, 166, 179, 225, 263, 267, 313, 323*

Panzergruppe Afrika, *38, 222*

Divisions: 15 Panzer Division, *23, 38, 40, 52, 100, 102, 104, 107, 114, 177, 220, 222, 236, 243, 251, 253, 255, 263, 265, 267, 272, 275, 289, 325, 355*

21 Panzer Division (previously 5 Light Panzer), *23, 38, 40, 52, 102, 104, 107, 114, 146, 177, 220, 222, 236, 243, 248, 251, 253, 263, 267, 275*

90 Light Division (previously ZBV Afrika (Special Purposes) Division), *35, 38, 52, 71, 177*

Regiments: 5 Panzer Regiment, *102*

8 Panzer Regiment, *230, 246*

Rifle Regiment, *143*

361 Afrika Regiment, *128, 141, 146, 177*

Units: Geissler Advance Guard, *323*

Knabe Advance Guard, *323*

33 Reconnaissance Unit, *284*

Medical: Regimental Aid Post, Sidi Rezegh, *360*

Germany: information sources, *71, 220*

invasion of Egypt, *28, 35*

invasion of Greece and Crete, *18, 28, 43, 44, 47, 74*

invasion of Russia, *32, 35*

POW camps, *376, 386, 399*

surrender, *401*

Giorgis, General Fedele de, *335*

Godwin-Austen, Lieutenant General Alfred, *50, 79, 91, 107, 111, 171, 179, 190, 196, 280, 304, 317, 414*

Gollan, Stanley ('Shorty'), *260*

Gott, General William, *121, 282*

Graziani, Rodolfo, *2, 5, 11, 13*

Greece, *9, 18, 23, 28, 43, 44, 47, 74, 76, 84, 111, 133, 420*

Gregg, Victor, *352*

Grigg, Major Arthur, *230, 233, 235*

Gulf of Bomba, *2*

Gunn, Zeta, *372, 374*

H

Habata, *222*

Hafid Ridge, *109*

Halfaya, *11, 30, 54, 66, 86, 114, 121, 166, 225, 228, 323, 333, 335*

Hammond, Phillip ('Phil'), *133, 136, 139, 306, 308, 313, 424*

Harawira, Padre Kahi, *331*

Hargest, Brigadier James (Jim), *44, 79, 82, 179, 220, 225, 228, 230, 233, 235, 323, 378, 381, 383, 386, 388*

Hargreaves, Sergeant John, *329*

Heaps, Eric, *424, 426*

Heaps, Hugh, *426*

Heaps, Noel, *424, 426*
Helmieh, *350*
Helwan, *350*
Heron, Sergeant James (Randel), *123, 125, 201, 376, 378, 396, 399, 401, 424*
Hetherington, John, *284, 286*
Hitler, Adolf, *5, 9, 23*
Horne, Thomas, *424, 426*
Horrell, Major Henry, *91*
hospital ships, *363, 368, 370, 372, 374, 393, 396*
hospitals, *365, 396*
  German, *360, 363, 378*
  Italian, *378, 388*
  No. 1 New Zealand General Hospital, *350, 352*
  No. 2 New Zealand General Hospital (mobile), *352, 357, 372, 393*
  No. 3 New Zealand General Hospital, *350, 363, 370, 372*
  Tobruk, *363*

I

Indian army, *25, 317, 320*
  4 Indian Division, *50, 54, 58, 95, 164, 166, 220, 222, 225, 228, 235, 236, 329, 331, 333, 409*
  5 Brigade, *11, 325* Medical: Casualty Clearing Station, Sidi Omar, *365*
Inglis, Brigadier Lindsay, *62, 66, 79, 94, 179, 204, 207, 209, 243, 253, 267, 269, 272, 289, 292, 294, 301, 308, 414*
Iran, *2, 4*
Iraq, *2, 32*
Italian air force, *5, 9, 16*
Italian army,
  Gazala area, *326, 329*

relationship between Italians and Germans, *355*
strength, *52*
Tobruk, *28, 35, 60*
Italian army formations: 21 Army Corps, *38*
Armoured Corps, *38*
Bersaglieri battalions, *190, 214, 218*
Divisions:, *214*
Trieste Motorised Division, *38*
132 Ariete Armoured Division, *38, 52, 102, 220, 251, 253, 263, 265, 267, 269, 275, 282*
Bologna Division, *38, 263*
Brescia Division, *38, 263*
Pavia Division, *38, 263*
Savona Division, *38, 111, 114, 222*
Trento Division, *38, 263*
Engineers, *109*
Italian navy, *13*
Italy: declaration of war on Britain, *4*
interest in Libya, *2, 4*
invasion of Greece, *9, 23*
invasion of Libya, *5, 9, 11, 13, 16*
POW camps, *376, 381, 386, 388, 391, 396, 420*

J
Jason (Sebastiano Veniero), *383, 386*
Jones, Frederick, *44, 47, 60*
Jordan, William (Bill), *84*
Joyes, Corporal Ralph, *191*

K
Kippenberger, Lieutenant Colonel Howard, *79, 84, 94, 95,*

141, 175, 181, 191, 194, 292, 294, 301, 355

Klass, Lieutenant David, *360, 363*

L

Latham, Brigadier H.B., *171*

Latona, *35*

Lee, Private Alton, *141, 424, 426*

Libya: first Libyan campaign, *5, 9, 11, 13*
  history, *2*
  military significance, *2, 4*
  see also Crusader campaign,

Libyan Desert, *66*

Loughnan, Corporal Robert, *66, 255, 258, 260, 365, 368, 370*

Loughnan, Ian, *294, 396, 399, 401*

Luxford, Major Jack, *284, 286, 306*

M

Maadi, *74*

Maaten Baggush,
see Baggush,

Mackay, Major General Iven, *13, 21*

Maddalena, *222*

Malloy, Captain J., *133*

Malta, *32*

Manella, General Petassi, *21*

Marada, *333*

Marshall, Bombardier Francis, *294, 296*

Mason, Staff Captain Wynne, *228, 230, 235*

Mathewson, B.J., *214*

Matruh Stakes, *222*

Maxwell, Lieutenant Colonel D.T., *82*

MBE (Military Division), *393*

McIver, Charlie, *426*

McIver, Graeme, *426*

McIver, Leslie ('Les'), *424, 426*

McNaught, Lieutenant Colonel Gifford, *125, 128, 131, 133, 136, 177*

medical facilities and treatment of wounded, *350, 352, 355, 357, 360, 363, 365, 368, 370, 372, 374*

  see also hospitals; New Zealand army formations; and under British army formations, Mediterranean, *2, 4, 23*

Menastir, *111, 228, 235, 323, 325*

Mentioned in Dispatches (MiD), *16, 326*

Mersa Matruh, *5, 16, 58, 69, 71, 350, 365, 368*

Mgherreb, *329*

Miles, Brigadier Reginald, *82, 272, 289, 294, 386, 388, 414*

Military Cross, *143, 326, 363*

Milliken, Major Thomas, *214*

Mingar el Hosci ridge, *326*

Minqar el Zannan, *350*

Money, Lieutenant Jack, *248, 251*

Montgomery, General Bernard, *401*

Moorehead, Alan, *32, 114*

Morshead, Major General Leslie, *25, 28*

Murphy, W.E., *118, 228, 301, 370, 414*

Musaid, *164, 166, 225*

Mussolini, Benito, *2, 4, 5, 9*

N

Navarini, General Enea, *38*

Neale, E.R., *426*

Neame, General Philip, *25, 388*

Nelley, Eugene Charles ('Charlie'), *217, 416, 420, 421*

Nelley, Joseph, *420*

Nelley, Private Louis Matthew ('Lou'), *184, 217, 275, 416, 420*

Nelley, Ted, *420*

Nelley, Walter ('Wally'), *420*

Neumann-Silkow, Major General Walter, *38, 220, 325*

New Zealand Army: equipment, *43, 44, 47, 62, 76*

New Zealand Army
2 New Zealand Division, *16, 222, 225, 240, 243, 311, 313*
 and armoured offensive, *97, 100, 102, 104, 118, 121*
 Crusader campaign achievements, *412, 414*
 Crusader campaign planning, *44, 47, 50, 54, 58, 60, 62, 164*
 in Greece and Crete, *18, 43, 44, 47*
 intelligence officers, *89, 104, 133, 177, 248, 251*
 orders, departure and approach march, *79, 82, 84, 86, 89, 91, 94, 95*
 Sidi Rezegh, *146, 164*
 training, *5, 9, 16, 44, 47, 58, 66, 74, 76, 79, 82, 84, 86, 404, 412*
 Administration Group, *263*
 19 Army Troops Company:, *16*
 Artillery, *272, 275, 333, 416*
 4 Field Regiment, *184, 194, 275, 294*
 5 Field Regiment, *230, 416*

6 Field Regiment, *111, 125, 133, 141, 184, 196, 294, 296, 416*

7 Anti-Tank Regiment, *111, 141, 230, 416*

43 Light Anti-Aircraft Battery, *111*

Brigades, *82* (see also 4, 5 and 6 Brigades, below),

Divisional Cavalry, *76, 79, 82, 84, 102, 107, 111, 225, 255, 258, 260, 272, 323, 325, 333, 335*

Divisional Headquarters, *84, 107, 169, 179, 186, 199, 253, 255, 260, 263, 267, 269, 272, 275, 296, 308, 311, 325, 352*

Divisional Reserve, *246, 267*

Divisional Signals, *9, 76*

Engineers, *9, 76, 82*

6 Field Company, *296*

8 Field Company, *111, 186, 248, 282, 301*

Infantry battalions, *82*

27 (Machine Gun) Battalion:, *79, 82, 123, 196, 201, 284, 286, 306, 313, 424, 426*

9 Platoon, 3 Company, *133, 136, 139, 141, 175, 201, 204, 284, 306, 308* (see also under Brigades 4, 5 and 6, below),

Medical: advance dressing stations (ADSs), *230, 350, 357, 360, 365*

casualty clearing stations (CCSs), *350*

field ambulances, *350, 365*

6 Field Ambulance, *89, 111, 352, 357, 365*

field hospitals, *350*

Medical Dressing Station (MDS), *260, 315, 350, 352, 355, 357, 365*

Mobile Surgical Unit, *355, 365*

New Zealand Army Nursing Service (NZANS), *350, 352, 372, 374*

regimental aid posts (RAPs), *260, 320*

Railwaymen, *11*

Transport: 4 Reserve Mechanical Transport (RMT), *5, 11, 13, 16, 326, 333*

New Zealand Army

2 New Zealand Division, 4 New Zealand Brigade, *5, 11, 84, 94, 107, 123, 175, 177, 181, 186, 253, 255*

Bardia–Tobruk, *79, 109, 111, 121*

Belhamed, *190, 191, 194, 199, 201, 204, 207, 238, 243, 253, 255, 265, 267, 272, 277, 280, 289, 292, 294, 296, 299, 386, 404, 406*

casualties, *386*

Ed Duda, *204, 207, 209, 217, 243, 296, 311*

Gambut, *166, 169*

medical support, *365*

Sidi Rezegh, *246, 248, 253*

withdrawal from Belhamed, *296, 299, 311*

Zaafran, and withdrawal, *179, 296, 299, 301, 308, 311, 313*

Infantry Battalions, *4*

18 Battalion, *79, 181, 190, 191, 194, 201, 204, 207, 238, 243, 277, 280, 289, 296, 315, 320, 323, 326*

19 Battalion, *79, 82, 169, 181, 190, 207, 209, 212, 238, 240, 246, 280, 296, 315, 326*

20 Battalion, *79, 82, 84, 111, 169, 175, 181, 184,*

190, 191, 194, 201, 204, 207, 238, 292, 296

New Zealand Army, 2 New Zealand Division, 5 New Zealand Brigade, 82, 84, 94, 111, 123, 357

Bardia area, 166, 169, 220, 225, 228, 230, 233, 235, 263, 313, 315, 323, 325

Capuzzo, 109, 121, 166, 169, 220

Gazala area, 326, 329, 331, 333

medical support, 365

Sidi Azeiz, 109, 121, 166, 220, 225

Trigh Capuzzo, 79, 107

Infantry Battalions: 21 Battalion, 79, 109, 111, 114, 123, 166, 169, 171, 177, 184, 186, 191, 196, 199, 201, 204, 212, 214, 218, 248, 269, 272, 282, 306, 372, 416

22 Battalion, 79, 109, 111, 220, 228, 235, 236, 323, 325, 329, 331, 333

23 Battalion, 79, 91, 109, 166, 220, 225, 228, 235, 323, 326, 329, 333

28 (Maori) Battalion, 79, 84, 166, 225, 228, 235, 323, 325, 329, 331, 355

New Zealand Army, 2 New Zealand Division, 6 New Zealand Brigade, 79, 82, 84, 94, 123, 164

border area, 107, 109, 111

casualties, 139, 141, 146, 148, 386, 416

medical support, 357, 360, 365

Point 175, 139, 141, 146, 148, 166, 169, 175, 177, 179

Sidi Rezegh, 121, 123, 169, 181, 184, 186, 190, 191, 196, 199, 201, 204, 212, 214, 217, 218, 222, 238, 246, 248, 255, 263, 265, 267, 269,

272, 275, 277, 280, 282, 284, 286, 299, 301, 386, 404, 406, 414

transport, 282, 289

withdrawal from Sidi Rezegh and Zaafran, 301, 304, 306, 308, 311, 313

Infantry Battalions: 24 Battalion, 82, 123, 125, 133, 136, 141, 175, 177, 181, 184, 186, 191, 196, 199, 201, 212, 214, 217, 246, 248, 272, 275, 282, 284, 313, 357, 416, 420, 421, 424

24 Battalion, 82, 123, 125, 128, 131, 133, 136, 139, 141, 177, 181, 186, 191, 196, 199, 201, 212, 248, 272, 275, 282, 306, 313, 357, 416

26 Battalion, 82, 91, 111, 123, 141, 143, 146, 177, 181, 184, 191, 196, 199, 201, 212, 214, 217, 218, 248, 275, 277, 282, 284, 306, 313, 357, 416

New Zealand Expeditionary Force 2nd (2NZEF): First Echelon, 4, 350

reinforcements, 44

Nichols, Lieutenant Colonel John ('Crasher'), 320

Nieuw Amsterdam, 372

Niven, Bombardier Michael, 230

Norrie, Lieutenant General Willoughby, 50, 52, 54, 58, 60, 102, 107, 141, 171, 269, 280, 282, 304, 306, 308, 311

North Africa, 4, 23, 32, 47

O

Oasis Group, 50, 333

O'Connor, Major General Richard, 4, 5, 9, 13, 18, 23, 25, 28, 388

Omar fortresses, 79, 220

Operation Sommernachtstraum (Midsummer Night's Dream), 40

Oranje, *363, 374*
Osborn, George, *5*

P

Page, Colonel J.R.('Rusty'), *196, 199, 212, 214*

Palestine, *71, 331*

Paterson, Lance Corporal Clement ('Clem'), *82, 89, 94, 97, 100, 109, 181, 207, 209, 240, 315, 329, 335*

Peart, Lieutenant Colonel Joseph (Jan), *296, 320*

Pepper, Lieutenant Cyril, *143, 146*

Pienaar, Brigadier Dan, *269, 280, 282, 304*

Pizey, Lieutenant Commander E.F., *383*

Playfair, Major General Ian, *118, 141*

Point 175, *121, 125, 128, 131, 133, 136, 139, 141, 143, 146, 148, 166, 169, 171, 175, 177, 179, 181, 184, 186, 190, 191, 194, 196, 199, 201, 204, 207, 209, 212, 214, 217, 218, 220, 222, 225, 228, 230, 233, 235, 236, 238, 240, 243, 246, 248, 251, 253, 255, 258, 260, 263, 265, 267, 269, 272, 275, 277, 280, 282, 284, 286, 289, 292, 294, 296, 299, 301, 304, 306, 308, 311, 313, 315, 317, 320, 323, 325, 326, 329, 331, 333, 335, 350, 352, 355, 357, 360, 363, 365, 368, 370, 372, 374, 376, 378, 381, 383, 386, 388, 391, 393, 396, 399, 401, 404, 406, 409, 412, 414, 416, 420, 421, 424, 426*

Point 182, *329, 331*

Point 187, *177*

Polglase, Private Clarence ('Dick'), *372, 374*

Polish army, *320*
  1 Polish Carpathian Infantry Brigade, *35, 50, 329, 331*

prisoners of war: Australian, *378*

British, *25, 114, 186, 378, 381, 388, 416*

escapes, *294, 355, 357, 363, 388, 391, 393, 396*

German, *28, 30, 107, 109, 111, 125, 131, 133, 136, 139, 166, 175, 179, 181, 186, 190, 209, 243, 246, 248, 251, 260, 267, 317, 335, 352, 355, 368, 416*

Indian, *378*

Italian, *11, 13, 109, 196, 284, 311, 326, 368, 416*

New Zealand, *43, 131, 230, 233, 246, 275, 277, 284, 292, 294, 301, 313, 331, 333, 335, 355, 360, 363, 365, 376, 378, 381, 383, 386, 388, 391, 393, 396, 399, 401, 416, 420*

South African, *143, 209, 378*

Prole, 'Bun', *136*

Pussell, Corporal Osbert, *16*

R

Ravenstein, Major General Johann von, *38, 40, 220, 222, 248, 251, 253, 255, 263, 299, 368, 370*

Ritchie, Major General Neil M., *175, 240, 317, 320*

Robertson, Brigadier Horace, *23*

Rommel, Lieutenant General Erwin, *38, 52, 86, 97, 102, 109*

and advance of 4 and 6 New Zealand Brigades, *16, 18, 21, 23, 25, 28*

November, *171, 175, 177, 179*

Battle of the Salient, *28, 30*

Crusader campaign impact, *404*

Crusader campaign wrapping up, *315, 317, 323, 325, 329, 331, 333*

Easter Battle, *23, 25*

Egyptian frontier raid, *220, 222, 225, 228, 230, 233, 235, 236, 414*

Point 175, *131, 143*

Sidi Rezegh, *104, 114, 177, 238, 240, 243, 246, 248, 251, 253, 255, 258, 260, 263, 311*

Sommernachtstraum, *40*

Tobruk, *35, 38, 40, 58, 60, 71, 100, 102, 171, 175*

and treatment of wounded, *363*

Royal Air Force (RAF), *18, 21, 28, 47, 62, 71, 194, 236, 243, 265, 331, 401*

see also British Army; Desert Airforce,

Royal Navy, *331, 399*

Rugbet en-Nbeidat, *125, 128, 131, 177, 181, 186, 306*

recommendation, *233*

S

Schmidt, Lieutenant Heinz Werner, *38, 143, 243, 333*

Scobie, Major General Ronald M., *35, 181, 196, 209, 317*

Seebohm, Captain Alfred, *71*

Sheferzen, *225*

shipping: Axis losses in Mediterranean, *38, 40*

hospital ships, *363, 368, 370, 372, 374, 393, 396*

Shuttleworth, Lieutenant Colonel Clayden, *136, 177, 184, 275*

Sidi Azeiz, *86, 102, 107, 109, 111, 121, 166, 169, 220, 225, 233, 236, 378*

Sidi Barrani, *5, 9, 11, 13, 18, 30, 350*

Sidi Bu Amed, *325*

Sidi Clif, *76*

Sidi Mahmoud, *365*

Sidi Omar, *50, 86, 95, 97, 114, 121, 225, 228, 365*

Sidi Rezegh, *62, 66, 69, 370*

airfield, *102, 114, 184, 282, 284*

Allied attacks, defence and withdrawal, *50, 100, 102, 133, 146, 164, 166, 169, 190, 191, 196, 199, 201, 204, 212, 214, 217, 218, 238, 240, 246, 255, 265, 267, 269, 272, 275, 277, 280, 282, 284, 286, 299, 301, 376, 409, 414*

German capture and recapture, *104, 107, 114, 118, 121, 128, 166, 222, 225, 246, 253, 255, 265, 267, 269, 272, 275, 277, 280, 282, 284, 286, 311, 313, 315, 404, 406*

prisoners of war, *376, 383, 386*

Rommel at, *238, 240, 243, 246, 248, 251, 253, 255, 258, 260, 263*

strategic point, *66, 69*

treatment of wounded, *352, 355, 360, 363, 365*

see also Totensonntag (Sunday of the Dead),

signals intelligence (SIGINT), *9, 18, 23*

Sirte, *23*

Smith, Sergeant H.L., *304, 306*

Sollum, *11, 13, 16, 28, 30, 54, 66, 86, 164, 166, 225, 228, 323, 331, 333, 335*

South African Air Force, *71*

South African Army, *74, 320*

1 South African Division, *50, 58, 62, 94, 95, 164*

2 South African Division, *325*

1 South African Brigade, *240, 243, 248, 263, 267, 269, 272, 280, 282, 284, 289, 296, 304, 414*

3 South African Brigade, *333*
5 South African Brigade, *141, 143, 146, 169, 171, 269, 296*
1 Transvaal Scottish Battalion, *311*
Spence, Padre George, *181*
Staveley, Captain John ('Jock'), *89, 357, 360, 363*
Straker, Major Thomas, *233, 235*
Suez Canal, *2, 16, 74*
Sümmerman, Major General Max, *38*
Sunday of the Dead (Totensonntag), *121, 123, 125, 128, 131, 133, 136, 139, 141, 143, 146, 148*
supply dumps, *40, 69, 71*
Syria, *32*

T

tanks: Allied tactical problems, *406, 409, 412*
British tank numbers, *52, 54, 62, 118, 171*
German tank numbers, *52, 54, 62, 71, 118, 171*
Italian tank numbers, *52*
models, *52, 60*
training, *406, 412*
see also anti-tank weapons,
Taylor, Private, *141*
Tevini, Count Carlo, *391, 393, 396*
Thomson, Captain Frederick, *326*
Thorgrim, *368*
Tiger convoy of tanks and Hurricane fighters, *28*
Tiger position, *107*
Tobruk, *13, 18, 21, 23, 25, 28, 30, 32, 35, 38, 40, 315, 317, 320, 329*
corridor, *190, 240, 243, 246, 248, 251, 263, 265, 272, 277, 289, 296, 299, 313, 360, 414*

garrison, *23, 25, 28, 35, 52, 86, 107, 114, 164, 240, 243, 255, 267, 272, 296, 313, 317, 320, 414*

garrison link-up with New Zealand Division, *50, 54, 107, 179, 181, 190, 191, 196, 199, 201, 209, 212, 222, 238, 304, 414*

medical evacuations to, *363, 365, 368, 414*

relief of, *28, 30, 32, 35, 47, 62, 74, 164, 171, 320, 404, 409, 414*

Tobruk Bypass Road, *69, 190, 191, 194, 317, 320*

Tomlinson, Captain Edgar, *123, 136, 217*

Totensonntag (Sunday of the Dead), *121, 123, 125, 128, 131, 133, 136, 139, 141, 143, 146, 148*

Trigh Capuzzo, *69, 79, 107, 111, 121, 123, 125, 175, 184, 186, 190, 199, 228, 251, 253, 301, 317, 320, 323*

Trigh el-Abd, *97, 100, 225*

Tripoli, *16, 18, 23, 30*

Tripolitania, *2, 18*

Tripp, Steve, *16*

Tummar East, *11*

Tummar West, *11*

Tutbury, Arch, *277*

U

Ultra intelligence material, *9, 18, 23, 28, 38, 71, 331*

United States, *32, 76*
  'Black Code', *71*

Upham, Lieutenant Charles, *82*

Uren, Martyn, *76, 79, 84, 184*

V

Via Balbia, *69, 164, 255, 323, 326*

Victoria Cross, *114*

Vietina, Massimiliano, *23*

W

Wadi esc-Sciomar, *121, 125, 128*

Wadi Sehel, *267*

Walker, Laurie ('Pooky'), *136, 139, 306, 308*

War Cabinet, New Zealand, *62*

Wavell, General Sir Archibald, *4, 5, 9, 16, 23, 25, 28, 30, 44*

Weir, Colonel, *294*

Wesney, Captain Arthur ('Archie'), *146, 214*

Westphal, Colonel Siegfried, *222, 236*

Whakarau, Private Iver, *331*

Wilder, Brigadier Allan, *325*

Williams, Violet, *424, 426*

Wilson, Major Harold, *125, 133*

Winfield, Ray, *136*

Wintle, Frank, *421, 424*

Women's Royal Air Force (WRAF), *401*

Y

Young, Major Leslie, *391, 393, 396*

Z

Zaafran, *179, 181, 190, 194, 207, 246, 255, 280*